How to Write BETTER RÉSUMÉS and COVER LETTERS

Third Edition

Patricia K. Criscito, CPRW

President and Founder
ProType, Ltd., Colorado Springs
and author of Barron's e-Résumés,
Résumés That Pop!,
Interview Answers in a Flash,
and Guide to Distance Learning

BARRON'S

The résumés in this book are real résumés used by real people to get real jobs. The names and contact information have been changed to protect their privacy.

All website addresses in this book were current on the date of publication. Because of the dynamic nature of the Internet, URLs can change. If you cannot find a site with the published address, use a good search engine to locate one that is up to date.

All inquiries should be addressed to:
Barron's Educational Series, Inc.
250 Wireless Boulevard
Hauppauge, New York 11788
www.barronseduc.com

Library of Congress Catalog Card No.: 2013003689

ISBN: 978-1-4380-0147-0

Library of Congress Cataloging-in-Publication Data

Criscito, Pat, 1953–
How to write better résumés and cover letters / Patricia K. Criscito, CPRW – 3rd edition.
        pages cm
Includes bibliographical references and index.
ISBN: 978-1-4380-0147-0 (alk. paper)
1. Résumés (Employment) 2. Job hunting. I. Title.

HF5383.C742 2013
650.14'2–dc23   2013003689

PRINTED IN THE UNITED STATES OF AMERICA
9 8 7 6 5 4 3 2 1

Contents

About the Author

Pat Criscito is a Certified Professional Résumé Writer with more than 30 years of experience and résumé clients in 42 countries. As the president and founder of ProType, Ltd., she has written more than 15,000 résumés in her career and speaks nationally on the subject, appearing regularly on television and radio shows, as well as at Harvard, Yale, Tulane, SMU, Thunderbird, and other major universities.

Pat is also the author of Barron's *Résumés That Pop!* (a comprehensive idea book for designing your résumé for paper and electronic uses), *e-Résumés, Interview Answers in a Flash,* and *Guide to Distance Learning.* She is a contributing writer to *The Wall Street Journal, The Boston Globe, Colorado Springs Business Journal,* and other publications.

Because of her research, Pat is always on the cutting edge of job-search science. She interviews human resource managers and recruiters across the country and understands what they are looking for in a résumé and how to get a résumé read. In her books, Pat teaches you how to be successful in your job search and how to create and use electronic résumés, LinkedIn profiles, and e-folios. In this book, she passes on her expert knowledge of the résumé-writing process from an insider's perspective.

Pat is a member of the National Résumé Writers' Association *(www.nrwa.com)* and sits on their board of directors. She teaches résumé writers how to write and design résumés to reflect the unique personal brands of their clients. For more information and to access the hyperlinks from this book in a handy online format, visit *www.patcriscito.com.* You will also find downloadable versions of all the forms in this book at the same site.

Meet the
Perfect Résumé

The job market itself defines the *perfect résumé*, which means résumés must evolve along with it. This new edition of *How to Write Better Résumés and Cover Letters* provides you with the latest résumé science, which means a lot of it will focus on the creation and use of résumés, including for e-mail, the Internet, e-folios, LinkedIn profiles, blogs, and social networking. However, we can't ignore the paper version of your résumé for use in networking, interviewing, mailing to a well-researched list of companies, and the few times you will mail or fax a résumé in response to a job advertisement.

Whether you are a seasoned executive trying to condense a lifetime of experience onto two pages or a recent graduate struggling to find enough data to file a one-page résumé, this book will provide you with everything you need to create the *perfect* personal branding instrument for your unique job search.

William Arruda, founding partner and president of the Reach Branding Club *(www.reachbrandingclub.com)*, says, "Personal branding is a revolution in the way we manage our careers. It means identifying and communicating what makes you unique, relevant, and compelling so you can reach your goals. It's about differentiation, about using what makes you unique to stand out from the myriad others who offer seemingly similar knowledge, skills, and abilities. Personal branding means using who you *are* to get what you want from life." To create a résumé that reflects this uniqueness, you need to highlight your unique promise of value, and this book will guide you through that process.

So just what is the perfect résumé? The *perfect* résumé is the one that fits your personality in both design and wording, tempered, of course, by the unique expectations of your industry and tailored to maximize the technologies of the Internet. It must contain the keywords of your industry, so your résumé appears at the top of a list of candidates in an electronic keyword search. It must be formatted to work

> *The perfect résumé is the one that fits your personality in both design and wording, tempered by the expectations of your industry and tailored to maximize the technologies of the Internet.*

on the Web, but the wording also must be dynamic and interesting to the human reader who will ultimately decide whether or not you deserve an interview.

Your paper résumé must be designed and written in such a way that it stands out in a stack of résumés on a busy executive's desk, since even electronic résumés are ultimately printed. It will help you get that all-important interview by making a strong first impression with a reader, and then by keeping that attention with dynamic sentences that convey your knowledge, skills, and abilities. It's that simple.

Having said that, you should know that writing your résumé is often one of the most difficult things you will ever do! Think about it … You must turn your life history into a one- or two-page advertisement that highlights a lifetime of experience, accomplishments, and education. Since we have been taught all of our lives to be modest and not to brag or be prideful, most people find this ultimate "pride" piece difficult to write.

Even if you have already made a first attempt at writing a résumé, it may not meet the expectations of today's technology or discerning hiring manager. The National Résumé Writers' Association *(www.nrwa.com)* publishes a test to help job seekers decide whether their résumés are ready for a job search. With their permission, let's evaluate your old résumé's effectiveness. Put a checkmark by every box that applies to you.

- ❏ My résumé uses the same marketing techniques used by companies to sell my unique "personal brand" to employers.
- ❏ My résumé is packed with industry-specific language and crucial keywords to ensure it will be searchable in an electronic database.
- ❏ My résumé emphasizes and quantifies my achievements/results to show not only what I have done, but also *how well* I have done it.
- ❏ My résumé reflects what I'm really good at doing, my unique value proposition.
- ❏ My résumé uses varied action verbs and powerful marketing phrases.
- ❏ My résumé contains superior grammar, spelling, sentence structure, and punctuation.
- ❏ My résumé emphasizes how I will benefit employers and meet their precise needs.
- ❏ My résumé engages the reader from the outset (on the first third of page one) and maintains interest throughout.
- ❏ My résumé clearly communicates my job target and the key strengths I bring to the table within the first few lines of text.
- ❏ My résumé uses accomplishment statements in a compelling way, using numbers when possible to quantify my achievements.

❑ My résumé communicates and targets my key transferable skills.

❑ My résumé minimizes my potential weaknesses and turns negative "red flags" into positive assets—things like gaps in employment, recent graduate with little real-world experience, lack of key skills for a new industry, self-employment, reentering the job market after a long time raising children, and older worker facing possible age discrimination, among others.

❑ My résumé uses an eye-catching, inviting, and original design (not a template).

❑ My résumé includes MS Word, PDF, and plain text versions to enable use with e-mail, Internet, and e-forms.

❑ My résumé uses the most effective format, style, and strategy for my particular situation.

❑ My current résumé is getting enough (or the right type of) interviews.

How did you do? If you checked 14–16 boxes, your résumé-writing abilities appear to be sound. You can still benefit from some of the strategies and tips in this book, or you might want to avail yourself of a critique from a professional résumé writer to be sure you didn't miss anything important.

If you checked 11–13 boxes, you have some distinct abilities that will help you write a résumé more solidly than most. Without the help of this book, however, you may leave out some critical components that can cost you interviews. Optimize your results by following all 12 steps in this book.

If you checked fewer than 11 boxes, you definitely need this book! You will miss opportunities that may be perfect for you unless you apply all the suggestions listed.

Writing the Perfect Résumé

Millions of paper and electronic résumés are distributed every day, and they all serve one purpose—to entice potential employers to open their doors for an interview. Every résumé is simply a marketing tool—your own personal advertisement to promote your personal brand. Just as the value of money is determined by what is printed on a piece of paper—there is a big difference between $1 and $100 bills—so is the value of your résumé determined by its content and format.

When writing the perfect résumé, you must ensure you include the things hiring managers and recruiters want to see on a résumé. According to a survey by CareerBuilder.com, that includes evidence of relevant work experience (77%), skills put into action (45%), problem-solving and decision-making capabilities

(56%), leadership (44%), oral and written communication skills (40%), team building (33%), and performance and productivity improvement (31%).

You must also avoid the things they find irritating—spelling errors (59%), inaccurate information (29%), lack of customization to the position (30%), too much irrelevant information (21%), and résumés longer than two pages (21%), as well as formatting errors, lack of organization, and irrelevant personal interests.

In my own résumé-writing practice, I designed a 12-step process over the years to help me clarify the experience, accomplishments, skills, education, and other background information of my clients and then to condense that person's life onto paper to create the perfect advertisement, always keeping in mind both the reader and the industry's expectations.

I shared that experience with my readers in a shortened form in the first edition of *Résumés in Cyberspace* (later titled *e-Résumés*). My 12-step writing process was then excerpted from the book in *The Wall Street Journal's National Employment Business Weekly* and was selected by their editors for one of the "Ten Best Articles of the Year" awards.

With this book, I wanted to give you the whole story, to teach you how to create the perfect résumé from beginning to end. In this book you will find insider information from the world of résumé writers. You will learn the following:

- How to focus your résumé (Chapter 4, Step 1)

- How to define educational experiences to your advantage (Chapter 5, Step 2)

- How to research other sources to help you describe your past experience (Chapter 6, Step 3)

- How to fill your résumé with the buzzwords of your industry and make your résumé pop up in a keyword search in an electronic résumé database (Chapter 7, Step 4)

- How to organize your experience and describe your duties (Chapter 8, Step 5)

- How to emphasize your accomplishments (Chapter 9, Step 6)

- How to refine your information to the most relevant experience (Chapter 10, Step 7)

- How to develop dynamic, attention-getting sentences that will grab and keep your reader's attention (Chapter 11, Step 8)

- How to rearrange the information on your résumé so your reader is forced to see your most important items first (Chapter 12, Step 9)

- How to include related information to strengthen your qualifications (Chapter 13, Step 10)

- How to create a personal branding statement that will knock your reader's socks off (Chapter 14, Step 11)

- How to put it all together, including positioning, design, functional versus chronological résumés, executive résumés, and curriculum vitae (Chapter 15, Step 12)

Electronic Résumés

However, this book won't stop there. To manage your career today, you need both a paper résumé and electronic versions that can be used for attaching to e-mail messages, posting to websites, and filling out e-forms on the Internet. Chapter 2 will cover how to create and when to use plain text files, MS Word files, and PDF files.

You will learn how to use an electronic résumé effectively to ensure that it is selected from the thousands of résumés that companies receive every year. Just as one example, JetBlue Airways receives 130,000 résumés a year, from which they must choose only 3,000 qualified people. You want to be one of the few chosen and not the many rejected.

Then I will add the latest information on how to use blogs, e-folios (personal websites), and social networking sites (Twitter, LinkedIn, Facebook, YouTube, and MySpace) to build your online identity in Chapter 3.

Since more than 80% of recruiters and hiring managers conduct a Google search on applicants before interviewing them, you must learn how to manage your online identity. That means controlling every word you write on the Internet and in e-mails, and choosing Web tools that will enhance the position of information *you choose* to appear when your name is Googled.

Cover Letters

What is a good résumé without an equally good cover letter? The answer is nothing. If your cover letter doesn't whet the hiring manager's appetite, your résumé may not get read at all.

Every résumé you send out, whether by mail, fax, or e-mail, needs a good cover letter. The last chapter will share some of the more common types and give you guidelines for including the right information that will entice a hiring manager to continue reading.

You will also see examples of recruiter-specific letters, dynamic and story cover letters, thank-you letters after an interview, and even a resignation letter, which all job seekers are dying to write.

Get Ready, Get Set, Write!

You have a wealth of résumé examples in this book from which to choose. Each chapter will provide you with sample wording to guide your creative process. If you find descriptions that work for you, please feel free to use them as a foundation for the words on your own résumé.

That doesn't mean that you should use every sentence verbatim. Accuracy is paramount in a résumé. Never use wording that you cannot explain or justify in an interview.

Unfortunately, cheating on résumés has become distressingly common. A study of 2.6 million job applications, conducted by the Society of Human Resource Management (SHRM), showed that 55% of all job applications contained false information, 44% lied about their work experience, 23% fabricated credentials or licenses, and 41% lied about their education. An FBI study found that approximately half a million people falsely claimed to have college degrees. Further studies show that nearly one-third of job applicants list dates of employment that are inaccurate by more than three months.

Don't get caught in that trap. A SHRM survey found that 96% of companies conduct some type of background screening, which can include reference checks, pre-employment drug/alcohol screening, fingerprinting, credit and driving history reports, INS verification, and background checks for criminal or terrorist activities.

Throughout the book, you will find forms to help you collect information for your résumé. Please feel free to copy them as needed. If you would like to download PDF or MS Word versions of the forms, please go to *www.patcriscito.com* and follow the links to my books. When you see the title of this book, there will be hyperlinks to download the files. There are also lists of the websites provided in the book so you can quickly hyperlink to each site.

Now, let's get down to the business of writing that *perfect* résumé!

Electronic Résumés

2

The Internet has changed the way the world does business, and job searching is no exception. On the Internet, you can find job openings anywhere in the world in a matter of seconds. According to The Conference Board, there were 4,425,000 unduplicated online job advertisements on 1,200 major Internet job boards in 2012. The International Association of Employment Websites (*www.employmentwebsites.org*) lists more than 65,000 premier job sites on the Internet that meet their strict membership requirements out of 100,000+ sites worldwide.

There have been massive changes in the recruiting industry over the past decade. Recruiting and job seeking transitioned from paper based to electronic, and huge online job boards spurred a massive increase in online résumé submissions. Over the past few years, job boards have been contracting, consolidating, specializing, and evolving to the point where it's difficult to predict just how many will be left five years from now.

Advances in Web 2.0 technology have propelled hiring managers into real-time Googling of applicants, and applicants can now see job openings as soon as they hit the Web. Applicants can use social media, blogs, e-folios, and visual CVs to advertise themselves. This real-time Web makes it even easier to brand yourself and to keep the content you want employers to see on the first page of a Google search.

Résumés themselves have changed just as dramatically. Instead of paper résumés, digital résumés have become the main contact medium for more than 75% of the nation's employers. The only thing that hasn't changed is the purpose of a résumé. It is still an advertisement to promote your personal brand.

To make certain you have the right tools for today's job search, this chapter will cover three types of electronic résumés. The first type is a generic computer file that you create specifically to cut and paste your résumé into those frustrating

> *The Internet has created a nationwide network that requires a new set of job-hunting skills.*

e-forms on the Internet—a text version. Sometimes these text files are what job sites expect you to "browse" for and upload.

The other two electronic résumés include your MS Word document and Adobe Acrobat PDF file, which you use to attach to e-mails or upload when a website asks you to "browse" for a résumé.

We will deal with a fourth type of electronic résumé in the next chapter, an HTML résumé that is posted on the Internet at your own website, e-folio, visual CV, and/or blog.

Your personal website can include a digital video if you are comfortable with the medium and skilled in front of a camera. For instance, if you are a television broadcaster, news anchor, actor/actress, or model, then you already know how to maximize the media, so you just need to find the technical help to create the kind of digital file you need and upload it to the Internet, either to your own personal website or to YouTube, which you can link to from your e-folio.

Video interviews are more frequently used by recruiters to save the travel costs of bringing a candidate to the company. To be successful on video, you need to feel comfortable with the medium, have a polished image, wear non-distractive clothing, watch what is in your background, sit close to the camera, speak slowly, keep your answers or comments brief, and try not to yawn.

Recently, staffing experts Gerry Crispin and Mark Mehler of CareerXroads published a tongue-in-cheek view of the job seeker's electronic path to a job, which I share here with their permission.

1. First, the candidate likely told some friends on Facebook they were looking for a new job. So far so good.

2. A friend might have then suggested asking Siri to search Google.

3. And perhaps somebody paid off Siri to forward him to Indeed, which led him to Job Central, which linked him to a great position on the career site of a firm in his commute range.

4. The candidate then went to LinkedIn and found a friend of a friend who worked there and had gone to the same school as he did.

5. Wanting to be cool, he followed the employee on Twitter, then put him in his "must meet" circle on Google+, and soon found out that he (the employee) would be at a meet-up nearby where they accidentally-on-purpose met.

6. Dropping the name of the friend they both knew in common, they found other common ground—they both pinned Italian recipes on Pinterest—

and the now new friend (the employee) agreed to be his referral for an open position.

That could be you!

The Plain Text Résumé

When you type words onto a computer screen in a word processing program (like MS Word), you are creating what is called a file or document. When you save that file, it is saved with special formatting codes like fonts, margins, tab settings, and so on, even if you didn't add them. Each word processing software saves its files in its own native format, making the file readable by anyone else with the same software version or with some other software that can convert that file to its own native format—think MS Word or Corel WordPerfect.

Only by choosing to save the document as a generic, plain text file can your document be read by anyone, regardless of the word processing software he or she is using. This is the type of file you should create in order to cut and paste your résumé into an e-form.

A plain text file is simply words—no pictures, no fonts, no graphics, no tabs, no bold, no italics, etc.—just plain words. If you print this text, it looks very boring, but all the words that describe your life history are there, just as they are in the handsome paper résumé you created to mail to a potential employer or take to an interview.

You can use this file to post your résumé onto the Internet at a company's website or to a job bank in answer to an online job posting (such as at *www.careerbuilder.com)*. In any case, the file ends up in the same type of computerized database in which the e-mailed résumés have been stored.

Steps for Creating a Text Résumé

To create a plain text version of your résumé, don't use any special bells and whistles when you type it in a word processing program. That means don't use boldface, underline, italics, fonts, font size, margin settings, and so on. Tabs will disappear when you convert your file to text, so use your spacebar to move words over instead of tabs. Rather than trying to force lines into bulleted phrases, I recommend using paragraphs and generous white space on a text résumé.

Also be careful of the "smart quotes" that many word processing programs automatically place when you press the " key on your keyboard. These special characters will not translate when you save your file as plain text. That includes mathematical symbols, em-dashes, en-dashes, and any character that does not appear on your keyboard.

Your choices for bullets are also limited to the characters on your keyboard. Some of the better symbol choices to highlight lines of text are ~, *, or +. You can use special characters from your keyboard to create dividers, like a series of ~~~~~ or ----------- or ===== or ********.

Do not set full justification on a text résumé. Instead left justify all lines so the right margin is ragged.

You can't control how e-forms will format your message at their end. When you type your résumé text, let your sentences "wrap" to a new line so the pasted text will adjust itself to the width of the electronic form on the Internet. Use the "enter" key to add extra white space between paragraphs and sections not at the end of lines within a paragraph. That way, you can be sure the lines will break correctly and your text résumé will look neat on the recruiter's screen.

Don't worry about the page breaks that your word processor shows you. They won't matter once the text is pasted into an electronic form on the Internet, since the text adjusts itself to fit the available space.

A text résumé can be longer than one page, but remember that you have one screen full of space (about 15–30 lines) to grab your reader's attention and motivate him or her to click down to the next screen. If you have written your résumé as I recommend in this book, your most important information will be in the top half of page one already.

If you have created a neat, formatted paper résumé and have saved it on your computer, it is easy to strip it of all the codes by saving it as a plain text file. In most word processing software, you can select "Save As" from the "File" menu and choose "Plain Text" (or "MS DOS Text" in some versions). Remember to save the file under a new name with a ".txt" extension. You don't want to save over your formatted paper résumé and lose all that hard work! See the screen shot on the next page for the process in Microsoft Word.

In Corel WordPerfect, the best file type to select is "ASCII (DOS) Generic Word Processor," which maintains the wrap at the end of lines. If you choose "ASCII DOS Text" in WordPerfect, the file will be saved with hard returns at the end of every line of text and it won't wrap correctly when pasted into an e-mail or e-form on the Internet. Just as in Microsoft Word, after you have saved the file as a ".txt" file, you must then open it again and clean up the text.

Now that you have a generic file on your computer screen, you need to be careful how you save that file, or your word processor will still add hidden codes that will make your file jumbled on the Internet. You must always remember to

"Save As" from the "File" menu or your word processor's default format will take over. Repeat the instructions above for saving the file as an "ASCII (DOS) Generic Word Processor" in Corel WordPerfect or "Plain Text" in Microsoft Word.

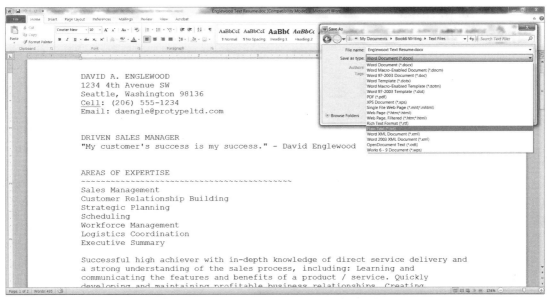

Screen shot of Microsoft Word used with permission of Microsoft Corporation

On the following pages are sample résumés created in word processing programs but saved as plain text files and then cleaned up. You will notice that they are nothing special to look at and are more than one page long, but hiring managers are accustomed to seeing these generic files and aren't expecting beauty. Their company's applicant tracking software will change the font (which you can't control), so your résumé won't look quite as bad as it does on your screen.

RENA D. SMITH
1234 Wild Trap Drive
Colorado Springs, Colorado 80925
Home: (719) 555-1234
Cell: (719) 555-5678
E-mail: rena.smith@protypeltd.com
LinkedIn: www.linkedin.com/in/rdsmith

PROFILE
~~~~~~

Proven team leader with a strong background in telecommunications customer service. High-energy professional who enjoys the challenge of solving complex problems. Experienced supervisor with a reputation for team building, coaching, and mentoring.

Strengths: detail oriented, flexible, analytical, self-motivated, and articulate. Experienced in Windows, MS Word, Excel, Internet Explorer, and Visio software.

EXPERIENCE
~~~~~~

QWEST (Formerly US WEST Communications), Denver, Colorado
Excelled in supervisory positions for this telecommunications leader over a 25+ year career. Awarded numerous certificates, stock options, and bonuses for excellence in service. Achieved President's Club twice, an honor reserved for the top 10 percent of employees nationwide.

LEAD PROCESS ANALYST
Federal Government Division, Colorado Springs, Colorado (2010 to present)
Provide tier-two technical support to sales personnel in all 50 states. Handle escalated and chronic problems for federal government customers, including missed deadlines, facility issues, and special projects. Required to respond within one hour of being contacted and to provide constant feedback to all parties involved. Collaborate with internal departments and nationwide customers to manage large projects. Serve as a member of the Emergency Response Team for 14 states in the Qwest network. On call 24/7. Received recognition for exceptional service. Fill in for supervisors and peers during absences. Assist in coaching customer relations managers in the Federal Government Customer Care Group. Received a Certificate of Appreciation for coordinating the NATO project in 2011.

PROCESS MANAGER
Construction/Engineering Staff, Denver, Colorado (2007 to 2010)
Evaluated whether the Perigon initiative (a legacy system upgrade) and its four component projects will improve productivity, cost effectiveness, contractor accountability, accuracy and quality of work, and the ability to interface with current systems. Created 30 user guides to provide standard methods and procedures for each type of user. Assisted in deploying the new systems in 14 states, including user demonstrations and training programs. Worked closely with creative services to develop a training video to educate users on new systems; responsible for scripting, editing, music and graphic selection, and content. Collaborated with field, construction, and engineering staff to ensure a smooth transition of work and to develop productivity measures for system users.

CONSTRUCTION MANAGEMENT CENTER SUPERVISOR
Colorado Springs, Colorado (2006 to 2007)
Supervised the Construction Management Center for the southern and western Colorado territories. Processed 400 to 500 construction jobs a month, including scheduling, monitoring, updating, tracking, and ordering of materials for the office and outside plant cable. Supervised ten analytical associates, two clerical contractors, an administrative assistant, network technician, and job force manager. Worked closely with engineers, senior executives, and other internal/external customers to maintain work flow and certification standards. Responsible for reports, held orders, designed services, and database maintenance. Served as management's representative to the union; responded to discrimination, performance, and attendance issues.

CENTRAL OFFICE MANAGER
Colorado Springs, Colorado (1999 to 2006)
Managed the daily operations of a 1,500-square-mile territory with 24 offices and three area codes that included Colorado Springs, Glenwood Springs, and Idaho Springs. Supervised, coached, and trained 17 technicians, ensuring safety, productivity, and quality performance. Coordinated the scheduling and completion of all central office jobs. Responsible for meeting design service and delayed order commitments. Managed several projects to convert switches from analog to digital and to upgrade, add, or remove central office and power equipment. Succeeded in reducing staff overtime by changing work schedules to better meet customer demand and by cross-training technicians.

NAC/MPAC MANAGER
Colorado Springs, Colorado (1998 to 1999)
Managed the Number Assignment Center (NAC) and the Machine Performance Assignment Center (MPAC). Supervised a system support group of 15 employees responsible for assigning telephone numbers and tracking central office equipment. Collaborated with engineers to add or replace central office equipment.

EDUCATION
~~~~~~
REGIS UNIVERSITY, Colorado Springs, Colorado (2006 to 2019)
Courses in business management

CONTINUING EDUCATION
Computers: Microsoft Word, Excel, PowerPoint, Internet Explorer, Outlook
Leadership: Quality Team, Leadership Renewal, Team Problem Solving, Initial Management Course, Team Building, Project Management, Labor Relations
Training: Train the Trainer, Detailed Quality Engineering

AFFILIATIONS
~~~~~~
Executive Women International, vice president and various committees. Coordinated the national conference hosted by the Denver chapter. Selected the location, lodging, meals, hospitality room, and conference agenda.

Silver Key, board of directors, seven years.

MATTHEW C. GELLER
1234 Knoll Lane, Apt. 123
Colorado Springs, Colorado 80917
Home: (719) 555-1234
Cellular: (719) 555-5678
E-mail: mcgeller@protypeltd.com

BACKGROUND
==
Experienced Engineer with a strong background in these areas:
* Electro-mechanical systems
* Research and development
* Hydraulics and pneumatics
* Robots and robotic controllers
* Lasers and optics
* Servo systems
* Precision measuring instruments
* Extremely close tolerances

Eight years of experience servicing medical equipment in the field and
factory, including x-ray, mammography, hematology, and immunoassay
systems. Experienced with FDA inspections and regulations for the
inspection of prototype medical equipment. Extensive expertise in module
integration at the system level. Collaborated with R&D engineers to build
and test prototyped enhancements to existing systems.

STRENGTHS
==
Adaptable engineer who can readily transfer skills and bring a fresh
perspective to any industry. Effective communicator with the ability to
provide exceptional customer service at all levels. Experienced trainer
with extensive hands-on and classroom technical experience. Proficient in
Windows, MS Word, Excel, PowerPoint, Outlook, and Internet Explorer.

MEDICAL EXPERIENCE
==
ENGINEERING SERVICE TECHNICIAN (2006 to 2009)
Lorad, Inc., Danbury, Connecticut
Directed a team of eight electro-mechanical technicians in the construction and testing of mammography and x-ray equipment. Spent 50 percent of
time providing field service to downed equipment in a large territory with
ten hospitals. Collaborated with R&D engineers on design improvements and
prototype enhancements for new product lines. Met with customers to determine liability for warranty problems and negotiated settlements. Trained
new technicians, field engineers, and customers on equipment and tool
repair. Helped write assembly and repair procedures for factory and field
service personnel. Installed and monitored systems at hospital beta test
sites. Provided technical phone assistance to service engineers. Performed
system upgrades in both field and factory settings.

SENIOR ENGINEERING SERVICE TECHNICIAN (2001 to 2006)
Miles, Inc., Tarrytown, New York
Led a team of 15 electro-mechanical, electrical, and test technicians in
the research and development of hematology and immunoassay systems.
Conducted quality control inspections of in-production and finished
modules. Managed materials and production control for the entire product
line. Worked closely with design engineers on product improvements and
prototype development. Responsible for troubleshooting and repairing all

14

electro-mechanical, cable, hydraulic, and pneumatic problems. Wrote all training manuals for new electro-mechanical assemblies. Trained domestic and international field engineers on electro-mechanical systems and served as an expert resource for field service engineers. Transferred systems from an R&D environment to the production plant in Puerto Rico. Trained, installed, and retrofit legacy systems. Accountable for controlling inventory of parts and maintaining repair logs of systems. Installed systems at beta testing sites for FDA approval; collaborated with FDA inspectors on revisions to new systems before production release.

TECHNOLOGY EXPERIENCE
===
SENIOR FIELD SERVICE ENGINEER (2004 to 2012)
SVG Lithography, Wilton, Connecticut / ASML, Tempe, Arizona
Stationed at an Intel chip-manufacturing site in Colorado Springs to troubleshoot and maintain SVG lithography equipment (valued at $10 million) from component to system levels. Installed new tools as they arrived at the site, and performed lithographic testing to ensure tools met customer specifications. Performed system upgrades and modifications at the request of customer and/or factory. Provided technical phone assistance to other sites and managed all warranty issues. Diagnosed and repaired computerized electro-mechanical systems. Maintained and tracked precision-calibrated tools used for system repairs. Trained new employees on all tool phases from module replacement to troubleshooting down to the component level. Interviewed, made hiring recommendations, supervised, and evaluated ten engineering technicians. Wrote training manuals for certain modules and documented repair procedures. Developed an automated journal system that tracked weekly repair time using Excel.

Key Accomplishments: Helped identify a duct work error that was costing Intel $100,000 per shift because of contamination blowing up from the sub-fab. Saved Intel $250,000 by changing motor coils in the system rather than replacing the entire module. Cleaned vacuum ports, which prevented replacement of the system, saving Intel an additional $250,000. Received a Silicon Valley Group award in recognition of outstanding contributions to the MSX and REA build process.

EDUCATION
===
UNDERGRADUATE STUDIES (2009 to 2012)
Duchess Community College, Poughkeepsie, New York

PROFESSIONAL DEVELOPMENT
General Industry Safety and Health (10 hours, 2001)
* OSHA/SVG Safety
* Lockout/Tag Out
* Physical Hazards
* Job Hazard Analysis
* Chemical Hazards
* Hazardous Energies
* Egress and Fire Protection
* Electrical Safety
* Personal Protection/PPE

Micrascan Training (2006)
* Computerized Electro-mechanical Systems
* Environmental Control Systems

How to Compose and Send an E-mailed Résumé

You may be thinking, "I can do this. I'll just skip this section." Don't! Even though the process itself is pretty basic, there are a few tricks of the trade that you should not miss, so please read this section completely.

First, add a cover letter to your e-mail message. Remember that e-mail is intended to be quick, so don't precede your pasted résumé with a long-winded cover letter. A simple paragraph or two that highlights your best qualifications and tells your reader where you heard about the position is all you need. I recommend that you limit your cover letter to no more than two paragraphs, although there are exceptions to every rule in the career business. Here's a sample cover letter that you can paste above your résumé in an e-mail:

> *I found your posting for a Customer Service Manager (Job #12343) on the Internet at Indeed.com and would appreciate your serious consideration of my qualifications.*
>
> *I have more than 13 years of operations management experience that included budget analysis and tracking ($13 million), expense control, staffing, training, and customer service. I have succeeded in significantly controlling costs and maximizing productivity in all my jobs. I could also bring to this position my team spirit, ability to manage multiple priorities with time-sensitive deadlines, and strong communication skills.*
>
> *Pasted below is the text version of my résumé and attached is the MS Word document as your advertisement requested. I look forward to hearing from you soon.*
>
> *Sincerely, Jane Doe*

Next, the subject line is a valuable tool for introducing who you are and what you do. Don't neglect this line. You can use it for your objective statement, to reference the job opening for which you are applying, or to show that you are updating a résumé you have sent previously. Never leave a subject line blank, since that is the hallmark of spam (junk mail). I know that I never open e-mail messages sent to me without a subject line, and I've heard the same comment from many recruiters.

Finally, now you add the text of your résumé. You can type your entire résumé into an e-mail message from scratch, but why would you do that when you have already typed it, spell checked it, and used your word processor's grammar function? When you are composing a cover letter and/or résumé for e-mail, it is always much better to start with your word processor since you can use its powerful grammar and spell check features to make certain your document is perfect before e-mailing it to a potential employer.

After you have created this perfect résumé in your word processor and saved it in plain text format, open the file again in your word processor. On the "Home" tab, choose "Select" and then "Select All" and then "Copy." See the two screen shots on the next page.

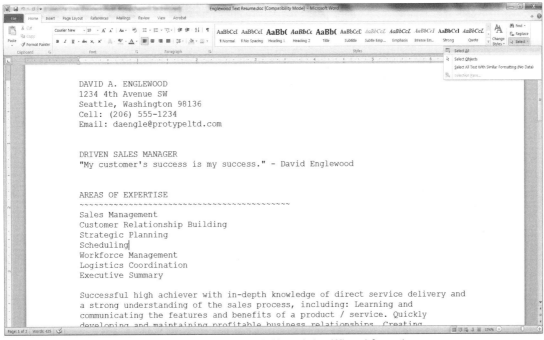

Screen shot of Microsoft Word used with permission of Microsoft Corporation

Screen shot of Microsoft Word used with permission of Microsoft Corporation

Return to your e-mail software. After you have typed in the address where you will be sending your message and added your subject line, click on the message box so your cursor is active in the large white space. Then select "Paste" on the "Home" tab. Your text will appear in the message box. See the screen shots on the next page to visualize the process in Microsoft Outlook.

Screen shot of Microsoft Outlook used with permission of Microsoft Corporation

Now you are ready to attach your Word file and click on "Send." It is as simple as clicking on the paper clip and telling Outlook where to find the file you want to attach. That file can be stored on your hard drive, a CD-ROM, flash drive, or some other digital storage medium.

Screen shot of Microsoft Outlook used with permission of Microsoft Corporation

Once you select the file, it is automatically attached to your e-mail message and is ready to send. Most e-mail programs will automatically log on for you and send your message, or you can schedule it to send later.

One last thing you should do is test the whole process to make sure you have it right. Send the résumé to yourself or a friend, print it, and see what it looks like. Also look at it on your computer screen. If the text and spacing don't translate correctly, this is the time to fix them. Save it again and then try the e-mail one more time. Once it is perfect, you are ready to use the file in e-mail and on the Internet.

MS Word and PDF Résumés

You may be asking why you can't just attach a Microsoft Word file to the e-mail message and forget about this cut-and-paste thing. First of all, when you attach a file to an e-mail message, the recipient of your e-mail will see only what you have typed in the subject line and your brief cover letter in the message box saying that your résumé is attached. If he doesn't have time to double click the attached file to open it immediately, then he will click on "Download Now" to save your résumé on his hard drive. Later, he will have to remember that he has a file to view, recall where he saved it on the hard drive, and then open MS Word in order to view your résumé. Wouldn't you much rather have him begin reading the text of your résumé the minute he opens his e-mail? If he wants to see the formatted version, he can always download your PDF file or MS Word document and look at it later.

There was a time when applicant tracking software could not interpret Adobe Acrobat PDF files, so résumés sent in that format were never added to the databases. That has changed. The majority of these software systems have become capable of importing PDF files and extracting the information into their applicant tracking systems. Résumés created using Adobe InDesign, Corel WordPerfect, Microsoft Works, or Microsoft Publisher should be printed to PDF or converted to MS Word before sending to a hiring company. In an Orange County Résumé Survey, 62.70% of recruiters preferred receiving résumés in MS Word (.doc or .docx) format and 36.10% preferred Adobe Acrobat (.pdf).

If you don't have Microsoft Word software, there are several free programs available online that can save your information in Word or PDF format. Try Google Docs *(docs.google.com)*, ZoHo Writer *(writer.zoho.com)*, Open Office Suite *(download.openoffice.org)*, or Microsoft Office Web Apps *(office.microsoft.com/en-us/web-apps/)*.

Sending plain text embedded in an e-mail message is relatively painless, but attaching word processed files can get complicated. First, both you and your recipient must have the same (or newer) version of the software used to create your "pretty" résumé. For instance, if you created a résumé in Microsoft Word 2010 and your recipient has Word 95, she won't be able to open the file at all.

What if you used a unique font to design your Word résumé, but your recipient's computer doesn't support that font? Then your résumé will adjust to a new default font, and your résumé will look different from how you created it. The newer versions of MS Word and Corel WordPerfect now allow you to embed TrueType and OpenType fonts (but not Adobe Type 1 fonts) in documents, which helps prevent this problem. However, you must set up each document in MS Word 2010 by selecting the "File" tab and then click on "Options," "Save," and "Embed fonts in the file." In WordPerfect X6, you check the "Embed fonts using TrueDoc" box on the "Save As" option. The only negative is that this makes your file quite large, which can cause its own problems when trying to upload to some websites.

There are many things you can't control when sending e-mail. You can't control whether the recipient's printer definition will reformat your MS Word file. And you can't control how your recipient's e-mail software decodes your MS Word file. In order to send files across the network of computers that make up the Internet, binary files must be encoded in a special way before they are sent and then decoded when they are received at the other end. Each file is broken into tiny packets of information and sent across various parts of the Web. At the recipient's end, those packets must be put back together again … and in the right order!

Most e-mail software will automatically encode an attached file, so it is invisible to you. However, sending between different platforms (PCs, Macintosh, UNIX) can sometimes cause problems with decoding.

There are so many things you can't control when sending MS Word and other binary files across the Internet that you want to take the safest route possible. And that route is to cut and paste your plain text file into the body of the e-mail message. Then it is okay to attach an MS Word document or PDF file to the e-mail. Your reader can choose to download it or not, but you haven't lost anything because your résumé is being read right on the screen.

Uploading Your Résumé to the Internet

Once you have the plain text, MS Word, and PDF versions of your résumé stored on your hard drive, you are ready to upload the appropriate one to job boards on the Internet, create profiles, and set up job alerts/agents.

First, upload your résumé to company websites that interest you. Then choose niche job sites that are specific to your industry or specialty. Find them with keyword searches on Google or Yahoo. Lastly, I recommend setting up accounts with one or two job aggregators—like *www.simplyhired.com, www.jobster.com*—and big job boards—like *www.indeed.com, www.careerbuilder.com,* and *www.usajobs.opm.gov.* Some of the big job boards—like *www.monster.com*—are so huge and so full of junk résumés and stale job openings that recruiters are turning to niche sites, free sites *(www.craigslist.com)*, and social networking media to post their jobs. Instead of paying to post jobs on Monster or Career-Builder, recruiters are gravitating toward career sites where they pay only when a candidate has pulled up their ad and either clicked through to the company's website or applied through the career site itself. It won't take long for the mega-career sites to adapt to this pay-per-click format, but for now, you should cover all of your bases.

On job boards and company websites, you will have the option of uploading the MS Word file of your résumé, filling out their online résumé builders, or cutting and pasting your ASCII text résumé into e-forms on their websites. For the last two options, open your plain text résumé in MS Word, highlight the portions of your résumé that you need for each block on the e-form, and then paste the text into the form. There is no reason to retype information that has already been spell checked.

CareerBuilder offers you the option of browsing and uploading your résumé, which most of us would assume would be an MS Word file. However, if you do upload a formatted, "pretty" résumé, it will look jumbled when you go to preview it. CareerBuilder is actually looking for a plain text file.

Regardless of where your résumé is saved on the Internet, refresh it every month by changing a word or two and resaving it. Some sites have a "refresh" button so you don't have to change anything. Just click the button once per month and your résumé will be back on top of the heap.

While you are at it, create a profile at each site and set up a job agent that will send job openings to you every day or every week that match your keywords and geographic preferences.

Don't just post your résumé and wait for employers to find you, which happens less than 7% of the time. Creating job agents allows you to take control of your search by responding to each job that interests you.

There are privacy issues to consider when setting up these accounts. The threat of identity theft, job scams, and exposure to spam are real issues on the Web, although it happens much less often than you think. Use your common sense when you look for jobs online, including work-at-home offers. Job-hunting scams rank fifth on the Better Business Bureau's top ten scams and rip-offs, so you should evaluate each job advertisement with a healthy dose of skepticism. If it sounds too good to be true, it probably is.

Expect to get a lot of junk e-mail after setting up accounts with job boards. You will get spam, work-from-home offers, get-rich-quick schemes, and true scams, but they are easy to spot and sort out. If you have a favorite e-mail address that you want to keep forever, you might want to consider setting up a separate e-mail account just for your job search so you can trash it once you are finished looking for a job. Then you won't continue to get inundated by spam and other junk e-mail.

So, what Internet resources should you use to reach the right recruiters and hiring managers? If you are an active job seeker who is either unemployed or actively looking for a new job, post your résumé on job boards, résumé databases, and social networking sites. Develop an e-folio and/or blog. Look for print advertising and job fairs.

Passive job seekers, on the other hand, are reached by recruiters through referrals, networking, blogs, e-folios, résumé databases, niche websites, professional associations, social networking sites, and even competitive intelligence. Passive job seekers are already working and are usually the star performers working for other companies.

Career professionals like me have known for years that hiring managers and recruiters discriminated against applicants who were not currently employed, but it has only been in the past five years that you will find them admitting it openly. There isn't anything illegal about focusing a search on passive job seekers, so it will help your search if you keep your job until you've found another one. If your résumé says you are presently working, you will have a much better chance of being considered a serious applicant. As long as the economy is in a recession and there are many more job seekers than job openings, employers will consider those still holding a job the cream of the crop.

If you have applied for a job online and are now sitting around waiting to hear from an employer, then you might want to consider a new CareerBuilder tool. *HireINSIDER* gives you insight into the jobs you've applied for by providing you with information about other people who have applied to the same job, including

- **Number of Applications**—How many people have applied? Were you first or last?
- **Years of Experience**—Are you competing against senior or entry-level candidates?
- **Education Level**—What types of education are you up against? Master's degree? Bachelor's degree?
- **Current Salary**—How much is your competition making now?
- **Top Majors**—What did your competition study in college?
- **Cover Letter Usage**—Is everyone submitting a cover letter? Should you submit one?

Katharine Hansen's Quintessential Careers Annual Report emphasizes that face-to-face job search techniques are more important than ever. She recommends stepping away from your computer to network with warm bodies. Deploy a combination of job boards, social media, and networking. You should remain vigilant about the downsides of job boards and learn how to use them most effectively. It's easy to spend too many hours trolling job sites instead of doing the harder work of calling and meeting people, so monitor yourself closely and cast as wide a net as possible.

Today, more than ever, job searching is about who you know and who knows you. It's also about identifying the needs of potential employers and demonstrating that you can fill these needs. The next chapter will address your online branding presence in the form of a personal website, e-folio, and/or a blog, which will allow you to connect your proven knowledge, skills, and abilities with the needs of those employers.

e-Folios, Blogs, Visual CVs

3

Imagine a musician playing her latest composition, a teacher incorporating a video of his teaching style, a poet reading clips from her poetry, or an entertainer demonstrating his latest dance steps. The creative juices are flowing! Web-based, HTML résumés and e-folios are the perfect places to showcase skills that are better seen (or heard) in all their glory, but that's not the limit.

If you are a C-level executive, self-employed consultant, computer programmer, website developer, politician, graphic designer, artist, sculptor, chef, actor, model, animator, cartoonist, poet, writer, or anyone who would benefit by the photographs, graphics, animation, sound, color, or movement inherent in a Web-based portfolio, then you should definitely read this chapter.

If you don't fall into one of these categories, read the rest of this chapter anyway, because you will be surprised how an e-folio can enhance your job search and help you manage your career even while you are currently employed. If you want to control what a hiring manager sees when you are "Googled," then a well-designed and promoted e-folio and/or blog are your answer. They allow you to control your online image and differentiate yourself. Having an online presence should be a critical piece of your career management plan.

Before we get into the details, though, let's talk about the various names for these online forms of your résumé so you don't become confused. According to Webster, a portfolio is "a hinged cover or flexible case for carrying loose papers, pictures, or pamphlets," "a set of pictures (as drawings or photographs) usually bound in book form or loose in a folder," or "a selection of a student's work (as papers and tests) compiled over a period of time and used for assessing performance or progress." Well, substitute the case or book for a website and the student's work for your work and you have an e-folio.

I held a contest among the nearly 500 members of the National Résumé Writers' Association to find the perfect name, but even though Cheryl Minnick (a career adviser at the University of Montana, Missoula) came close with CareerDocs,

> *If you are "Googled," then a well-designed and promoted e-folio and/or blog are your answer to being found.*

25

e-folio couldn't be beat, so I will use the word *e-folio*. You might find an e-folio called CareerDocs, Visual CV, CareerFolio, Portfolio, Personal Branding Portal, CareerDock, Professional Portal, Career Hub, and various versions of Web Resume (without the accents).

A Web Résumé or an e-Folio?

A Web résumé is simply your paper résumé converted to a website using HTML codes. It is rather basic without a lot of extra information. Instead of having a single page on your website, however, a Web résumé is usually divided into sections that are accessed through hyperlinks from an introductory page—Career Objective, Summary, Skills, Experience, Education, Affiliations, and so on. You can add information that you couldn't include in your paper résumé, but the more information you add, the more like an e-folio your Web résumé will become.

If you have more information about your career than you can practically include in a résumé, then an e-folio is a great option for making this additional information available to a potential employer. An e-folio provides visible evidence of your knowledge, skills, abilities, and core competencies. It features links to proofs of performance that control how your target audience views your unique value proposition. Make sure your website looks professional, though. You want to establish a virtual rapport with your site visitors so you can emotionally connect with them.

You've heard the old saying "A picture is worth a thousand words." That is the primary advantage of e-folios. They are more tangible with links to PDF files, scanned images, podcasts, and video downloads. You can talk about what you've accomplished in words (either on paper or verbally) from now until doomsday, but nothing makes an impression like tangible, visual backup, especially today when so many recruiters and hiring managers are skeptical of claims made on résumés.

Another advantage of an e-folio is the first impression it makes. Dr. John Sullivan, head professor of Human Resource Management in the College of Business at San Francisco State University, says that "because portfolios take some effort, they demonstrate a degree of commitment on the part of the candidate that is not required in a résumé ... so it improves the quality of new hires."

Most of us think of artists, models, actors, and photographers when we think of a portfolio, but that's not the case today. Everyone should maintain a portfolio. More and more employers are asking to see concrete evidence of the experience, skills, education, and accomplishments shown on your résumé, especially during the interview.

An e-folio allows you to present additional details that expand on your résumé, such as the following:

- Case studies
- Project lists
- Career highlights
- Consulting gigs
- Leadership initiatives
- Volunteer experience
- Photographs
- Professional affiliations
- Board positions
- Your blog and archives
- Links to your favorite blogs

- Credentials
- Education
- Certifications
- Achievements
- Skills and strengths
- Patents
- Honors and awards
- Endorsements
- Upcoming events
- Technical competencies
- Sales statistics

- Media interviews
- Presentations
- Demonstrations
- Speaking engagements
- Publications
- Book reviews
- Newsletters
- Links to favorite blogs/sites
- Frequently asked questions
- A recommended reading list
- Writing samples

Keep an "I Love Me" File

For years, in my own practice, I've been advising my clients to keep an "I Love Me" file with things that expand on or support the outline that is inherent in their résumés, including:

- Performance evaluations
- Job descriptions
- Letters of recommendation
- Thank-you notes from customers, vendors, or supervisors
- Sales statistics
- Growth charts
- Writing samples
- Awards and honors
- Scanned product images
- Photographs
- Three-dimensional items (like packaging or products)

If you have collected this information during your entire career, then you have the foundation for an e-folio that will help you sell your special abilities and manage your entire career. If you haven't, then create an e-folio with whatever you do have or can get your hands on now. It's never too late to start collecting for your "I Love Me" file.

Your e-folio or visual CV cannot take the place of your paper résumé, plain text résumé, and MS Word or PDF file. In today's busy world, most recruiters and hiring managers have so little time to read résumés that they are turning to applicant tracking systems to lighten their load. Unless they are highly motivated, they won't take the time to search for and then spend 15 minutes clicking their way through a multimedia presentation of someone's qualifications, often called a visual CV. To see some examples of visual CVs using SlideShare, go to this website: *workawesome.com/career/top-10-powerpoint-resume-presentations-on-slideshare/*. Or check out *http://re.vu/* for another way to create a visual CV.

The real purpose of an e-folio is to manage your online reputation and to provide extra information for when a potential employer is trying to narrow down his or her applicant pool. You can even direct the hiring manager to your website during an interview. You are more likely to be Googled at the weeding-out stage, which is either just before an interview offer or after the interview. That is when an e-folio becomes truly valuable. It might just tip the scales when a hiring manager is trying to choose between you and someone else.

You should always direct your reader to your e-folio by listing the URL on your résumé, letterhead, personal business card, and e-mail signature. Place your URL in the appropriate field on job boards and social networking profiles so recruiters can click on the link to get more information about you—information that you control.

Quick Response (QR) codes serve the same purpose but with a different format. A QR code provides an image that can be photographed with a cell phone, which leads someone directly to any URL on the Internet—preferably your e-folio. There are many free QR code generators on the Internet, and you can learn more about how to use them by putting "how to create a QR code" into any search engine. Google provides page after page of "how to" guides and code generators, so I won't go into those details here.

One caveat about e-folios, blogs, and visual CVs. Don't expect to get a job offer by simply creating an e-folio and waiting for a recruiter to find you. You must still be proactive in your job search by signing up for job agents on the major job boards, applying for each job that interests you, and networking in the real world like crazy.

e-Folios for More Than Job Hunting

Besides keeping your résumé in front of recruiters by being on the Internet all of the time, a well-planned e-folio is great for formal employment interviews, networking, informational interviews, performance assessments and evaluations on your current job, admission to colleges and universities, easily accessed information for your references, and an archive that lets you download your résumés from anywhere in the world (think Hurricane Katrina), among other functions. It is a professional self-marketing tool that can help you manage your entire career.

An e-folio is especially useful for entrepreneurs and consultants, since it can serve as a marketing tool for whatever products or services they sell. If you think about it, though, we should all be treating our careers as "entrepreneurial" ventures. When you take control of your career as a business owner controls his or her company, you make conscious choices about how to market your product—in the case of your career, that's you. Your résumé becomes your print advertising, and your e-folio is your online brochure that persuades a "buyer" to call you instead of the "competition."

An e-folio is also a great career management tool that you don't have to save just for your job search. Imagine preparing for your annual performance evaluation with your current employer by reviewing the accomplishments you have collected in your "I Love Me" file and putting together either a paper-based or Web-based portfolio. When it is time to sit down with your supervisor and talk about what you have achieved this year, you can take control of the discussion by making a "sales presentation" of your accomplishments and tangible examples of work samples. What an impression you will make! You've got a raise!

Don't wait for your annual evaluation to think about using this tool. Many companies have implemented performance assessment programs that are ongoing with periodic meetings throughout the year to assess goals, milestones, and incremental achievements toward objectives.

If your company isn't that progressive and barely uses annual performance evaluations, let alone performance goal setting, then make yourself stand out in the crowd of other employees by being proactive. Develop your e-folio or paper portfolio and set the meeting with your supervisor yourself. Take charge of your career path and show your entrepreneurial spirit. Remember that entrepreneurship is all about "ownership," and you can own your career whether or not you own the business for which you work. This kind of independent thinking is often rewarded with promotions and/or pay increases that reflect your value to the company. It also makes your job more secure, since you have proven value to your employer. With downsizing the norm in today's workforce, the more valuable you are, the less likely you are to be laid off. Companies are in the business of making money. If you make your employer more money than you cost to keep around, it just makes business sense that you will be retained.

When developing an e-folio, avoid proprietary/confidential employer information, personal information, family photographs, or negative comments about previous employers. If your website developer recommends a design that includes automatic background music or a lot of Flash programming, think twice before agreeing. They tend to be irritating to site visitors.

It is easy to overdo an e-folio or visual CV. It is sometimes hard to narrow down the items you want to include, so people have a tendency to make their e-folios much too long. Dr. Sullivan feels that a world-class portfolio has the following five characteristics:

1. It must be scannable in 15 minutes or less.
2. It sells you with your work and your ideas.
3. It is customized for each job and each company.
4. It includes and highlights your accomplishments.
5. It excites the viewer.

Portfolio Ideas by Job Type

Everybody's e-folio will be different, especially across industries and job titles. Even when two people share the same position in the same company, they shouldn't expect the contents of their e-folios to be the same. We each have our own unique backgrounds, qualifications, and accomplishments. However, there are some basic items that will appear in all e-folios:

1. A home page that highlights your unique value proposition with a tagline and/or vision statement, executive summary, areas of expertise, contact information, your blog, and links to archives. If you use work samples, photographs, graphic images, or testimonials on your e-folio, get permission to use them first. Integrate social media links, video, audio, or anything that enhances your professional image.

2. A résumé—Your résumé (or bio in some cases) generally serves as the foundation of your e-folio. If it is well written, your résumé determines the basic outline for your website and helps you decide what sections to include. Don't simply rehash your résumé verbatim in your e-folio, however, or there is no point to your website. Summarize and expand on your résumé with job descriptions, employer reviews, work samples, problem-solving examples, organizational charts, leadership examples, customer survey results, proposals, business plans, and so on.

3. Proofs of performance—These can be charts or graphs if your accomplishments are quantifiable (like in sales and positions with P&L responsibility where you can show your bottom-line results), copies of publicity, articles you have written, photographs, videos, company newsletters, white papers, special projects, newspaper or magazine articles, thank-you letters from supervisors/customers/vendors, performance evaluations with key accomplishments highlighted, honors, awards, archived blog articles, volunteer or community affiliations, and so on. If any of the information you want to use is copyrighted by someone else, you will need to get written permission to use it on your website first.

4. Credentials—This is where you back up your education, special training, licenses, certifications, and other credentials with scanned images of your diplomas, certificates, transcripts (for some positions), and other proof documents. Lists of major course work and select projects might be included if you are a recent graduate with little experience.

5. Recommendations—Scan your letters of reference from past employers, current supervisors, key customers or vendors, and other people who know your work well. Highlight key phrases or simply type a list of quotes with the person's name, job title, and company. These third-party recommendations validate what you say about yourself in your own documentation.

Once your e-folio has the five basics, you can add other things to make it unique. Rather than repeat the items above for every industry, the lists below are in addition to your résumé, credentials, recommendations, and proofs of accomplishments (although some items fall into this category just to give you more ideas). Use your imagination. These lists are just jumping-off points for your own creativity, which is really what you are trying to display in your e-folio anyway.

Accounting & Finance

- Charts showing improvements in revenues, profits, ROI, EBITDA, etc.
- Special projects, i.e., automation projects, business performance optimization
- Mergers, acquisitions, joint ventures, and divestitures
- Client and/or industry specialties
- List of accounting software expertise

Administrative Assistant

- Lists of technical competencies
- Processes and procedures you improved
- Examples of various document preparation skills—correspondence, spreadsheets, PowerPoint presentations, forms, organizational charts, etc.
- Photos, agendas, budgets of events planned
- Letters of appreciation
- Certificates from classes, workshops, seminars, conferences

Antiques & Art Dealer

- Areas of expertise
- Select finds and sources
- Valuation/appraisal experience
- Restoration experience with photos
- International travel
- Import/export
- Apprenticeships and other hands-on experience
- Education and credentials
- Letters or comments from clients

Apartment Manager

- Photos of properties
- Size and types of units (luxury, family, senior citizen)
- Amenities
- Construction or renovation
- Occupancy rates
- Special promotions, events, and open houses
- Activities for residents
- Graphics representing impact on the bottom line

Architect

- Drawings, photographs, blueprints
- Styles
- Honors and awards
- Media coverage
- Professional affiliations
- Presentations
- Letters from satisfied customers and builders
- Acknowledgments from peers
- Parade of Homes participation

Artist (includes painters, sculptors, illustrators, designers, cartoonists, or anyone producing a visual art)

- Mediums
- Education and special training
- Photographs of artwork
- Published works
- Reviews in magazines, newspapers, and other publications
- Lists and photographs of exhibitions
- Representations
- Museum collections
- Descriptions of style and artist philosophy
- Hyperlinks to online displays of artwork

Athlete

- Sports
- Media coverage
- Records and times
- Competitions
- Honors and awards
- Coaches, trainers

Attorney

- Areas of specialty
- Credentials—diplomas, licenses, etc.
- Track record of success
- Client testimonials
- Lists of significant cases
- Legal precedents established
- Bar and court admissions
- Presentations
- Professional affiliations
- Pro bono work
- Volunteer board positions

Chef

- Menus
- Photographs of plated dinners and banquet presentations
- Thank-you notes from customers
- Certificates of completion from special training programs
- Participation in stages and international programs
- Reviews in magazines, newspapers, and other publications
- Honors, awards, contests, chef's tables

Computer Professional

- Photographs of software packages or manuals
- Examples of a unique or difficult code and its result
- Screen shots of GUI interfaces
- Charts and graphs that show increases in productivity or profitability as a result of the finished product
- Technical skills divided into types
- Special projects
- Technical documents produced

Construction

- Areas of specialty
- Photos of completed projects
- Honors, awards, Parade of Homes, etc.
- Proof of licenses and bonding
- Letters from satisfied customers
- Community participation
- Professional affiliations

Customer Service Representative

- Letters from satisfied customers
- Awards for exceeding quotas
- Customer service scores
- Contributions to sales growth
- Personality tests (like Myers-Briggs) that show an aptitude for working with people

Diplomat

- Negotiations, conflict resolutions, treaties
- Languages, cultures
- Special events
- Media coverage
- White papers, publications
- Pictures with famous people
- Noteworthy speeches and other presentations

Economist

- Credentials are very important in this industry—education, degrees, training
- Areas of expertise—energy, inflation, imports, employment, monetary policy, consumer theory, markets, profits, costs, public policy
- Examples of research and analysis
- Expertise with statistical analysis software
- Sample spreadsheets, graphs, charts
- Publications
- Presentations
- Publicity

Editor

- Education and special training
- Writing samples
- List of own published works
- Types of editing—fiction, creative nonfiction, trade, nonfiction
- Editing samples—both hard copy and digital
- Titles of books edited

Engineer

- New products developed
- Drawings
- Schematics
- White papers
- Research
- Patents awarded or pending
- Products redesigned and their financial impact
- Project planning, management, results
- Integration of advanced technologies
- Education and credentials
- Media attention
- Honors and awards

Event Planner

- List of functions
- Venues
- Entertainment
- Menus
- Photos of decorations
- Thank-you letters and other kudos
- Print promotions, invitations, newspaper coverage
- Video clips

Executive

- Executive summary
- Management philosophy
- Charts and graphs reflecting impact on the bottom line, performance improvement data, expansions
- List of business competencies showing levels of expertise
- Description of a major problem, your solution, and the result
- Leadership examples, recruitment and leadership of successful management teams
- Evidence of strategic planning and long-term business development
- Participation in joint ventures, mergers, acquisitions, divestitures, etc.
- Organizational charts showing subordinate personnel and areas of responsibility
- Affiliations and professional memberships with any leadership positions

Firefighter

- Certifications
- Areas of expertise
- Education and training
- Professional development
- Community involvement
- Special projects
- Professional affiliations
- Promotion record

Flight Attendant

- Photographs—head shot and full-body shot
- Special training
- Letters of appreciation from customers
- Recognition from supervisors
- Routes—domestic or international
- Languages and cross-cultural experience

Florist

- Lots of photographs that show quality of work
- Examples of different styles and types of arrangements
- Artistic designs using other media besides flowers
- Comments from satisfied customers

Groomer

- Photographs, photographs, photographs!
- Show dogs and champions
- Styles
- Humane treatment philosophy

Health Care

- Impact on quality of care and outcome initiatives
- Expansion of health care services and programs
- Implementation of advanced health care support technologies
- Proof of accreditation
- Letters of appreciation
- Licenses, credentials, continuing education
- Teaching, in-services, workshops
- Professional affiliations

Hospitality

- Lists or photos of hotels or restaurants managed
- Growth charts showing proof of impact on the bottom line
- Occupancy rates
- Letters of appreciation from satisfied guests
- Property improvements/construction/renovation
- Operating improvements
- News coverage
- Grand openings

Human Resources

- Measurement of recruiting success
- Employee benefits packages, expand services, lower costs
- Interview worksheets
- Motivational and training programs
- Union negotiations
- Documentation of faster hiring or better retention
- Proof of lower costs for the hiring process
- Industry association participation
- Implementation of new technologies to manage the hiring process
- Measurable improvements in organizational performance/productivity

Inventor or R&D

- Areas of expertise
- Patents
- Photographs of inventions
- Professional associations
- Presentations and academic assignments
- Publications and white papers
- Media coverage

Jeweler

- Photos! Photos! Photos!
- Design specialties—rings, necklaces, bracelets
- Testimonials from customers

- Materials expertise—gold, silver, platinum, precious stones, stone cutting, jewelry repair

Manufacturing

- Proof of product development
- Charts and graphs showing process improvements
- Implementation of new technologies, robotics, and processes
- Safety improvement
- Improvements in quality; award of quality certifications
- Increases in production yield/output and worker productivity
- Reductions in operating costs and overhead expenses
- Schematics, blueprints, designs, technical drawings

Marketing

- Marketing plans
- Advertising programs (video, print, voice)
- New media productions (websites, CD-ROMs)
- Focus group design and results
- Proposals
- Photographs
- Results, results, results!

Mechanic

- Areas of specialty
- Photos of body work or design
- Certifications
- Testimonials from satisfied customers
- Location of shop with map

Minister

- Religious philosophies
- Family photos
- Personal information about children and spouse
- Sermon outlines
- List of topics
- Letters and comments from church members and leaders
- Presentations and special teaching assignments
- Media coverage
- Video clips or radio broadcasts

Model

- Photos, photos, photos!
- Copies of magazines or newspaper coverage
- Fashion show advertisements and runway shots

- Specialty areas
- Languages, singing, acting, musical instruments, sports, etc.
- Videotapes of commercial spots, movie appearances, etc.

Museum Curator

- Special events with invitations, photos, media coverage
- Lists and photos of special exhibits
- Fund-raising results
- Speakers acquired
- Permanent exhibits and acquisitions
- Capital improvements
- Advertising and promotions, including brochures, museum literature, television, radio, and print campaigns

Musician

- Recordings of performances and/or compositions made into sound files for the e-folio and CD-ROM
- Reviews in magazines, newspapers, and other publications
- Conservatory and special training programs
- Performances
- Honors, awards, contests

Nonprofit Sector

- Fund-raising
- Event planning
- Capital campaigns
- Volunteer management
- Areas of specialty
- Low turnover of employees and volunteers
- Publicity, media coverage

Photographer

- Photos! Photos! Photos!
- Genre specialties
- Recognitions, honors, awards
- Exhibits (both solo and group)
- Purchases—museum, gallery, business, individual
- Media reports and reviews

Physician, Nurse, or Other Health Care Practitioner

- Licenses and other credentials
- Degrees
- Research projects
- Grants, awards, and honors

- Patient testimonials
- Philosophies
- Academic appointments and teaching assignments
- Publications
- Presentations
- Professional affiliations
- Community service

Police Officer

- Special projects and committees
- Community involvement
- Areas of expertise
- Education and special training
- Awards and honors

Professor

- Education and credentials are very important
- Courses developed and taught
- Research and development
- Professional presentations
- Publications—books, journals, and other periodicals
- Special committees and projects
- Student evaluations
- Administrative responsibilities
- Awards, honors, and other recognition
- Community involvement

Project Manager

- Lists of projects
- Outcomes
- Processes—needs analysis, resource allocation, project scheduling, product development, budgets, implementation
- Letters from satisfied customers (internal and external)

Radio Broadcaster

- Audio clips of shows, promos, jingles, etc.
- Expertise with digital editing equipment and other technology
- Examples of original scripts, journalism, and other writing
- Community outreach
- Promotions

Real Estate Agent

- Sales achievements—graphs, awards, honors
- Areas of specialty

- Success stories with photographs
- Client comments

Recent Graduate

- Diplomas
- Scholarships, grants, awards, honors
- Samples of class papers, projects, reports, videos
- Transcripts or lists of relevant courses
- Course descriptions to add keywords and depth
- Teacher evaluations
- Community service projects
- Clubs, honor societies, fraternities, sororities, and leadership

Sales

- Types of products sold, customers, and territories
- Documented achievements—increased revenue or profits
- Charts and graphs
- Significant account acquisition
- Number of leads generated and converted
- Closing ratio
- New territory or market development
- Sales honors, awards, trips, etc.
- Letters from customers
- Sale team-building exercises
- Training and motivation programs developed and presented
- Results, results, results!

Scientist

- Areas of specialty
- Special projects
- Inventions
- Patents
- Professional affiliations
- Honors, awards, or other special recognition
- News reports
- White papers
- Research
- Grants
- Presentations

Social Services

- Areas of specialty
- Credentials, licenses, diplomas
- Testimonials from clients helped

- Professional affiliations
- Volunteer work

Speaker

- Video of key presentations
- Areas of expertise
- Topics, prices, and schedules
- Honors, awards, accolades
- Future speaking engagements
- Past audiences
- Invitations to share your expertise
- Thank-you letters
- Membership in speaker organizations
- Photographs of you in action
- Brochures from events

Superintendent (of Schools)

- Leadership philosophy statement
- Certifications
- Strategic plans
- Measurement of student achievement
- Fiscal accountability
- Capital campaigns, grants, fund-raising
- Community interaction
- Program development
- Continuous quality improvement initiatives
- Other key initiatives
- Professional development
- Honors and awards
- Community service
- Continuing education
- Publications
- Research

Teacher

- Teaching philosophy statement
- Lesson plans, syllabi, curricula
- Photographs of bulletin boards, classroom decorations, and learning aids
- Staff development projects, training other teachers
- Measurements of student achievement
- Examples of special challenges and how you overcame them
- Degrees, transcripts, continuing education—credentials are very important
- Examples of community partnerships, legislative or volunteer work, special committees

- Student portfolios or other proof of your legacy
- Affiliations and professional memberships

Technology

- Lists of technical competencies
- Development of new technologies and their impact on the organization
- Financial benefits, including savings, cost reductions, revenue gains, etc.
- Patents awarded or pending
- Technology transfer programs
- Involvement in emerging technologies

Television Newscaster

- Lists of major stories covered
- Writing examples
- Video clips
- Areas of specialty—hard news, breaking news, feature stories
- Professional head shots
- Promotional materials created by the station

Translator

- Writing examples
- Lists of special projects
- Areas of specialty
- Languages and levels of proficiency
- Teaching or tutoring programs developed and presented
- Letters of appreciation

Web Designer

- Examples of websites to show off your designs
- Link to pages to emphasize what makes them unique—Java scripts, flash graphics, e-commerce features
- Letters from satisfied clients
- List of technical competencies
- List of projects and clients with hyperlinks to their sites

Writer

- Poems
- Excerpts from published works
- Media coverage
- Reviews
- Copies of articles in newspapers and magazines or hyperlinks to the online version of the article

e-Folio Sample

Kirsten Dixson, co-author of *Career Distinction: Stand Out by Building Your Brand*, develops unique, executive-level portfolios that she calls "personal brand portals." Kirsten agrees that "an e-folio is much more effective when it does more than just reiterate a person's paper résumé." She is also adamant that the design of the website does not detract from its message.

Kirsten believes that a good e-folio will do the following:

1. Position your unique value to your audience in a controllable way.
2. Feature links to proofs of performance/accomplishments.
3. Showcase thought leadership in the person's industry.
4. Integrate social media.

With Kirsten's permission, on the following pages you will find examples of two sophisticated e-folios, one with a blog and one without. For more samples, check her website at *www.kirstendixson.com*.

When you develop a website for the first time, deciding what message you are going to convey and then laying out the flow of the site to facilitate delivery of that message is the key to an effective finished product. Patricia Moriarty (the sample e-folio that follows) is a specialist in education and technology curriculum integration, so her website focuses on her knowledge, skills, and abilities in this arena. Her site is laid out using the outline beginning on the next page.

Introduction

- A summary paragraph of history and qualifications.

- A list of areas of expertise.

- A keyword list of personal attributes or strengths.

- The introduction is the place for your personal branding statement, the unique value you bring to the job.

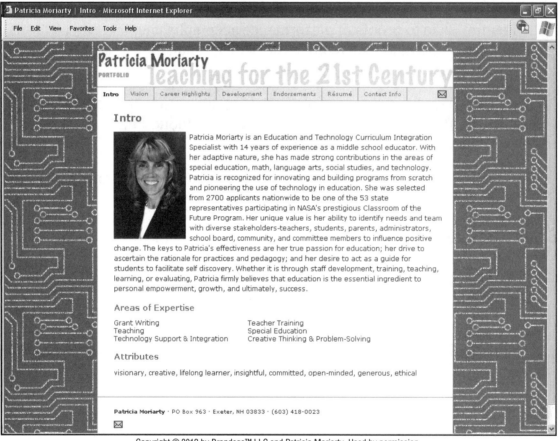

Vision

- A statement of personal philosophies about that work, which reveals values, vision, goal, purpose, etc.

- Notice that every page of the website contains the following:

  – Full links to every other page of the site.

  – Full contact information at the bottom of the page to make it easier for a potential employer to call.

  – A little envelope that jumps directly to a contact form that the viewer can use to send an e-mail immediately.

- The point is to make the site easy to navigate.

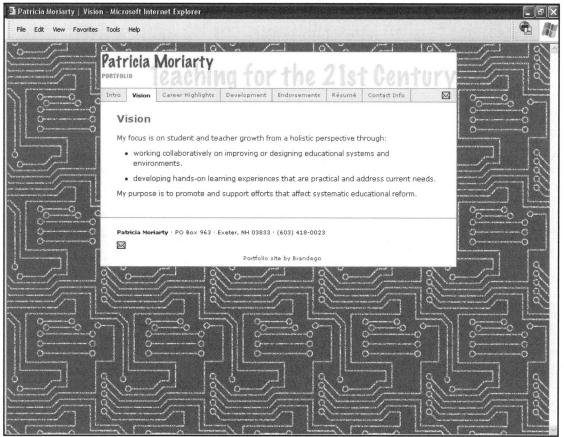

Career Highlights

- This section is not just a reiteration of the résumé. I especially like the fact that you don't have to use the "Back" button to return from the scanned images to the main page.

- Details of the NASA Classroom of the Future Program:
  - Challenge, Action, Results (CAR) statements
  - Scanned image of the citation
  - Scanned image of a newspaper article

- Details of the Technology Literacy Program:
  - CAR statements
  - Scanned image of a Compaq training certificate
  - Scanned image of a newspaper article

- Details of a New Hampshire Special Education Grant:
  - CAR statements
  - Quote from the parent of a former student

- Details of a State Work-to-School Grant:
  - CAR statements
  - Scanned image of a newspaper article

- Details of her study abroad:
  - CAR statements

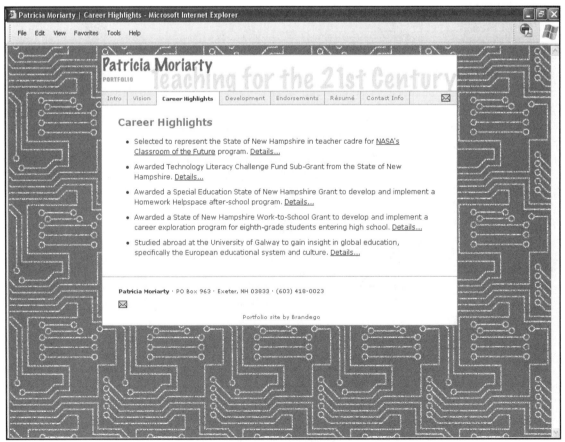

Development

- Formal Education:
  - Scanned images of master's degree
  - Scanned images of bachelor's degrees
- Ongoing Professional Development:
  - Scanned images of various certificates

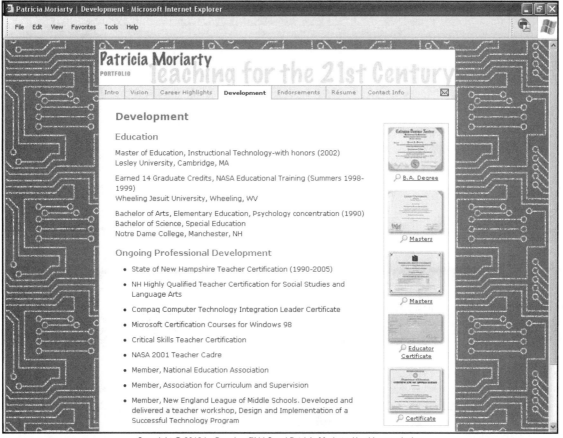

Endorsements

- Quotes from former students
- Quote from a parent of a former student
- Quotes from colleagues
- Quotes from an administrator

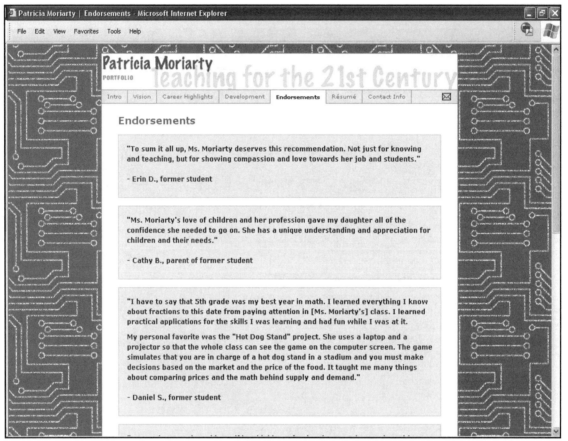

Résumé

- The complete paper résumé is re-entered here using HTML formatting.

- The reader can choose to download a PDF or plain text version of the résumé. Even though this screen shot allows the reader to download an MS Word file, I don't recommend making the MS Word version of your résumé available this way. Someone could download your formatted résumé and use it to steal your identity or tweak it to use the content or style. If a recruiter needs an MS Word file, he or she can always call you to request it.

- The text file can be downloaded by the viewer for input into computerized applicant tracking systems.

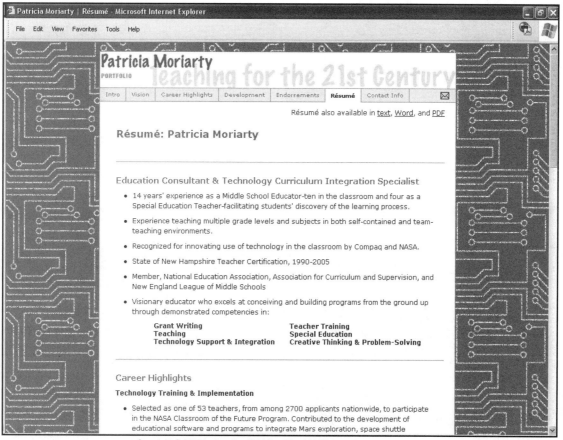

Contact Info

- In addition to the full mailing address and telephone numbers at the bottom of the page, this page provides a form that the viewer can complete and e-mail directly.

- If you have only a cellular number, always identify it as a cell phone so the viewer knows they can try to reach you during business hours.

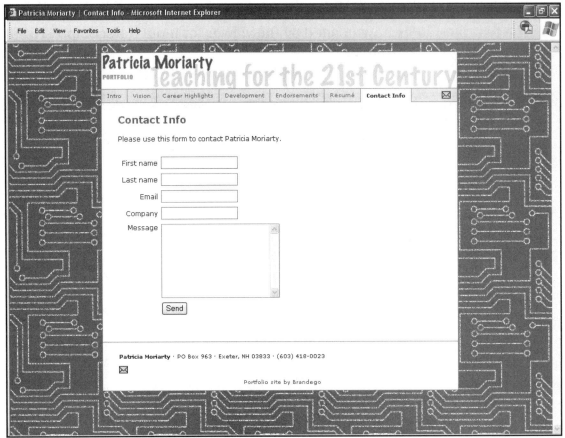

Blogs for Personal Branding

The word *blog* is a rather new invention. It didn't exist before 1999. According to Webster, *blog* is short for *weblog*, which means "a website that contains an online personal journal with reflections, comments, and often hyperlinks provided by the writer."

Blogs are more revealing and authentic than résumés. Blogs are interactive spaces where you can see inside a prospect's head—their ability to think, write, communicate, and innovate. A blog gives an employer more of your essence and helps you to distinguish yourself. If your industry has a bazillion blogs, then it could hinder your job search if you don't have one, too.

As I mentioned earlier, the vast majority of potential employers will Google you either before issuing an interview invitation or after the interview to narrow down applicant choices. That means you need to Google yourself to see if there is anything negative about you on the Web. If you do find something bad, you can try to get it removed, but it isn't always possible.

There are services on the Internet that will research your online reputation, help you repair it, and then manage your online brand for a fee. I have no personal experience with these services, but if you have a bad online reputation, it might be worth researching these companies by Googling the following terms: *online brand management* or *online reputation management*. Your best bet, though, is to bury negative search results with more recent, positive links to an e-folio and/or a blog.

A blog is both an electronic business card and a tool for reinforcing the credentials on your résumé. A blog doesn't replace your résumé; it simply gives it credibility. Katharine Hansen, PhD, says in her Quintessential Careers website, "A good blog can establish you as a thought leader in your field by projecting confident expertise and current commentary about emerging trends." Dr. Hansen recommends "blogging with purpose" and "interviewing leading experts in your field and blogging about them to raise your profile."

Blogs may work best in certain fields, like high-tech, marketing, writing, and C-level management, but anyone can have a blog. If you are a successful blogger, you will stand out from the crowd of bloggers in your industry, so be persistent.

Search engines love blogs because they are updated frequently and are often cross-linked to other blogs and websites. That means your e-folio with a blog can rank higher in organic searches than almost any other mention of your name when you are Googled. Bloggers often link to each other's postings, so there is the potential for viral publicity and exposure to audiences you never even considered.

You don't have to be a Web designer to create a simple blog or website. Some of the applications available for blogs include TypePad, WordPress, Google Blogger, Movabletype, Posterous, Drupal, Joomla, Vignette, Blogger, and BlogHarbor. Some are more difficult to use than others, so take advantage of their free videos and trial periods to see which one works best for your level of technical experience.

If you create a blog, you must be a good writer. A blog should be engaging and perfect in grammar, spelling, and punctuation. If that is not one of your skills, then consider hiring a writer to help you fine tune your articles. If you aren't willing to commit to keeping up a blog, then create an e-folio, comment on other people's blogs whenever you can, subscribe to e-lists, and write articles or book reviews.

It's a good idea to outline your content and categories in advance. Write a week or two of posts before your website goes live. That way you won't feel pressured to write an article every day in the beginning. You should make a habit of posting an article to your blog once a week at the very least. Two or three times a week or daily are the best. Search for blogs in your industry by using *www.technorati.com.* Find subject-matter experts in your field and follow them for a while to get inspiration. But stay away from controversial topics.

Be careful about writing blog posts about your current employer or you may find yourself unemployed. Check with your HR department about the company's blogging policies. Avoid writing something that might be construed as embarrassing or negative. Don't talk about specific projects, trade secrets, compensation, benefits managers, colleagues, or proprietary, confidential, or competitively sensitive information about your employer.

Lastly, include the Web address of your blog on your résumé, letterhead, business cards, e-mail signatures, and social networking profiles. Syndicate your blog using RSS software. The better known you are, the more likely you are to turn up on page one of a Google search.

Christian Anscheutz's e-folio is a great example of using a blog as a career management tool to raise visibility and credibility for one's personal brand. On this page and the next two, you will notice how he built his e-folio around a blog that is industry focused. If you click on the first "Posts" tab, you will find his blog content. Christian has used Google+ as his e-folio/blog platform.

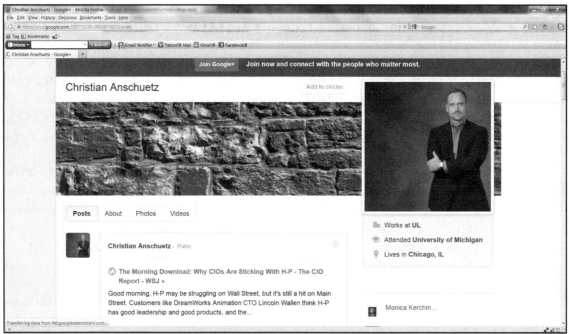

Also on the "Posts" tab, you will find a video incorporated into a blog post (see the first screen shot on the next page). This is a great use of multimedia technology in a blog. He also used graphics from the *Wall Street Journal* when he quoted articles from the newspaper in his blog. The name alone generates confidence in what Christian has written, but a picture speaks a thousand words.

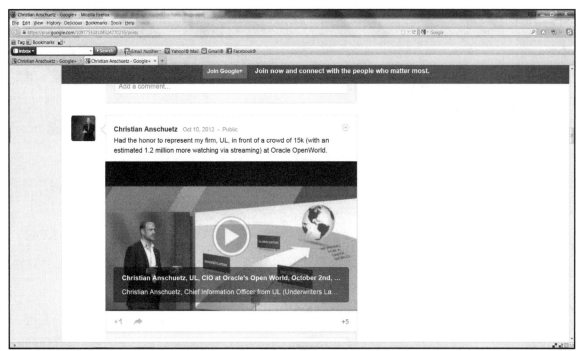

Under Christian's "About" tab, you will find his profile with extracts from his résumé. You will notice that, under his photograph, he has given a few biographic facts that appear on each page, regardless of the tab selected—current employer, college attended, and where he lives (see the screen shot at the bottom of the previous page). His employment history continues on down the page, ending with links.

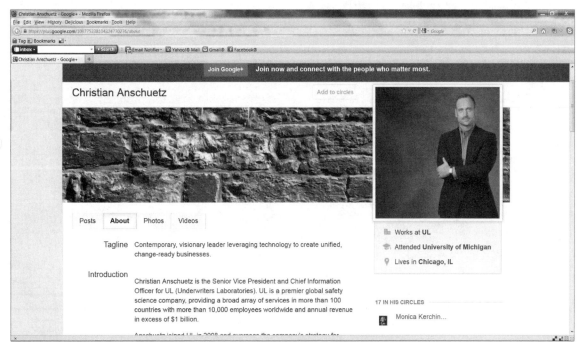

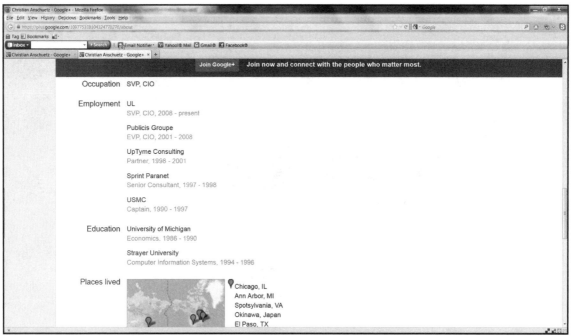

At the end of the "About" tab, there are hyperlinks to his LinkedIn account, his bio, Facebook page, and other supporting information. Readers can download his PDF résumé or sign up for his blog feed. See the screen shot below.

Search Engine Optimization

Search Engine Optimization (SEO) is the use of keywords and other techniques designed to bring a website to the top of a search in Google, Yahoo, Bing, and other search engines.

Optimizing the content of your website is about using keywords in such a way that you show up in the results when it matters.

SEO isn't just about your website content anymore. Twitter feeds, Facebook comments, blog posts, and more are now being picked up by search engines. Optimizing your social media channels and blog can increase the number of indexed pages. It is a fact that people who blog have 434% more indexed pages than those who don't.

So, what gets the attention of search engines? Fresh, well-written content that changes frequently. Search engines are primarily popularity contests. Google gives each Web page a number called a "PageRank." The more sites that link to your page and the higher the PageRank of those sites, the higher your page will display in search engine results. The same goes for blogs. The more popular and "fresh" the blog, the higher it ranks, so add to your blog frequently and comment on other people's blogs. Including your full name in your website's titles and other meta tags will make it easier for search engines to rank you.

Peter Brown, an SEO expert and Web traffic analyst, suggests five ways to draw traffic to your website and raise your SEO score:

1. **Article Marketing**—Write 300-word articles that explain your site and how it will benefit the visitor. Submit them to article directories, like *ezinearticles.com*, *goarticles.com*, or *articlesbase.com*. Write at least five articles initially, and then follow up with an article a day or at least one a week.

2. **Backlink Building**—Search for websites similar to your own and propose a link exchange to their Webmaster. Search engines judge a site's popularity by the number of links pointing to it. They assume that your site offers something worth linking to if other people want to link to your site.

3. **Search Engine Optimization**—Set up meta tags in the HTML coding of your website and use keywords in your page titles. Make sure that 5–7% of your site's content includes targeted keywords, which is known as your page's keyword density. To research what words people are searching for, go to *www.wordtracker.com* or *www.keyworddiscovery.com*. Enter a few sentences about the content of each page in the description field of the HTML code.

4. **Social Bookmarking**—When a visitor to your site likes your site's content and goes to a social bookmarking site (like *digg.com*, *delicious.com*, *technorati.com*, *stumbleupon.com*, *reddit.com*, etc.) and then tags your site's content with keywords, others can then find your site through that tag. Submit your site to a dozen or more social bookmarking sites by using *onlywire.com*.

5. **Pay-Per-Click Advertising**—You can pay for Web traffic, but it can be very expensive. Google AdWords is the leader in pay-per-click advertising. Extremely broad keywords can cost a lot, so make your keywords highly targeted if you decide to go this route.

To gauge your SEO efforts, go to *google.com/analytics* to measure how many people visit your site and how they got there. *Siteexplorer.search.yahoo.com/mysites* allows you to monitor the number of outside links to your site and where they originated. Xinu *(xinureturns.com)* runs a battery of diagnostic tests on your site to evaluate your title tags and keywords.

Using Social Networking Sites

Social media sites (like LinkedIn, Facebook, MySpace, Twitter, and YouTube) are quickly growing as a recruiting method for passive candidates, particularly executives who aren't actively looking for a job but have specialized skills and experience that is difficult to find. Often, the most talented and sought-after recruits are those currently employed. One of the benefits of Internet social networking technology is that it can increase the diversity of the talent pool available to recruiters.

Oracle found CFO Jeff Epstein via LinkedIn in 2008. Since Home Depot started using social networking sites for recruiting, it has cut in half the time it takes to fill a job opening. Social networking sites are used by 47% of recruiters before actually contacting the applicant for the first time, and 41% use social networking sites before the first formal interview. Another 37% use these sites before making an offer.

Companies are increasingly using Twitter to broadcast their job openings. This might mean the death knell for job boards, but they are integrating social-media functions to create hybrid sites that take advantage of the best features of both. For instance, Jobster has joined forces with employers to enhance its career networking platform on Facebook. Recruiters can promote specific job openings and tap into referrals at Jobster.

The vast majority of recruiters conduct a Google search on applicants before interviewing them, and 60% of all online users are now members of a social network. That means recruiters are almost guaranteed to see your e-folio, as well as your LinkedIn, Facebook, MySpace, Twitter, and YouTube profiles. For that reason, your social media profiles should be customized to reflect your personal brand so they become billboards that showcase your talents.

Does your Facebook page have incriminating photos, dubious comments, and questionable friends? Then remove them now and password protect the family and friends area to keep the public out. Don't let your children or other people use your computer to bookmark "favorite" videos and Web pages or to Tweet others. If a YouTube video gets linked to your Facebook account, you could end up appearing to endorse things that could harm your personal brand.

LinkedIn Profiles

Of all the social networking sites, LinkedIn is intended to be the most career oriented, so use it to the max. According to Jessi Hempel writing in *Fortune* magazine, "Facebook is for fun. Tweets have a short shelf life. If you're serious about managing your career, the only social site that really matters is LinkedIn. More than 187 million members have created LinkedIn profiles … and these include your customers, your colleagues, your competitors, your current boss, and possibly the person about to interview you." Professionals are currently signing up to join LinkedIn at a rate of approximately two new members per second, so that number becomes larger every day.

One caveat. LinkedIn doesn't work for everyone. It isn't as effective for teachers, cashiers, administrative support, or seasonal workers as it is for corporate executives and hard-to-fill IT, engineering, supply chain, and global sourcing positions, ones usually filled by recruiters and not with simple classified ads.

LinkedIn also allows you to connect your online professional interactions in one place—join groups on the site (companies, school alumni, affiliations), offer advice, and link your e-folio, blog, and Twitter account to your LinkedIn profile.

Your LinkedIn profile is very important and should lead recruiters to your website, e-folio, visual CV, or blog. You can customize the URL of your public profile on LinkedIn to make it appropriate for your job search. Enter "customize my public profile URL" in the help menu for full instructions.

So, how can you make your social networking profiles stronger? Think of your profile as an introduction and not a résumé. You can always embed a link to the PDF file of your résumé if someone wants more information. Use your own, unique voice when you write this "elevator pitch." Develop a tagline that reflects your "brand." The line of text under your name is the first thing people see, so make it count. Add references from past and current colleagues who can address your accomplishments. Sign up for LinkedIn groups that reflect your professional interests, and participate by posting comments, answering questions, linking to relevant websites, and recommending others.

Take a look at the sample LinkedIn profile starting on the next few pages. It includes Julio's experience, education, areas of expertise/skills, recommendations, groups, résumé, shared connections, answers to questions, advertisements, contact information, and a status bar that can be linked to Twitter feeds. This sample LinkedIn profile is courtesy of Rosa Elizabeth Vargas of Creating Prints in Denver *(www.creatingprints.com)*.

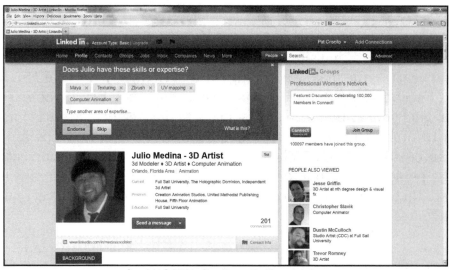

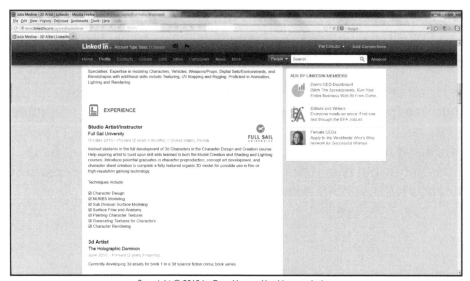

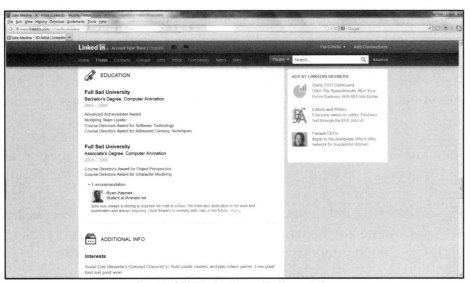

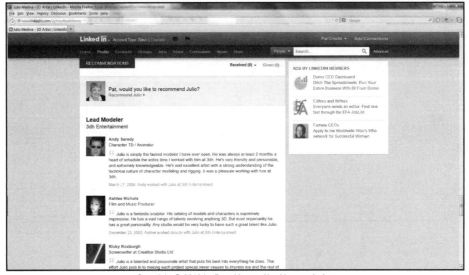

The "Specialties" field of LinkedIn is a great place to list your industry buzzwords, passion, values, and even humor. This section is searchable, so think carefully about your career goals when you decide which words to include here. Explain your experience in the profile succinctly. In the "Additional Information" section, round out your profile with a few key interests. Make sure you link to your e-folio and/or blog.

All social networks can help you tap into your Six Degrees of Separation. You can search for people you know, and the people they know, and the people they know … until you reach someone in your dream company. Even if you aren't connected, you can research people who either worked there in the past or work there now to determine what sorts of background and education it took to be successful there. Then contact that person to pick his or her brain.

Don't forget to use all of the social networking sites to research the company before your interview. What's good for the goose is good for the gander.

Step 1
Focus

4

The first step in writing the perfect résumé is to know what kind of job you will be applying for. A résumé without a focus is never as effective as one that relates to a specific job description. If you don't know what you want to be "when you grow up," now is the time to see a career counselor. He or she can help you define where your skills and interests lie through tests and interest inventories.

You can either pay a professional career counselor for these services or approach your college's career services center for help. Some colleges and universities work only with currently enrolled students, whereas others provide their services to anyone who ever graduated from their institution. Some of these services are free and others are available for a fee.

For help in finding your alma mater's career services center, check the list of websites at the end of this chapter. To look into the credentials of a career counselor or coach, check the following websites:

- International Coach Federation, *www.coachfederation.org*
- Certified Career Coaches, *www.certifiedcareercoaches.com*
- Career Coach Institute, *www.careercoachinstitute.com*
- Career Counselors Consortium, *www.careercc.org*
- The Coach Connection, *www.findyourcoach.com*
- Professional Association of Résumé Writers and Career Coaches, *www.parw.com*
- Noomii Professional Coach Directory, *http://www.noomii.com/career-coaches*

If you are an active duty member of or are separating from a military service or are a reservist or a member of the National Guard, you are eligible for free career counseling through your service's transition assistance program. There are professional career counselors available on military bases, or you can use their online assistance program at *www.taonline.com*.

> *A résumé without a focus is never as effective as one that relates to a specific job description.*

Your Passion

Do you have a purpose for your life, something that drives you every day when you get out of bed? Or do you feel like something is missing, like you are just going through the motions every day? Marcia Bench of the Career Coaching Institute *(www.careercoachinstitute.com)* is convinced that "You will experience success in your life to the extent that you are clear about your life purpose."

Knowing your passion can help you determine the focus of your résumé. To help you find that focus, Marcia has developed a list of Clues to Your Life Purpose, which I will list here in shortened form with her permission. For more information on the clues, check Marcia's website, *www.careercoachinstitute.com/pdf/DiscoveringYourLifePurpose2.pdf.*

Clue 1: What do you love to do? That is, when you have spare time, how do you like to spend it?

Clue 2: What parts of your present job or life activities do you thoroughly enjoy?

Clue 3: What do you naturally do well? What has always come easily to you?

Clue 4: What are your ten greatest successes to date (in your eyes)?

Clue 5: Is there a cause about which you feel passionate?

Clue 6: What are the ten most important lessons you have learned in your life?

Clue 7: Are there some issues or perceived problems that have occurred over and over again? Out of one of these repeated issues may come your greatest lessons.

Clue 8: What do you daydream about doing? It is in your subconscious mind that your beliefs reside, as well as your deepest desires for success and fulfillment.

Clue 9: Imagine you are writing your epitaph. What things do you want to be remembered for at the end of your life? What things will your life be incomplete without? If you had only six months to live, what would you do differently from what you are now doing?

Clue 10: What would you do if you knew you could not fail?

You should take the answers to the ten clues and evaluate them for any themes. Those themes can then be distilled down into an essence, the core of your purpose that is relatively unchanging. They represent your core values and core mission, which can be used to define your core competencies, the things you do very well. They will help you focus your résumé and give it a "theme."

After gathering this information and developing your focus, the next step is to decide what needs a potential employer might have that would benefit from your core competencies. Your résumé will be evaluated by its readers to see if you can solve their company's problems and whether or not you will be worth your pay. You need to focus the information more on *who you are* than on *what you want*. I will talk more about this in Chapters 9 and 14.

Your Brand

Research by the Gallup organization suggests that the most effective people are those who understand and operate in their areas of natural talent, a.k.a. passion or unique value proposition or personal "brand."

Branding has been used in the corporate world since the first product was created and marketed, but the concept has only recently been applied to individuals. Just like for a business, your personal brand is what distinguishes you from other people. Think of Coke and Pepsi. They are not selling a bubbly brown water. They are selling their *brand*, what each one represents, their unique features (taste, bottle shape, logos) and benefits (refreshing, thirst quenching, satisfying).

By determining your passion, and consequently your *brand*, you can become a career activist, setting your own career direction by determining short- and long-term goals that have meaning for *you* and implementing them by acquiring the education, training, and experience you need to succeed. You are truly in charge of your career rather than being the victim of your employer's whims.

"By being your own career boss, you decide which positions you will take, how much effort you will invest in each job, and how you will handle the challenges you'll inevitably encounter. You control how you present yourself and your intellectual and emotional assets," say Kirsten Dixson and William Arruda in their book, *Career Distinction: Stand Out by Building Your Brand (www.careerdistinction.com)*. "Just doing your job, and even doing it well, is no longer enough. Every day, in everything you do, you tell the world about yourself, your values, your goals, and your skills. In fact, you already have a brand—even if you don't know what it is and even if it isn't working for you the way you'd like it to. Clarify and [purposely] create your personal brand in order to achieve career distinction. Then, communicate that brand unerringly to those around you."

Peter Weddle, career researcher and consultant *(www.weddles.com)*, feels, "Career activism is essentially a pair of commitments you make to yourself; bringing the best you can be to work each day and improving your personal best every day. Those promises provide the only real security there is in today's volatile and perilous workplace ... because you are relying on yourself."

Your passion, or brand, and how it relates to your industry's needs, becomes the focus for your résumé. Louise Kursmark, well-known career author and president of Best Impression Career Services *(www.yourbestimpression.com)*, believes, "Truly powerful résumés need to convey a person's brand—what it is about him or her that is unique and differentiating. I strive to include branding statements in the summary of a résumé. Then, throughout the résumé, I show themes and trends during the person's career that reinforce the brand image, which creates a cohesive document that helps to distinguish the person from the competition."

Career Planning Internet Resources

The Internet is also a great source for do-it-yourself help in finding your passion. Although often not as effective as seeking help from professionally trained counselors, it can sometimes give you at least enough information to help you determine a focus for your résumé. Here are some of the career planning and assessment sites I recommend:

Campbell™ Interest and Skill Survey (fee based) . . . . *psychcorp.pearsonassessments.com/HAIWEB/ Cultures/en-us/Productdetail.htm?Pid=PAg115*

Career Intelligence Assessments . . . . *www.career-intelligence.com/assessment/career_assessment.asp*

Career Interests Game, University of Missouri . . . . *career.missouri.edu/students/majors-careers/ skills-interests/career-interest-game/*

Career Direct (fee based) . . . . *careerdirectonline.org/*

Career Explorer . . . . *www.careerexplorer.net/aptitude.asp*

Career One Stop Skills Inventory . . . . *www.careeronestop.org/SKILLS/SkillCenterHome.asp*

CareerBuilder Career Assessment . . . . *www.careerpath.com/career-tests/*

CDD Questionnaires . . . . *kivunim.huji.ac.il/cddq/*

College Board Online . . . . *bigfuture.collegeboard.org/majors-careers*

Columbia University Center for Career Ed . . . . *www.careereducation.columbia.edu/services/assessment*

iMap My Career (fee based) . . . . *secure.imapmyteam.com/MyCareer/CP.aspx*

iSEEK Skills Assessment . . . . *www.iseek.org/careers/skillsAssessment*

Job Profiles.com . . . . *www.jobprofiles.org*

JobHuntersBible.com . . . . *www.jobhuntersbible.com/counseling/index.php*

Keirsey Character and Temperament Sorter . . . . *www.keirsey.com*

Live Work Transitions . . . . *www.lifeworktransitions.com/exercises/*

LiveCareer Free Career Interest Test . . . . *www.livecareer.com/career-test*

MAPP Assessment . . . . *www.assessment.com/*

Mind Tools . . . . *www.mindtools.com/*

Myers Brigg Type Indicator (fee based) . . . . *www.myersbriggs.org/*

NextSteps.org, Youth Employment Center . . . . *www.nextsteps.org*

North Carolina State University . . . . *www.ncsu.edu/career/students/explore/assessments.php*

O*NET Interest Profiler . . . . *www.mynextmove.org/explore/ip*

QueenDom: The Land of Tests . . . . *www.queendom.com*

Quintessential Careers . . . . *www.quintcareers.com/career_assessment.html*

The Objective Statement

Now that you know what you want to do for a living, take a blank piece of paper and write that focus/objective at the top. This will become the title of your résumé or be used in the first line of the profile section of your résumé to give your reader a general idea of your area of expertise.

True objective statements are not required on a résumé, and often the cover letter is the best place to personalize your objective for each job opening. There is nothing wrong with using an objective statement on a résumé, however, provided it doesn't limit your job choices. As an alternative, you can alter individual résumés with personalized objectives or résumé titles that reflect the actual job title for which you are applying. Just make sure that the rest of your information is still relevant to the new objective.

Adding an objective statement to a résumé you will post on your personal website/e-folio, careerbuilder.com, indeed.com, monster.com, or other job site can severely limit your possibilities. It is better to be a bit more generic in stating your goals, although you still need to stay true to your passion/brand. In other words, if you want a sales or marketing position and you are willing to consider multiple industries, it is better not to state the industry or specialty of your expertise in your objective.

Having said that, never write an objective statement that is so imprecise that it says nothing at all about your focus. In your paper résumé, you should name the position you want so specifically that, if a janitor came by and knocked over all the stacks of sorted résumés on a hiring manager's desk, he could put yours back in its right stack without even thinking about it. That means saying

A marketing management position with an aggressive international consumer goods manufacturer.

instead of

A position that uses my education and experience to mutual benefit.

Here are some examples of specific objective statements for various industries:

- **AIRLINE PILOT:** Career as a United Airlines Flight Officer.

- **APPRAISER (entry-level):** Registered appraiser seeking an apprenticeship with a progressive appraisal service specializing in commercial real estate.

- **CHEF:** An executive chef position in a gourmet à la carte restaurant.

- **CUSTOMER SERVICE:** A customer service position in the airline industry, preferably in the Chicago area.

- **ELECTRICAL ENGINEERING:** A position in electrical engineering at the technician/integration level.

- **FACILITY MANAGEMENT:** A high-level facility/safety program management position.

- **FLIGHT ATTENDANT:** A career as a flight attendant with Southwest Airlines.

- **GENERAL MANAGEMENT:** A management position where an MBA and 12 years of experience can be combined with positive interpersonal skills, initiative, and the capacity to motivate others.

- **HEALTH CARE MANAGEMENT:** To be an integral part of the management of a progressive, visionary health care organization.

- **INTERNATIONAL MANAGEMENT:** A senior management position in a marketing or related capacity for a multinational company with operations in Latin America.

- **MARKETING:** A challenging marketing and/or public relations position that utilizes international experience in a dynamic company whose vision is truly global.

- **MARKETING MANAGEMENT:** A marketing management position with the opportunity to develop and implement marketing strategies that will promote innovative products and/or services. Or: A management position in international sales/marketing in the entertainment industry.

- **MEDICAL ASSISTANT:** A position as a medical assistant that will also utilize back office skills gained in five years of experience. Or: To work in a medical office where I can utilize my skills in both back and front office procedures.

- **PARKS AND RECREATION:** A permanent parks and recreation position that will utilize my knowledge, skills, and experience in outdoor education, natural resource interpretation, and/or park maintenance.

- **PHARMACEUTICAL SALES:** Eager to make the transition into pharmaceutical sales where a dynamic personality and strong work ethic could be used to grow market share and increase the profitability of a territory. Or: A challenging and rewarding career in pharmaceutical sales.

- **RESPIRATORY THERAPIST:** Registered Respiratory Therapist desiring a position with a progressive hospital that needs proven leadership, teaching, and clinical skills.

- **RETAIL SALES REP:** A retail kiosk coordinator position with Verizon Wireless.

- **SALES / ACCOUNT EXECUTIVE:** A sales and marketing position with the opportunity for advancement into management. Or: An account executive position focusing on new business development opportunities.

- **SEMICONDUCTOR MANUFACTURING:** A position with Intel as a Process Engineering Technician. Or: A position as a clean-room operator or an entry-level maintenance technician position.

- **SOFTWARE DEVELOPMENT:** A challenging position in software requirements analysis, testing, or training. Or: An entry-level, object-oriented software development position.

- **SPORTS MANAGEMENT:** A challenging position in sports management and/or training in a hotel or resort.

- **SYSTEMS ENGINEERING:** A systems engineering position combining outstanding customer and communication skills with leading-edge information technology experience. Particularly interested in emerging system requirements engineering and architecture methodologies, strategic planning for information technology, and business process re-engineering for technology insertion.

- **TRAINING:** A challenging opportunity in corporate or industrial training.

You will notice that occasionally the job title is capitalized as if it were a proper noun. You have some creative license when you write and design a résumé, just like advertising copywriters do. You can choose to capitalize the job title to make it stand out, or you can use the grammatical conventions of capitalizing it only when you personify the title, as I did in the airline pilot and respiratory therapist objectives.

College Career Service Centers

As I mentioned earlier, if you are presently a student at a college or university, your career services center is a great place to start a job search. In addition to skills and interest assessments, many of these schools maintain a résumé database of all their students that can be accessed by companies worldwide.

College career service centers are connected with many employers who list entry-level job openings and internships available to students of that particular school in job banks. Take advantage of those internships and other work experiences long before your graduation. Join student chapters of professional associations, like the American Marketing Association, American Geological Association, and so on. Doing so will produce marketable keywords that will help your electronic résumé pop to the top in a keyword search.

Sometimes colleges offer reciprocal services to students of other schools, but the only way to find out is to make a telephone call to the career center of the school nearest you. Alumni associations are another good place to start. There is an Internet site at *www.careerresource.net/carserv/* that is an excellent source for hyperlinks to hundreds of college alumni services. Check there first to see what type of support your alma mater provides. Colleges and universities often offer their alumni the same services as current students, but others limit free services to a year after graduation. Again, check your school just to make sure.

College career service centers may have a home page or a hyperlink from the university's main home page where you can find lists of the career resources available from your particular school. In addition, most major universities and colleges post their own job openings on the school's home page.

To locate online information about universities and colleges in general, including the addresses for their home pages, check the following resources:

Campus Explorer	*www.campusexplorer.com/*
Career Resource Home Page	*www.careerresource.net*
College View	*www.campusexplorer.com/*
Fifty States	*www.50states.com/college/#.ULxhVIZcGrg*
Index of American Universities	*www.clas.ufl.edu/au/*
Peterson's Education Center	*www.petersons.com/college-search.aspx*
U.S. Universities and Community Colleges	*www.utexas.edu/world/univ*

Résumé Sections

In the next chapter, we will begin the process of dividing your information into major headings. Before we start, let's review what those potential titles can be.

Your *objective statement* (should you decide to use one) can be titled as follows:

- Objective
- Goal
- Interests
- Career Objective
- Career Goal
- Job Target

Education is "Education," but it could also be one of these:

- Credentials
- Professional Development
- Continuing Education
- Training
- Some other variation

The *profile*, or *qualifications*, section of the résumé can be called the following:

- Profile
- Qualifications
- Highlights of Qualifications
- Expertise
- Strengths
- Summary
- Synopsis
- Background
- Professional Background
- Executive Summary
- Highlights
- Overview
- Professional Overview
- Capsule
- Keyword Profile

The *experience* section could be headlined with one of these terms:

- Experience
- Relevant Experience
- Professional Experience
- Work History
- Employment History
- Employment Summary
- History
- Professional History
- Related Employment
- Business Experience
- Employment Record
- Career History

When you pull out your *achievements* into a separate section, you can use any of the following subtitles:

- Accomplishments
- Key Accomplishments
- Representative Accomplishments
- Related Accomplishments
- Highlights of Accomplishments
- Achievements in the same combinations

You might have noticed the addition of *related* or *relevant* before some titles. Use these adjectives when you want to drop some of your experience and focus on a certain industry or job function. Remember, your résumé is just an advertisement. It's not intended to give your reader every ingredient in the soup can. Its purpose is to provide enough information to prompt a hiring manager to pick up the telephone and call you for an interview. You can leave off entire jobs in a résumé. By using the words *related* or *relevant,* you automatically tell your reader that there is more to the story but you have intentionally chosen to leave something out because you thought it would be a waste of the reader's time.

Step 2
Education

5

The second step in writing a résumé is to think about your education. That means all of your training and not just formal education (college, university, or trade school). The education section of your résumé will include degrees, continuing education, professional development, seminars, workshops, and sometimes even self-study.

Turn to the forms at the end of this chapter and list any education or training that you think might relate to your job search. If you participated in college activities or received any honors or completed notable projects that relate directly to your target job, then this is the place to list them. A business student might cite a marketing plan developed for a specific class, or a graphic designer might describe artwork created for a website and provide a link. Think also about relevant course work, volunteering, internships, clubs, honor societies, fraternities, and sororities.

Take advantage of internships, temporary jobs, and volunteering to gain valuable experience in your target industry. As little as five hours of volunteering or interning a week can add meat to your résumé. If you are working toward becoming a teacher, volunteer for after-school programs. If you want to be a nurse, then volunteer at hospitals, nursing homes, or hospices.

Showing high school education and activities on a résumé is appropriate only when you are under twenty and have no education or training beyond high school. Once you have completed either college courses or specialized technical training, drop your high school information altogether.

Which Came First ...

If you are a recent college graduate and have little relevant experience, your education section will be placed at the top of your résumé. As you gain more experience, your education almost always gravitates to the bottom.

There is an exception to every rule in the résumé business.

There is an exception to every rule in the résumé business, however, so use your common sense. If you are trying to change careers and recently went back to school to obtain new credentials, your education section will appear at the top of the résumé even if you have years of experience. Think about your strongest qualifications and make certain they appear in the top half of page one of your résumé.

How you choose to list your school and degree can make a difference in how the reader perceives the importance of each item. For instance, in the following education section, the name of the university is prestigious, so I chose to list it first so the reader would focus on the school. The job seeker had little real experience, so I provided valuable keywords by listing areas of study under each major. The GPA was relevant because he was competing for jobs through the school's career services center, which required GPAs on all résumés.

SOUTHERN METHODIST UNIVERSITY, Cox School of Business, Dallas, Texas
Bachelor of Business Administration, May 2012
- *Major in Management Information Systems* (166 credit hours, GPA 3.9): Database Design and Administration, Business Computer Programming, Advanced Programming Techniques, Systems Analysis Design, Information Systems in Organizations, and Telecommunication Design and Policy.
- *Minor in International Business:* Introduction to World Cultures, International Politics, International Economics, and the Global Perspective.
- *Awards:* SMU Scholarship, Who's Who Among Students in American Universities and Colleges.
- Selected for a special Electronic Commerce Honors Course that provided in-depth, hands-on experience in the use of the Internet to help companies achieve competitive advantage, transform relationships with customers, suppliers, and business partners, and empower global business.
- Completed a yearlong mentoring program with a senior executive at Southwestern Bell as part of the SMU Business Associates Program.
- *Honors:* Beta Gamma Sigma National Honor Society for Collegiate Schools of Business, Alpha Iota Delta honorary member of Decision Sciences Institute, Golden Key Honor Society, Financial Management Association National Honor Society, Alpha Chi National Honor Society.

When the degree is more important than the university where it was earned, list your education with the degree first. Prioritize your degrees in order of importance, like this:

PhD IN AEROSPACE ENGINEERING (2012)
University of Maryland, College Park, Maryland
- Dissertation: "The Optimization of Engine-Integrated Hypersonic Waveriders with Steady State Flight and Static Margin Constraints"
- Received a four-year postgraduate research assistantship in the Hypersonic Research Group

MASTER OF BUSINESS ADMINISTRATION, FINANCE (2012)
The Pennsylvania State University, University Park, State College, Pennsylvania
- Graduated *magna cum laude* with a GPA of 3.93
- Graduate Student Association Representative for the MBA program (2007–2011)
- Awarded a Graduate Assistantship in the Real Estate Department during the final semester

BACHELOR OF SCIENCE IN NURSING (2012)
Beth-El College of Nursing and Health Sciences, University of Colorado, Colorado Springs, Colorado
- Recipient of the Outstanding BSN Student Award for outstanding leadership, clinical, and academic achievement (May 2012)
- Handpicked by the university's nursing faculty to help teach Aging Simulations (February 2011)
- Beth-El College of Nursing nominee for the UCCS Student Achievement Award (May 2012)

The Devil's in the Details

Details, details, details … They really do matter. Something as simple as a date in your education can affect your job search. For instance, writing from–to dates (2009–2012) implies that you did not graduate. If you graduated with a degree, list only the year you graduated (2012). Computerized applicant tracking systems and Internet résumé databases are programmed to show that you have college study but not a degree if they see from–to dates.

If you are searching for a job that will use special language skills, cross-cultural experience, or international travel, the fact that you studied abroad or completed a foreign exchange program will be an important addition to your résumé. Study abroad falls under the "Education" category, whereas travel for recreation's sake could be included in a separate "International Experience" section on your résumé, if you are searching for a job that would make that experience valuable.

STUDIES ABROAD
Loyola University, Rome, Italy (Spring 2012)
- Classroom study integrated with European field experiences
ITESM, Monterrey, Mexico (Summer 2011)
- Intensive Spanish language and Mexican culture studies

When you did not complete a degree but have some college study, you can list the degree with the qualification that you have a certain number of credits left to finish, as in the first sample below, or classify the section as "Undergraduate Studies" like the second sample. Whichever method you choose, just make sure it is quite clear that you didn't graduate.

BACHELOR OF SCIENCE, MARKETING (2009–2012)
Hawaii Pacific University, Honolulu, Hawaii
- Two credits short of completing an undergraduate degree
- Selected for the Dean's List
- Relevant course work completed: Marketing Management, Public Relations, Marketing Research, Consumer Analysis, Principles of Advertising, International Marketing, Principles of Retail, Industrial Marketing, Production Management, Principles of Marketing

OR …

UNDERGRADUATE STUDIES

Pikes Peak Community College, Colorado Springs, Colorado
- Banking and Finance Program (2 semesters, full-time)
- Early Childhood Education (3 semesters, full-time)
- Course work included Communications I and II, Minorities, American Indian, Human Relations

Northern Virginia Community College, Fairfax, Virginia
- Liberal Arts Program (1 semester, full-time)
- Course work included English Composition, History/Western Civilization II

Colorado Mountain College, Glenwood Springs, Colorado
- Liberal Arts Program (1 semester, full-time)
- Course work included Introduction to Psychology, Physical Science

I am often asked whether or not to list GPAs on a résumé. My reply is, "If you have a GPA of 3.5 or above, it could help you. From 3.0 to 3.5 neither helps nor hurts you, in most cases. Anything from 2.9 or below can actually hurt your chances of getting an interview." I recommend that you list your GPA if you are a recent graduate whose résumé will be competing against the résumés of fellow students, provided it's a good GPA. Otherwise, leave it off.

As I've already mentioned, there is an exception to every rule in the résumé business, so use common sense. If nearly every résumé you see for your industry has GPAs listed, then you should list yours, too. For instance, in academic circles, a GPA is often important on a curriculum vitae.

Technical and Occupational Training

When you attend a trade school, you receive either a diploma or certificate. This type of schooling can be listed under the "Education" heading or under a separate heading called "Training" or "Technical Training." Following are some examples of various training sections.

MICROSOFT COMPUTER SYSTEM ENGINEER (MCSE) COURSE (2012)
Knowledge Alliance and Executrain, Colorado Springs, Colorado
- Networking Essentials, Administering Windows NT 4.0, Windows NT Core Technologies, Internet-working Microsoft NT using TCP/IP, Enterprise Technologies, Internet Information Systems

HEWLETT-PACKARD TRAINING (2010–2012)
- MBTI Business Assessment/Application, Understanding Team Development, Interpersonal Communications, Quality Systems, Conflict Management, Peer Appraisal, Applied One-on-One Task Analysis

ACADEMY GRAPHICS (2012)
- Introduction to CADD Systems for PCB Layout and Program File Editing

LICENSED MASSAGE THERAPIST (2012)
Colorado Institute of Massage Therapy, Colorado Springs, Colorado

EMT CERTIFICATION PROGRAM (2011–2012)
Memorial Hospital, Colorado Springs, Colorado
- *General Medicine:* Infants and Children, Chest/Abdomen Injuries, Eye/Face/Neck Injuries, Injuries to the Head and Spine, Musculoskeletal Injuries, Burns, Soft Tissue Injuries, OB/GYN, Allergies, CPR, Diabetes, Seizures, Syncope, Defibrillation, Pharmacology, Patient Assessment/Documentation, Geriatrics, Communication, History and Physical Exam, Medical/Legal/Ethical Issues
- *Emergency Medicine:* Multiple Casualty Incidents, Aeromedical Resources, Extrication and Immobilization, Hazardous Materials, Ambulance Operations, Moving Patients, Trauma Skills, Agricultural and Industrial Emergencies, Splinting, Bandaging and Dressings, Bleeding, Shock, PASG, Drowning, Near Drowning, Diving Emergencies, Environmental Emergencies, Poisoning, Respiratory Emergencies, Airway/Ventilation/Oxygen, Cardiac Emergencies
- *Psychiatric:* Behavioral Emergencies, Violent Patients, Drugs and Alcohol

Continuing Education

Continuing education, or professional development, shows that you care about lifelong learning and self-development, so think about any relevant training since your formal education was completed. *Relevant* is the key word here. Always look at your résumé from the perspective of a potential employer. Don't waste space by listing training that is not directly or indirectly related to your target job.

EMT CONTINUING EDUCATION (2011 to present)
American Medical Response, Colorado Springs, Colorado
- EMT Refresher Course (2012)
- CPR First Responder (2012)
- EKG Recognition and Interpretation (2011)
- Basic Trauma Life Support (2011)
- EMT Basic IV Course (2011)

INGERSOLL-RAND TRAINING PROGRAMS

Quality: Six Sigma, ASQ-CQM Refresher Course (Pareto charts, flow charts, cause-and-effect tools, checklists, control charts, histograms, scatter diagrams, activity network diagrams, affinity diagrams, interrelationships diagraphs, matrix diagrams, priorities matrices, tree diagrams), Management by Fact

Business: Quality of Leadership, Designing High-Performance Organizations, Project Management, Microsoft Project

CHEM NUCLEAR SYSTEMS TRAINING PROGRAMS
Computers: Global Information Systems (ARC INFO)
Business: Communication, Leadership
Environmental: OSHA Hazardous Materials (40 hours), CPR, Radworker II

GENERAL ELECTRIC TRAINING PROGRAMS

Manufacturing: Manufacturing Management Program (MMP), Manufacturing Studies
Quality: NQA-1 Lead Auditor, KT, Root-Cause Analysis, QC Course, TQM, SPC, WorkOut
Engineering: Verification, Design Files, Change Control, Interchangeability

PROFESSIONAL DEVELOPMENT (Education Career)

- Coaching and Team Building Skills for Manager and Supervisor, SkillPath (March 2012)
- Creating Writers Through Assessment and Instruction, Six-Trait Writing, Northwest Regional Educational Laboratory, Portland, Oregon (December 2004, April 2006, and February 2012)
- Reproducibles for Beginning Writers, Read-Write Connection (February 2012)
- Getting the Most from Microsoft Office (February 2012)
- Formats and Frameworks, Guided Reading and Writing, National Literacy Coalition (November 2011)
- TOP: Creating Writers, Portland State University, Portland, Oregon (Winter 2010)
- Creating Writers Through Assessment and Instruction, Six-Trait Writing (December 2010)
- International Institute of Assessment Leadership, Center for Performance Assessment (35 contact hours, July 2009)
- Teaching to the Standards (Summer 2008)
- Our Future: Expect the Best (Fall 2007)
- Interactive Volleyball Coaching (Summers 2006, 2007)
- Issues Affecting Change, Special Topics Education, Brigham Young University (Summer 2007)
- Volleyball Coaches Clinic, Brigham Young University (August 2007)
- Goals 2000: Performance Assessment (Spring 2007)
- Implementing Standards and Assessments (Fall 2006)
- Curriculum Development and Assessment (Fall 2006)
- Fellow, Colorado Writing Project, Level 1 (Summer 2006)

PROFESSIONAL DEVELOPMENT (Project Management)

- **Project Management Classes:** Process Groups, Managing Projects Within Organizations, Project Activity Planning

- **Leadership Classes:** Effective Mentoring, The Mark of a Leader, Hiring Considerations, Business Continuity Planning, Communicating a Shared Vision, AFSC Certificate to Operate Orientation Training

- **Security Classes:** Information System Security, Cryptography and Network Security, Security Management and Operations Security Practices, Security Architecture and Applications Security, Access Control and Physical Security, Computer Misuse Detection System: KANE Analysis and Audit Software, Defense Security Services: Automated Information System Security Procedures for Industry, Designing a Protection Profile: National Information Assurance Partnership, Information System Security Workshop: SecureInfo Corporation, Windows 2000 Security: DISA, Network Security I/II: DISA, Information System Security Scan: DISA, Smart Force Networking and Telecommunications Fundamentals

- **Network Classes:** Wireless Communication Basics, Architecture and Channels, Networks and Protocols, ISDN Protocols, Routing Protocols, Internetworking: Virtual LANs, Routing Fundamentals, OSI Model, TCP/IP, FDDI, ATM, IEEE Ethernet, LAN Media and Components, LAN Topologies and Techniques, Enterprise Operating Systems, Packet Switching, Analog Networks, Model and Interface Testing, LAN Fundamentals, WAN Technologies, Protocol Layers, Telecommunications Essentials, Data Communications

- **Executrain Classes:** Windows NT 4.0 to 2000, Microsoft TCP/IP on Microsoft Windows NT 4.0, NT Server 4.0 in the Enterprise, Microsoft Internet Information Server 4.0, Implementing and Supporting NT Server 4.0, Networking Essentials, NT 4.0 Workstation

PROFESSIONAL DEVELOPMENT (Nursing Career)
- Completed yearly accredited continuous education and monthly in-service workshops taught by doctors, drug companies, and equipment manufacturers.
- Received Category I credit for attending the Transcatheter Cardiovascular Therapeutics Symposium (TCT) (2010, 2012).
- Attended numerous conferences approved by the American Nurses Association.
- Completed two years of classroom and clinical experience in noninvasive vascular testing from Cevenar Vascular, Hartford, Connecticut.

PROFESSIONAL DEVELOPMENT (Benefits Management Career)
- Completed three parts of the Defined Contribution Course (PA, C1, C2), sponsored by the American Society of Pension Actuaries (ASPA) (2012).
- Attended the annual ASPA conferences and workshops (2010–present).
- Certified in flexible compensation instruction by the Employers Council on Flexible Compensation (ECFC), requiring five years of experience and a proficiency examination.
- Participated in annual ECFC conferences and workshops (2010–present).
- Completed 40 hours of continuing education per year required by the ASPA and Baird, Kurtz & Dobson (2010–present).

COLLEGE EDUCATION

Use this form to collect information on your formal college education. Write down everything you can think of, regardless of whether you use it on the final résumé. You will narrow the list later. There is a separate page included in this section for each degree.

DEGREE _____

SCHOOL _____

CITY AND STATE _____

YEARS ATTENDED _____

YEAR GRADUATED _____ GPA _____

MAJOR _____

MINOR _____

THESIS/DISSERTATION _____

_____

~ ~

SIGNIFICANT PROJECTS _____

_____

_____

_____

HONORS, AWARDS, SCHOLARSHIPS, ETC. _____

_____

_____

_____

ACTIVITIES (volunteer, leadership, sports, social groups, etc.) _____

_____

_____

_____

STUDY ABROAD (program, school, country, special areas of study) _____

_____

_____

COLLEGE EDUCATION

Use this form to collect information on your formal college education. Write down everything you can think of, regardless of whether you use it on the final résumé. You will narrow the list later. There is a separate page included in this section for each degree.

DEGREE _____

SCHOOL _____

CITY AND STATE _____

YEARS ATTENDED _____

YEAR GRADUATED _____ GPA _____

MAJOR _____

MINOR _____

THESIS/DISSERTATION _____

_____

~ ~

SIGNIFICANT PROJECTS _____

_____

_____

_____

HONORS, AWARDS, SCHOLARSHIPS, ETC. _____

_____

_____

_____

ACTIVITIES (volunteer, leadership, sports, social groups, etc.) _____

_____

_____

_____

STUDY ABROAD (program, school, country, special areas of study) _____

_____

_____

COLLEGE EDUCATION

Use this form to collect information on your formal college education. Write down everything you can think of, regardless of whether you use it on the final résumé. You will narrow the list later. There is a separate page included in this section for each degree.

DEGREE _____

SCHOOL _____

CITY AND STATE _____

YEARS ATTENDED _____

YEAR GRADUATED _____ GPA _____

MAJOR _____

MINOR _____

THESIS/DISSERTATION _____

_____

~ ~

SIGNIFICANT PROJECTS _____

_____

_____

_____

HONORS, AWARDS, SCHOLARSHIPS, ETC. _____

_____

_____

_____

ACTIVITIES (volunteer, leadership, sports, social groups, etc.) _____

_____

_____

_____

STUDY ABROAD (program, school, country, special areas of study) _____

_____

_____

COLLEGE EDUCATION

Use this form to collect information on your formal college education. Write down everything you can think of, regardless of whether you use it on the final résumé. You will narrow the list later. There is a separate page included in this section for each degree.

DEGREE _____

SCHOOL _____

CITY AND STATE _____

YEARS ATTENDED _____

YEAR GRADUATED _____ GPA _____

MAJOR _____

MINOR _____

THESIS/DISSERTATION _____

_____

~ ~

SIGNIFICANT PROJECTS _____

_____

_____

_____

HONORS, AWARDS, SCHOLARSHIPS, ETC. _____

_____

_____

_____

ACTIVITIES (volunteer, leadership, sports, social groups, etc.) _____

_____

_____

_____

STUDY ABROAD (program, school, country, special areas of study) _____

_____

_____

COLLEGE EDUCATION

Use this form to collect information on your formal college education. Write down everything you can think of, regardless of whether you use it on the final résumé. You will narrow the list later. There is a separate page included in this section for each degree.

DEGREE _____

SCHOOL _____

CITY AND STATE _____

YEARS ATTENDED _____

YEAR GRADUATED _____ GPA _____

MAJOR _____

MINOR _____

THESIS/DISSERTATION _____

_____

~ ~

SIGNIFICANT PROJECTS _____

_____

_____

_____

HONORS, AWARDS, SCHOLARSHIPS, ETC. _____

_____

_____

_____

ACTIVITIES (volunteer, leadership, sports, social groups, etc.) _____

_____

_____

_____

STUDY ABROAD (program, school, country, special areas of study) _____

_____

_____

VOCATIONAL/TECHNICAL TRAINING

Use this form to collect information on your vocational, technical, occupational, and military training. Write down everything you can think of, regardless of whether it relates to your job goal. You will narrow the list later.

NAME OF COURSE _____

PRESENTED BY (company, school, etc.) _____

RESULT (certification, diploma, etc.) _____

DATES ATTENDED _____

~ ~

NAME OF COURSE _____

PRESENTED BY (company, school, etc.) _____

RESULT (certification, diploma, etc.) _____

DATES ATTENDED _____

~ ~

NAME OF COURSE _____

PRESENTED BY (company, school, etc.) _____

RESULT (certification, diploma, etc.) _____

DATES ATTENDED _____

~ ~

NAME OF COURSE _____

PRESENTED BY (company, school, etc.) _____

RESULT (certification, diploma, etc.) _____

DATES ATTENDED _____

~ ~

NAME OF COURSE _____

PRESENTED BY (company, school, etc.) _____

RESULT (certification, diploma, etc.) _____

DATES ATTENDED _____

~ ~

VOCATIONAL/TECHNICAL TRAINING

Use this form to collect information on your vocational, technical, and occupational training. Write down everything you can think of, regardless of whether it relates to your job goal. You will narrow the list later.

NAME OF COURSE _____

PRESENTED BY (company, school, etc.) _____

RESULT (certification, diploma, etc.) _____

DATES ATTENDED _____

~ ~

NAME OF COURSE _____

PRESENTED BY (company, school, etc.) _____

RESULT (certification, diploma, etc.) _____

DATES ATTENDED _____

~ ~

NAME OF COURSE _____

PRESENTED BY (company, school, etc.) _____

RESULT (certification, diploma, etc.) _____

DATES ATTENDED _____

~ ~

NAME OF COURSE _____

PRESENTED BY (company, school, etc.) _____

RESULT (certification, diploma, etc.) _____

DATES ATTENDED _____

~ ~

NAME OF COURSE _____

PRESENTED BY (company, school, etc.) _____

RESULT (certification, diploma, etc.) _____

DATES ATTENDED _____

~ ~

PROFESSIONAL DEVELOPMENT

Use this form to collect information on your professional development and continuing education, including in-services, workshops, seminars, corporate training programs, conferences, conventions, etc. Write down everything you can think of, regardless of whether it relates to your job goal. You will narrow the list later.

NAME OF COURSE _____

PRESENTED BY (company, school, etc.) _____

DATES ATTENDED _____

~ ~

NAME OF COURSE _____

PRESENTED BY (company, school, etc.) _____

DATES ATTENDED _____

~ ~

NAME OF COURSE _____

PRESENTED BY (company, school, etc.) _____

DATES ATTENDED _____

~ ~

NAME OF COURSE _____

PRESENTED BY (company, school, etc.) _____

DATES ATTENDED _____

~ ~

NAME OF COURSE _____

PRESENTED BY (company, school, etc.) _____

DATES ATTENDED _____

~ ~

NAME OF COURSE _____

PRESENTED BY (company, school, etc.) _____

DATES ATTENDED _____

~ ~

NAME OF COURSE _____

PRESENTED BY (company, school, etc.) _____

DATES ATTENDED _____

~ ~

PROFESSIONAL DEVELOPMENT

Use this form to collect information on your professional development and continuing education, including in-services, workshops, seminars, corporate training programs, conferences, conventions, etc. Write down everything you can think of, regardless of whether it relates to your job goal. You will narrow the list later.

NAME OF COURSE _____

PRESENTED BY (company, school, etc.) _____

DATES ATTENDED _____

~ ~

NAME OF COURSE _____

PRESENTED BY (company, school, etc.) _____

DATES ATTENDED _____

~ ~

NAME OF COURSE _____

PRESENTED BY (company, school, etc.) _____

DATES ATTENDED _____

~ ~

NAME OF COURSE _____

PRESENTED BY (company, school, etc.) _____

DATES ATTENDED _____

~ ~

NAME OF COURSE _____

PRESENTED BY (company, school, etc.) _____

DATES ATTENDED _____

~ narrow ~ ~ ~ ~ ~ ~ ~ ~ ~

NAME OF COURSE _____

PRESENTED BY (company, school, etc.) _____

DATES ATTENDED _____

~ ~

NAME OF COURSE _____

PRESENTED BY (company, school, etc.) _____

DATES ATTENDED _____

~ ~

Step 3
Research

6

What if it has been years since you worked at a job and you can't remember what you did? What if it was just yesterday and you can't remember what you did?! Don't worry. You're not getting old. Most of us forget what we did yesterday, so now we need to come up with some strategies for finding ways to describe your work history.

This chapter will talk about resources for finding job descriptions. The next few chapters will then show you how to use them.

First, get your hands on a written description of the job you wish to obtain and for any jobs you have held in the past, as well as for your current job. If you are presently employed, your human resource department is the first place to look. If not, then go to your local library and ask for a copy of *The Dictionary of Occupational Titles* or the *Occupational Outlook Handbook*. These industry standard reference guides offer volumes of occupational titles and job descriptions for everything from abalone divers to zoo veterinarians (and thousands in between). You can also find them on the Internet (see next page). Here are some other places to look for job descriptions:

- Local government job service agencies

- Professional and technical organizations

- Search firms / recruiters

- Associates who work in the same field

- Newspaper advertisements for similar jobs

- Online job postings (which tend to have longer job descriptions than print ads, which is good)

You will find some great resources on the following websites, as well:

- America's Career InfoNet, *www.acinet.org*

Get your hands on written job descriptions.

- Dictionary of Occupational Titles, *www.oalj.dol.gov/libdot.htm*
- Exploring Occupations from the University of Manitoba, *www.umanitoba. ca/counselling/careers.html*
- JobProfiles.com, *www.jobprofiles.org*
- Occupational Outlook Handbook, *stats.bls.gov/ooh/*
- Occupational Outlook Quarterly, *www.bls.gov/opub/ooq/home.htm*

Performance evaluations, depending on how well they are written, generally list a description of your major responsibilities, a breakdown of individual tasks, and highlights of your accomplishments. You should *always* keep a folder at home of performance evaluations from every job you have ever held. If you haven't kept them up until now, please start.

Now, make copies of these performance evaluations so you can highlight them as you write your résumé. Use a different colored pen to highlight accomplishments, the things you did above and beyond the call of duty.

Also make copies of the job descriptions you discovered and mark the sentences that describe anything you have done in your past or present jobs. These job descriptions are important sources of keywords, so pay particular attention to nouns and phrases that you can incorporate into your own résumé.

Set these papers aside until Chapter 8, when it will be time to write everything down.

Step 4
Keywords

7

In today's world of electronic résumés, make sure you know the buzzwords of your industry and incorporate them into the sentences you are about to write. Keywords are the nouns, adjectives, or short phrases that describe any experience and education that might be used to find your résumé in a keyword search of an electronic résumé database, either on the Internet or in a company's own system. They reflect the essential knowledge, skills, and abilities (KSAs) required to do your job.

Since you will find a requirement to define your KSAs for many government jobs, let's stop here for a minute and talk about what KSAs really are. Your *knowledge* is information you have learned from both your work and personal life, including your education, special training, and experience. *Skills* are things you "do"—typing, computer programming, and cooking, among many others. *Abilities* are related to your unique talents and natural aptitudes. Abilities are the foundation of your passion, although your skills and knowledge play a part as well. You are the only person in the world who has your unique set of knowledge, skills, and abilities.

Now back to keywords. They are generally concrete descriptions such as these:

- cloud computing
- search engine optimization
- fiber-optic cable
- network
- project management
- Spanish
- international
- business development
- electronic health records
- customer retention
- cost reduction
- long-range planning
- organizational design

> *Keywords reflect the essential knowledge, skills, and abilities required to do your job.*

Even well-known company names (Microsoft, GE, Google, Time-Warner) and universities (Harvard, Yale, Princeton, SMU, Stanford, Tulane, Columbia, etc.) are sometimes used as keywords, especially when it is necessary to narrow down an initial search that calls up hundreds of résumés from a résumé database.

Acronyms and abbreviations here can either hurt you or help you, depending on how you use them. One example given to me by an engineer at a software development company was the abbreviation IN. Think about it. IN could stand for *intelligent networks*, *Indiana*, or the word *in*. It is better to spell out the abbreviation if there could be any possible confusion.

However, if a series of initials is so well known that it would be recognized by nearly everyone in your industry and would not likely be confused with a real word, then the keyword search will probably use those initials (i.e., IBM, CPA, UNIX). When in doubt, always spell it out at least one time on your résumé. A computer needs to see the combination only one time for it to be considered a "hit" in a keyword search.

In my research over the years, I have been surprised to find soft skills included in most job requisitions, which are used to develop the criteria to search electronic résumé databases. These soft skills are hard to prove and are often ignored by human readers, but if they become keywords for a search of a résumé database and your résumé doesn't contain those words, then your résumé will not pop up. A recent survey by CareerBuilder.com listed the most frequently searched soft skills as *oral and written communication*, *problem solving*, *leadership*, *team building*, *performance*, *productivity*, and *strategic planning*, among others.

This might seem surprising to you, since there have been many articles written over the past few years that say soft skills are the death knell of a résumé. It's a dilemma. Soft skill words are often ignored by HR managers, since they aren't verifiable. However, if they aren't on the résumé somewhere, your résumé won't pop up in a keyword search of an electronic résumé database. Résumé writers integrate soft skills as adjectives in a profile or in a separate section at the bottom of the résumé's last page, so they don't take up valuable space on page one. Regardless of what the articles say, if a soft skill is in a job description or advertisement, it needs to be on the résumé somewhere.

At the end of this chapter, you will find more examples of keywords for specific industries, although there is no such thing as a comprehensive listing of keywords for any single job. The computerized applicant tracking systems used by most companies allow the recruiter or hiring manager to personalize his or her list of keywords for each job opening, so it is an evolving process. You will never know whether you have listed absolutely every keyword possible, so focus instead on getting on paper as many related skills as possible, remembering to be absolutely honest and accurate, and integrate the keywords in an organic way so they are part of the natural conversation of the résumé.

The job descriptions and performance evaluations you found in Step 3 are some of the most important sources for keywords. You can also be certain that nearly every noun, and some adjectives, in a job posting or advertisement will be keywords, so make sure you use those words somewhere in your résumé, using synonyms wherever you can. Just make sure you can justify every word on your résumé—don't exaggerate. If you don't have the experience or skill, don't use the keyword.

The form at the end of this chapter will help you make a list of the keywords you have determined are important for your particular job search. Also list common synonyms for those words when you can. As you incorporate these words into the sentences of your résumé, check them off.

One caution. Always tell the truth. The minute a hiring manager speaks with you on the telephone or begins an interview, any exaggeration of the truth will become immediately apparent.

It is a bad idea to say, "I don't have experience with MS Word computer software" just to get the words *MS Word* or *computer software* on paper so your résumé will pop up in a keyword search.

In a cover letter, it might be appropriate to say, "I don't have five years of experience in marketing but can add two years of university training in the subject to three years of in-depth experience as a marketing assistant with Hewlett-Packard." That is legitimate reasoning, but anything more manipulative can be hazardous to your job search.

Today, it is getting harder for job seekers to game the systems that recruiters use to identify potential candidates. Some candidates have tried to hide keywords so they can't be seen by the naked eye by using white text on a white background, typing so small that it looks like a solid horizontal line, and even inserting Web coding in online résumés that's hidden from plain view. Newer applicant tracking and résumé database software are able to detect these tricks, discrediting the applicant. Some technology even penalizes job seekers who use keywords out of context by placing their résumé at the bottom of the search results.

Keywords in Electronic Résumés

Using the right keywords for your particular experience and education is critical to the success of your electronic résumé. Without the right keywords, your résumé will float in cyberspace forever, waiting for a hiring manager to find it. If your résumé contains all the right keywords, then you will be among the first candidates whose résumés are reviewed. If you lack only one of the keywords, then your résumé will be next in line after résumés that have them all, and so on.

Remember, your keywords are the specific terminology used in your job that reflect your experience and skills. For instance, *operating room* and *ICU* immediately classify the experience of a nurse, but *pediatric ICU* narrows it down even further.

Don't try to limit your résumé by using fewer words. If your information is longer than one page, a reader looking at a computer screen won't be able to tell, but the computer doing a keyword search will know if a word is not there. Recall, however, that you need to use a word only one time for it to be considered a "hit" in a keyword search. Try to use synonyms wherever possible to broaden your chances of being selected.

You should also understand the difference between a simple keyword search and a concept search. When a recruiter brings an e-mailed résumé onto the screen and sends the computer on a search for a single word like *marketing*—which one can do in any word processing program with a few clicks of a mouse or function key—he or she is performing a keyword search.

You are also performing a keyword search when you type a word or combination of words into the command line of a search engine like Yahoo! or Google (see example below). In that case, sometimes the computer searches entire documents for matches and other times it looks only at headers or extracts from the files.

Screen shot used with permission of Google.

A concept search, on the other hand, can bridge the gap between words by reading entire phrases and then using sophisticated artificial intelligence to interpret what is being said, translating the phrase into a single word, like *network*, or a combination of words, like *project management*.

For example, in a simple keyword search on *Manager of Product Sales*, ordinary software would return a match on a candidate's résumé that reads "worked for a Manager of Product Sales." A concept search can distinguish between this résumé and another candidate's résumé that indicated "served as a Manager of Product Sales."

The various software packages that extract data from electronic résumés are incredibly sophisticated. They can read the grammar of noun, verb, and adjective combinations and extract the information for placement on the form that will become your entry in a résumé database. Expert system extraction engines use a complex knowledge base of more than 200,000 rules and over ten million résumé terms. They recognize grammatical structure variations, including synonyms and context within natural language text.

They even know the difference between words by their placement on the page and their relationship to the header that precedes it—Experience, Education, or Computer Skills.

Because of this complicated logic, and because each company and each hiring manager has the ability to personalize the search criteria for each job opening, it is impossible to give you a concrete list of the thousands of possible keywords that could be used to search for any one job.

For instance, Sun StorageTek, a high-tech company in Louisville, Colorado, graciously conducted a keyword search of their résumé database for me and brought up the following criteria from two different hiring managers for the same job title. These are keywords extracted from real job requisitions written by hiring managers.

FINANCIAL ANALYST/SENIOR ACCOUNTANT

REQUIRED
- BS in finance or accounting with 4 years of experience or
- MBA in related field with 2 years of relevant experience
- certified public accountant
- forecasting
- strategic planning
- financial statement analysis

DESIRED
- accounting
- financial
- trend analysis
- results analysis
- trends
- develop trends
- financial modeling
- personal computer
- DCF
- presentation skills
- team player

REQUIRED
- BS in finance or accounting with 4 years of experience or
- MBA in related field with 2 years of relevant experience
- accounting
- financial reporting
- financial statement
- Excel

DESIRED
- ability
- customer
- new business
- financial analysis
- financial
- forecasting
- process improvement
- policy development
- business policies
- PowerPoint
- Microsoft Word
- analytical ability

Sample Keywords

You can see why it is so difficult to give definitive lists of keywords and concepts. However, it is possible to give you samples of actual keyword searches used by the recruiters at Sun StorageTek to give you some ideas.

Let me emphasize again that you should list only experience you actually have gained. Do not include the keywords on the following pages in your résumé just because they are listed here.

ACCOUNT EXECUTIVE

REQUIRED
- BS degree
- 3 years technical selling experience
- Fortune 500 account management experience
- sales
- storage industry
- solution selling

DESIRED
- Siebel
- quota levels
- Value-Added Dealers (VAD)
- Value-Added Resellers (VAR)

ACCOUNTING ANALYST

REQUIRED
- BA or MBA
- 2–4 years of experience
- asset management
- SAP
- accounting

DESIRED
- fixed assets
- capital assets
- corporate tax
- US GAAP

BASE SALES REPRESENTATIVE

REQUIRED
- 2–4 years of sales or contract management experience
- 2+ years of telemarketing or telesales experience

DESIRED
- Siebel
- storage industry

BUSINESS MANAGER, CENTRAL ARCHIVE MANAGEMENT

REQUIRED
- BS in engineering or computer science
- 10 years of related engineering and/or manufacturing experience
- strategic planning
- network
- product management
- program management

DESIRED
- business plan
- line management
- pricing
- team player
- CAM
- marketing
- product strategy
- vendor
- general management
- OEM
- profit and loss

DEVELOPMENT ENGINEER, ADVISORY

REQUIRED
- BS/BA, Master's desired
- 5–10 years mechanical engineering experience
- 10+ years experience in hardware design
- EMC/EMI debug
- mechanical design
- tape drive

DESIRED
- DFSS (Design for Six Sigma)
- ANSYS or Metlab
- mechanisms design
- shock
- vibration
- NARTE
- tape library
- data storage

BUSINESS OPERATIONS SPECIALIST

REQUIRED
- bachelor's degree
- 4 years of directly related experience
- production schedule
- project planning

DESIRED
- ability to implement
- CList
- data analysis
- off-shift
- team player
- automation
- ability to plan
- customer interaction
- VM
- JCL
- MVS
- UNIX
- analytical ability
- customer interface
- network
- skills analysis
- automatic tools

FINANCIAL ANALYST, STAFF

REQUIRED
- BS in Finance or Accounting
- 1–2 years related experience
- customer-focused experience
- excellent written communication skills
- collection
- financial forecast
- financial modeling
- financial reporting
- financial consolidation
- reconciliation

DESIRED
- international finance
- Hyperion consolidation software
- channel experience

ORDER SPECIALIST

REQUIRED
- BS degree
- 1–3 years experience
- order administration
- order fulfillment
- invoice processing
- Microsoft Word
- Excel

DESIRED
- database

PROJECT MANAGER, HR

REQUIRED
- bachelor's degree in human resources, business, or related field
- 6 years broad experience

DESIRED
- communication
- project management
- milestone development
- time management
- benchmarking
- recruiting
- long-range planning
- sourcing
- vendor management
- recruitment processing outsourcing

SOFTWARE ENGINEER— EMBEDDED, ADVISORY LEVEL

REQUIRED
- BS or MS degree in one of the computer sciences or engineering
- 12–14 years of experience minimum
- controller-architecture design experience
- disk controller
- software/hardware integration
- embedded systems
- system-level debugging
- object-oriented design
- script building

DESIRED
- open systems
- product development

SECRETARY III

REQUIRED
- high school education or equivalent
- 5 years of experience
- typing skill of 55–60 wpm
- interpersonal skills
- oral communication

DESIRED
- administrative assistance
- clerical
- data analysis
- file maintenance
- material repair
- PowerPoint
- project planning
- reports
- screen calls
- troubleshoot
- answer phones
- communication skills
- document distribution
- mail sorting
- Microsoft Word
- presentation
- publication
- schedule calendar
- secretarial
- appointments
- confidential
- edit
- material
- policies and procedures
- problem solving
- records management
- schedule conference
- telephone interview

SOFTWARE ENGINEER, SENIOR

REQUIRED
- BS/MS in engineering, computer science, or closely related field
- 8–9 years of experience

DESIRED
- C++
- hiring/firing
- prototype
- structured design
- code development
- methodology
- real time
- supervision
- communication skills
- experiment design
- problem solving
- software design
- testing

SYSTEMS ENGINEER, SENIOR

REQUIRED
- BS degree in related field
- 8–10 years of experience
- pre-sales
- systems engineering
- data storage

DESIRED
- systems configuration
- capacity planning
- data facility hierarchical storage manager (DFHSM)
- hierarchical storage controller (HSC)
- presentation skills

Sample Résumés with Keywords Highlighted

Let me show you how keywords can be extracted from an actual résumé. In the example on the following pages, the résumé has possible keywords highlighted using bold and italic letters. Résumés for different industries generate completely different keywords. The only keywords that might be the same are ones for "soft" skills.

Just because I've highlighted all possible keywords in a résumé doesn't mean that the hiring manager will write each one of them in a job requisition. Instead, this exercise is meant to help you become more aware of the nouns, adjectives, and sometimes verbs that *might* become keywords in a résumé database search, whether it is at Careerbuilder.com or in a company's private database of résumés.

You will also notice that I've highlighted the word only the first time it appears. To applicant tracking software, the number of times a word appears in a résumé or its position at the top, middle, or bottom of a résumé doesn't increase its importance. Relevance is more important than keyword density to these applications. For instance, your résumé will rank higher if you have more years of experience than the other candidates. The software extracts that information using the "from" and "to" dates on your job titles.

NOTE: Do not highlight keywords on your own résumé! They are highlighted on these examples solely as a tool to help you understand the concept of which words become keywords in a search.

Margaret DeVito

Post Office Box 12345
Colorado Springs, Colorado 80962

Cellular: (916) 555-1234
E-mail: megdevito@protypeltd.com

NONPROFIT ORGANIZATIONAL DEVELOPMENT

e-Commerce • Customer Relationship Management • Organizational Development • Program Management

Aligning information technology with business to create innovative solutions that drive change.

Accomplished business strategist with more than 12 years enhancing **operational efficiencies**, developing innovative solutions, and providing **organizational leadership** in **nonprofit** settings. Able to provide vision and direction for key technology development while aligning client needs with organizational goals. Strong ability to translate business needs into **technological requirements**. Skilled **program manager**, analytical **problem solver**, and organizational **leader** with extensive experience in the following:

- *Nonprofit Client Relationship*
- *Strategic Planning*
- *Client Experience Analysis*
- *Organizational Development / Change*
- *Process Re-engineering*
- *Team Building*
- *Vision Planning*
- *Community Needs Analysis*

EDUCATION

MASTER OF ARTS, ORGANIZATIONAL LEADERSHIP (2010)
Chapman University, Roseville, California
- Relevant course work: **Organizational Behavior**, Organizational Development, Organizational **Research**, Team Development, Self / Systems / Leadership, Storytelling in Leadership, Democracy / Ethics / Leadership.

BACHELOR OF SCIENCE, APPAREL AND MERCHANDISING (1992)
Colorado State University, Fort Collins, Colorado

NONPROFIT EXPERIENCE

SENIOR E-COMMERCE MARKETING SPECIALIST
Focus on the Family (nonprofit 501(c)(3)), Colorado Springs, Colorado (2011–present)
Provide leadership and expertise for the development of e-commerce solutions for the Focus on the Family **website**. Considered a super-user of the site's **software.** Currently analyzing top sellers by category and developing strategies for **cross-selling, upselling**, and **product merchandising**.
- Developed and implemented ongoing enhancement / **optimization strategies**, which increased revenue from the e-commerce site by $200,000 in three months.
- Analyzed and reviewed **site user data**, and identified areas of opportunity for increasing revenue.
- Trained others on **best practices** and implemented merchandising and technology strategies for the site.

VOLUNTEER / BOARD OF DIRECTORS
Crossroads Diversified Services, Sacramento, California (2007–2011)
Wellspring Women's Center, Oak Park, California (2008–2010
Volunteered to help nonprofit organizations close the growing digital divide between business and nonprofit entities. Introduced **technological capabilities** and created organizational **visions, missions,** and business strategies.
- Served as the secretary of the board of directors for Crossroads, a $3.0 million nonprofit entity providing job opportunities for people with disabilities or other barriers to getting work.
- Created a process and **operations manual** for the for-profit Sacramento Sirens women's professional football team, and helped to provide guidelines for their **501(c)(3) nonprofit foundation.**

BUSINESS EXPERIENCE

BUSINESS ESCALATION PROGRAM MANAGER
Hewlett-Packard / Compaq, Roseville, California (2005–2007)
Promoted to identify and implement plans to improve IT problem resolution for HP's global customers. Ensured that HP **storage products** met or exceeded **customer expectations** regarding availability and operability.
- Selected as one of the few HP / Compaq employees (6,000 out of 165,000) granted stock options and asked to stay during the merger.
- Created documentation to resolve **implementation issues** for a Fortune 500 retailer, ensuring the customer purchased additional **new products** after reviewing only the **prototypes**.

BUSINESS EXPERIENCE

Business Escalation Program Manager (continued)

- Resolved and closed 66% of *global escalations* on or ahead of schedule.
- Retained a major client (an $80 billion health care organization) after successfully resolving an escalation affecting 150 hospitals throughout the U.S. The client ordered an additional product with greater *enterprise storage capacity* at a price point of more than $5 million per order.
- Identified the needs of the combined HP / Compaq Enterprise Storage organizations *for knowledge management* to incorporate *organizational changes* and *process re-engineering.*
- Streamlined *shipping* escalation processes after 9/11 for the Roseville *manufacturing* site.

PROJECT MANAGER

Agilent (a former HP division), Colorado Springs, Colorado (2004)
Developed *project plans* to integrate Fort Collins IT teams into Agilent's centralized *help desk.*

- Provided improved support for customers and reduced IT *cost-of-delivery* for *customer support.*
- Developed *training plans* for the Colorado Springs site administrative assistant customers so they could learn how to effectively use the company's *e-mail application*. This information was used to address customer needs on future *application rollouts.*

MESSAGING SUPPORT MANAGER

Agilent (a former HP division), Colorado Springs, Colorado (2003–2004)
Managed the Messaging Call Center providing *Level 2 internal support* for *field* and *factory employees*. Provided client and *server support* using *Microsoft Outlook* and *Exchange Server* platforms for employee *e-mail* needs. Supervised up to 30 internal support staff and *contractors* at *distributed sites*.

- Led the IT outsourced e-mail team to reduce *call times* from 4 minutes to an average of 26 seconds within 30 days.
- Successfully managed a crisis caused by the large-scale Love Bug *computer virus* in May 2004.
- Contained call center *costs* for internal IT support by identifying and repairing a problem with *support tools.*

TEAM LEADER

Hewlett-Packard, Colorado Springs, Colorado (2002–2003)
Led the Colorado Springs IT help desk team (~1,800 employees) in providing first- and *second-level support*. Planned and monitored *delivery of services* to employees to ensure that *system* and *application business needs* were met.

- Ranked number one in *customer satisfaction* out of all U.S. HP internal site IT teams.

CUSTOMER SUPPORT ENGINEER

Hewlett-Packard (formerly Colorado Memory Systems), Loveland, Colorado (1995–2002)
Managed the Customer Care Center *Level 1 Agent tape backup systems* on *PCs* and *UNIX workstations* in the U.S. and Europe—lived four months in England. Worked on *Level 1 NT* and *UNIX servers*. Served as the HP *liaison* to Customer Care Center agents in England and the Netherlands.

- Received three awards from coworkers for outstanding *teamwork.*
- Key member of the Loveland Site United Way Campaign Team. Increased contributions from 41% to 86%.

PROFESSIONAL DEVELOPMENT

MARKETLIVE SUMMIT (2011)

- Attended a three-day *e-commerce* application seminar presented by MarketLive, Inc.

UNIX SYSTEM ADMINISTRATION, LEVELS 1 AND 2 (2006)

Sierra Community College, Rocklin, California

NT ADMINISTRATION CERTIFICATION (2002)

Front Range Community College, Fort Collins, Colorado

- Selected as one of 80 students out of 900 applicants for the term.

KEYWORDS

❑ Keyword:_____
   ❑ Synonym:_____
   ❑ Synonym:_____

❑ Keyword:_____
   ❑ Synonym:_____
   ❑ Synonym:_____

❑ Keyword:_____
   ❑ Synonym:_____
   ❑ Synonym:_____

❑ Keyword:_____
   ❑ Synonym:_____
   ❑ Synonym:_____

❑ Keyword:_____
   ❑ Synonym:_____
   ❑ Synonym:_____

❑ Keyword:_____
   ❑ Synonym:_____
   ❑ Synonym:_____

❑ Keyword:_____
   ❑ Synonym:_____
   ❑ Synonym:_____

❑ Keyword:_____
   ❑ Synonym:_____
   ❑ Synonym:_____

❑ Keyword:_____
   ❑ Synonym:_____
   ❑ Synonym:_____

❑ Keyword:_____
   ❑ Synonym:_____
   ❑ Synonym:_____

❑ Keyword:_____
   ❑ Synonym:_____
   ❑ Synonym:_____

❑ Keyword:_____
   ❑ Synonym:_____
   ❑ Synonym:_____

Step 5
Organize

8

Now that you have the basic information gathered for your résumé, you need to create a list of your jobs and write basic sentences to describe your duties. Start by using a separate page at the end of this chapter for each of the jobs you have held for the past 10 or 15 years. You can generally stop there unless there is something in your previous work history that is particularly relevant to the new job you are seeking.

Starting with your present position, list the title of every job you have held, along with the name of the company, the city and state, and the years you worked there. You don't need to list full addresses and zip codes, although you will need to know that information when it comes time to fill out an application. You should use a separate page for each job title even if you worked for the same company in more than one capacity.

By the way, you *can* use a computer. I've had people assume that they had to write this all out in longhand simply because I suggest a separate piece of paper for each job. You can download MS Word, WordPerfect, and PDF files of all the forms in this book by going to my website at *www.patcriscito.com.*

You can list years only (2010–present) or months and years (May 2010–present), depending on your personality. People who are detail oriented are usually more comfortable with a full accounting of their time. Listing years alone covers some gaps if you have worked in a position for less than a full year while the time period spans more than one calendar year. For instance, if you worked from December 2011 through May 2012, saying 2011–2012 certainly looks better. If you are concerned about gaps in your work history, then listing years only is to your advantage.

From the perspective of recruiters and hiring managers, most don't care whether you list the months and years or list the years only. However, regardless of which method you choose, be consistent throughout your résumé, especially within sections. For instance, don't use months some of the time and years alone within the same section. Consistency of

Consistency of style is important on a résumé.

style is important on a résumé, since it is that consistency that makes your résumé neat, clean, and easy to read.

Under each job on its separate page, make a list of your duties, incorporating phrases from the job descriptions wherever they apply. You don't have to worry about making great sentences yet or narrowing down your list. Just get the information down on paper.

This is the most time-consuming part of the résumé-writing process. Depending on how quickly you write/type, it could take an entire day just for this step. Anything worth doing, however, is worth doing right, so you will want to take the time to do this step right.

Unpaid Experience

Don't forget internships, practicums, and unpaid volunteer work in your experience section. Experience is experience whether you are paid for it or not. If the position or the knowledge you gained is relevant to your current job search, then list it on your résumé.

You can either include unpaid experience along with your paid experience or create a separate section just for your volunteer history, like this:

VOLUNTEER HISTORY

Junior League of Colorado Springs, Colorado Springs, Colorado (2008–2012)
Developed goals and action plans, promoted projects to the community, and recruited members. Provided information and training to other league members and educated members on placement opportunities and policies. Attended court hearings and made recommendations to social caseworkers to improve the quality of legal representation for abused children. Raised $30,000 in funds for community projects, reconciled financial statements, and arranged publicity.
- Court-Appointed Special Advocate (CASA) Program (August 2008–May 2012)
- Placement Adviser, Committee Member (June 2010–May 2012)
- Historian Committee, Chairperson (June 2011–February 2012)
- Membership Development Committee (August 2010–May 2011)
- Community Service Corps Committee (January 2008–May 2009)

Cheyenne Mountain Newcomers Club, Colorado Springs, Colorado (2008–2012)
Planned, organized, and coordinated activities for more than 300 members. Maintained membership records and coordinated printing and mailing of directories. Presided at all general and executive board meetings in president's absence.
- First Vice President (December 2011–May 2012)
- Second Vice President (July 2010–May 2011)
- General Meetings Chairperson (August 2000–May 2010)

EXPERIENCE—JOB NO. 1

JOB TITLE _____

NAME OF EMPLOYER _____

CITY AND STATE _____

DATE STARTED _____ DATE ENDED _____

SUMMARY SENTENCE (The overall scope of your responsibility, overview of your essential role in the company, kind of products or services for which you were responsible) _____

_____

_____

_____

_____

NUMBER OF PEOPLE SUPERVISED AND THEIR TITLES OR FUNCTIONS _____

_____

_____

_____

_____

DESCRIPTION OF RESPONSIBILITIES (Don't forget budget, hiring, training, operations, strategic planning, new business development, production, customer service, sales, marketing, advertising, etc.) _____

_____

_____

_____

_____

_____

_____

_____

_____

_____

_____

_____

_____

_____

_____

ACCOMPLISHMENTS (Leave this section blank until Step 6 in Chapter 9.) _____

_____

_____

_____

_____

_____

_____

_____

_____

_____

_____

_____

EXPERIENCE—JOB NO. 2

JOB TITLE _____

NAME OF EMPLOYER _____

CITY AND STATE _____

DATE STARTED _____ DATE ENDED _____

SUMMARY SENTENCE (The overall scope of your responsibility, overview of your essential role in the company, kind of products or services for which you were responsible) _____

_____

_____

_____

_____

NUMBER OF PEOPLE SUPERVISED AND THEIR TITLES OR FUNCTIONS _____

_____

_____

_____

_____

DESCRIPTION OF RESPONSIBILITIES (Don't forget budget, hiring, training, operations, strategic planning, new business development, production, customer service, sales, marketing, advertising, etc.) _____

_____

_____

_____

_____

_____

_____

_____

_____

_____

_____

_____

_____

_____

_____

_____

ACCOMPLISHMENTS (Leave this section blank until Step 6 in Chapter 9.) _____

_____

_____

_____

_____

_____

_____

_____

_____

_____

_____

_____

_____

_____

EXPERIENCE—JOB NO. 3

JOB TITLE _____

NAME OF EMPLOYER _____

CITY AND STATE _____

DATE STARTED _____ DATE ENDED _____

SUMMARY SENTENCE (The overall scope of your responsibility, overview of your essential role in the company, kind of products or services for which you were responsible) _____

_____

_____

_____

_____

NUMBER OF PEOPLE SUPERVISED AND THEIR TITLES OR FUNCTIONS _____

_____

_____

_____

_____

DESCRIPTION OF RESPONSIBILITIES (Don't forget budget, hiring, training, operations, strategic planning, new business development, production, customer service, sales, marketing, advertising, etc.) _____

_____

_____

_____

_____

_____

_____

_____

_____

_____

_____

_____

_____

_____

_____

_____

ACCOMPLISHMENTS (Leave this section blank until Step 6 in Chapter 9.) _____

_____

_____

_____

_____

_____

_____

_____

_____

_____

_____

_____

_____

EXPERIENCE—JOB NO. 4

JOB TITLE _____

NAME OF EMPLOYER _____

CITY AND STATE _____

DATE STARTED _____ DATE ENDED _____

SUMMARY SENTENCE (The overall scope of your responsibility, overview of your essential role in the company, kind of products or services for which you were responsible) _____

_____

_____

_____

_____

NUMBER OF PEOPLE SUPERVISED AND THEIR TITLES OR FUNCTIONS _____

_____

_____

_____

_____

DESCRIPTION OF RESPONSIBILITIES (Don't forget budget, hiring, training, operations, strategic planning, new business development, production, customer service, sales, marketing, advertising, etc.) _____

_____

_____

_____

_____

_____

_____

_____

_____

_____

_____

_____

_____

_____

_____

ACCOMPLISHMENTS (Leave this section blank until Step 6 in Chapter 9.) _____

_____

_____

_____

_____

_____

_____

_____

_____

_____

_____

_____

_____

EXPERIENCE—JOB NO. 5

JOB TITLE _____

NAME OF EMPLOYER _____

CITY AND STATE _____

DATE STARTED _____ DATE ENDED _____

SUMMARY SENTENCE (The overall scope of your responsibility, overview of your essential role in the company, kind of products or services for which you were responsible) _____

_____

_____

_____

_____

NUMBER OF PEOPLE SUPERVISED AND THEIR TITLES OR FUNCTIONS _____

_____

_____

_____

_____

DESCRIPTION OF RESPONSIBILITIES (Don't forget budget, hiring, training, operations, strategic planning, new business development, production, customer service, sales, marketing, advertising, etc.) _____

_____

_____

_____

_____

_____

_____

_____

_____

_____

_____

_____

_____

_____

_____

_____

_____

ACCOMPLISHMENTS (Leave this section blank until Step 6 in Chapter 9.) _____

_____

_____

_____

_____

_____

_____

_____

_____

_____

_____

_____

_____

EXPERIENCE—JOB NO. 6

JOB TITLE _____

NAME OF EMPLOYER _____

CITY AND STATE _____

DATE STARTED _____ DATE ENDED _____

SUMMARY SENTENCE (The overall scope of your responsibility, overview of your essential role in the company, kind of products or services for which you were responsible) _____

_____

_____

_____

_____

NUMBER OF PEOPLE SUPERVISED AND THEIR TITLES OR FUNCTIONS _____

_____

_____

_____

DESCRIPTION OF RESPONSIBILITIES (Don't forget budget, hiring, training, operations, strategic planning, new business development, production, customer service, sales, marketing, advertising, etc.) _____

_____

_____

_____

_____

_____

_____

_____

_____

_____

_____

_____

_____

_____

_____

ACCOMPLISHMENTS (Leave this section blank until Step 6 in Chapter 9.) _____

_____

_____

_____

_____

_____

_____

_____

_____

_____

_____

_____

_____

EXPERIENCE—JOB NO. 7

JOB TITLE _____

NAME OF EMPLOYER _____

CITY AND STATE _____

DATE STARTED _____ DATE ENDED _____

SUMMARY SENTENCE (The overall scope of your responsibility, overview of your essential role in the company, kind of products or services for which you were responsible) _____
_____
_____
_____
_____

NUMBER OF PEOPLE SUPERVISED AND THEIR TITLES OR FUNCTIONS _____
_____
_____
_____
_____

DESCRIPTION OF RESPONSIBILITIES (Don't forget budget, hiring, training, operations, strategic planning, new business development, production, customer service, sales, marketing, advertising, etc.) _____
_____
_____
_____
_____
_____
_____
_____
_____
_____
_____
_____
_____
_____
_____

ACCOMPLISHMENTS (Leave this section blank until Step 6 in Chapter 9.) _____
_____
_____
_____
_____
_____
_____
_____
_____
_____
_____
_____

EXPERIENCE—JOB NO. 8

JOB TITLE _____

NAME OF EMPLOYER _____

CITY AND STATE _____

DATE STARTED _____ DATE ENDED _____

SUMMARY SENTENCE (The overall scope of your responsibility, overview of your essential role in the company, kind of products or services for which you were responsible) _____

_____

_____

_____

_____

NUMBER OF PEOPLE SUPERVISED AND THEIR TITLES OR FUNCTIONS _____

_____

_____

_____

_____

DESCRIPTION OF RESPONSIBILITIES (Don't forget budget, hiring, training, operations, strategic planning, new business development, production, customer service, sales, marketing, advertising, etc.) _____

_____

_____

_____

_____

_____

_____

_____

_____

_____

_____

_____

_____

_____

_____

_____

ACCOMPLISHMENTS (Leave this section blank until Step 6 in Chapter 9.) _____

_____

_____

_____

_____

_____

_____

_____

_____

_____

_____

_____

EXPERIENCE—JOB NO. 9

JOB TITLE _____

NAME OF EMPLOYER _____

CITY AND STATE _____

DATE STARTED _____ DATE ENDED _____

SUMMARY SENTENCE (The overall scope of your responsibility, overview of your essential role in the company, kind of products or services for which you were responsible) _____

_____

_____

_____

_____

NUMBER OF PEOPLE SUPERVISED AND THEIR TITLES OR FUNCTIONS _____

_____

_____

_____

_____

DESCRIPTION OF RESPONSIBILITIES (Don't forget budget, hiring, training, operations, strategic planning, new business development, production, customer service, sales, marketing, advertising, etc.) _____

_____

_____

_____

_____

_____

_____

_____

_____

_____

_____

_____

_____

_____

_____

_____

ACCOMPLISHMENTS (Leave this section blank until Step 6 in Chapter 9.) _____

_____

_____

_____

_____

_____

_____

_____

_____

_____

_____

_____

_____

_____

EXPERIENCE—JOB NO. 10

JOB TITLE _____

NAME OF EMPLOYER _____

CITY AND STATE _____

DATE STARTED _____ DATE ENDED _____

SUMMARY SENTENCE (The overall scope of your responsibility, overview of your essential role in the company, kind of products or services for which you were responsible) _____

_____

_____

_____

_____

NUMBER OF PEOPLE SUPERVISED AND THEIR TITLES OR FUNCTIONS _____

_____

_____

_____

_____

DESCRIPTION OF RESPONSIBILITIES (Don't forget budget, hiring, training, operations, strategic planning, new business development, production, customer service, sales, marketing, advertising, etc.) _____

_____

_____

_____

_____

_____

_____

_____

_____

_____

_____

_____

_____

_____

_____

_____

ACCOMPLISHMENTS (Leave this section blank until Step 6 in Chapter 9.) _____

_____

_____

_____

_____

_____

_____

_____

_____

_____

_____

_____

_____

Step 6
Accomplishments

9

When you are finished with your work history, go back to each job and think about what you might have done above and beyond the call of duty. What did you contribute to each of your jobs? How did you measure your success? What were you most proud of? What made you feel good at the end of the day? Did you do any of the following?

- Exceed sales quotas each month?
- Save the company money by developing a new procedure?
- Generate new product publicity in trade press?
- Control expenses or cut overhead?
- Increase the company's market share?
- Expand business or attract/retain customers?
- Restore lost accounts?
- Improve customer satisfaction ratings?
- Improve the company's image or build new relationships?
- Improve the quality of a product?
- Do something that made the company more competitive?
- Make money? Was it a record?
- Improve net profit?
- Save money or time without compromising the company's products or services?
- Introduce new and better policies, procedures, processes, or systems?
- Increase efficiency or make work easier?
- Lower the company's debt?
- Increase productivity?
- Improve workplace safety?

> *Overused words lose their effectiveness, like a song played on the radio again and again.*

- Solve a problem?
- Create a business partnership?
- Improve recruiting systems?
- Train/mentor any personnel who were promoted?
- Lower employee turnover or improve morale?
- Bring new vision or direction to the company?
- Rate above average on performance evaluations?
- Get selected for a significant project(s)?
- Become recognized as a subject matter expert?
- Get recruited especially to solve a major problem?
- Face significant competition in the market?

Go back to the experience forms at the end of Chapter 8 and make a note of any accomplishments that show potential employers what you have done in the past, which translates into what you might be able to do for them in the future. This is not *bragging*, which is a prideful exaggeration. Instead, it is *advertising*, which is "to make known the positive features of a product (you)."

Quantify whenever possible. Numbers are always impressive. Be careful not to divulge confidential information about past and current employers, especially if they are privately held companies. Public companies have to reveal financial data anyway, so listing those numbers on your résumé isn't as much of a problem.

Don't duplicate wording throughout the résumé. If you use dollars in one case, use percentages in another. Overused words lose their effectiveness, like a song played on the radio again and again.

Remember, you are trying to motivate the potential employer to buy … you! Convince your reader that you will be able to generate a significant return on their investment in you. Try to focus on "before" and "after" examples. Identify a problem and explain how you corrected it using the CAR format—Challenge, Action, Result. Here is an example.

Challenge: Evaluated the sensor that optimized combustion in a coal-fired power plant—determined that power levels were low and inconsistent.

Action: Tuned the VCSEL-based laser that was at the heart of the process to optimize combustion.

Result: Succeeded in making the controlled burning processes cleaner, greener, more consistent, and capable of operating at higher power levels. Improved manufacturability.

If you were part of a team, it is sometimes difficult to express accomplishments without claiming full credit for the work of the entire team. You should refer directly to the role you played: "Led a team of six engineers…." or "Integral member of the team that…." or "Part of the sales team that doubled sales in one year." Even though over-claiming credit in the case of team projects is somewhat expected, especially in today's tight job market, I would recommend being as accurate as possible on every word of your résumé.

Sample Accomplishment Sentences

Following are some real accomplishments used by real people on real résumés. They are extracted from many different résumés, so don't be surprised if the bullets jump around within the sections. Each bullet is a separate accomplishment. They aren't used in a résumé as they are listed here.

Your achievements won't be identical, but you can use these sentences as a foundation for your own words. Many of the phrases can cross over various industries, but some are specific to a particular job or company.

ACCOUNTING
- Developed and implemented numerous improvements to financial reporting, budgeting, and internal controls that supported sales growth of 200%.
- Reduced charge-offs from .2% to .1% and receivables turnover from 50 to 42 days during this period.
- Over a five-year period, lowered overall borrowing costs by 1%.
- Identified $3.5 million in misused funds for return to the USOC.
- Personally recovered $1.423 million in 1997 out of a department total of $1.642 million.
- Audited $10 million in Olympic Games tickets, identifying opportunities to strengthen internal controls, improve operational efficiencies, and save hundreds of thousands of dollars.
- Conducted an analytical review of a $5 million inventory and spearheaded actions to revalue the inventory with material adjustments.
- Succeeded in delivering 25 complete systems to users, including the automation of a formerly paper-based order entry system that increased billing efficiency by 25%.
- Selected to serve on a statewide task force to develop a comprehensive internal controls program.

AVIATION
- Successfully set the standard for safe operations throughout the organization.
- Commended by upper management for mentoring and training junior pilots to improve their technical, tactical, and leadership skills.
- Designated to bring safety operations up to standard only two months before major inspections.
- Twice chosen to perform mid-level management responsibilities while only a junior officer.
- Handpicked to fly local general officers and visiting dignitaries.
- Developed and implemented improvement programs to correct flightline operating deficiencies.

ADMINISTRATIVE ASSISTANT / SECRETARY / CLERK

- Displayed a professional demeanor with a cheerful, positive attitude.
- Took reservations for a private beach and minimized conflicts in the schedule.
- Demonstrated an ownership attitude by completing tasks not specifically outlined but necessary for successful bank operations.
- Trusted with taking the initiative and making judgment calls during the manager's absence.
- Updated the filing systems and automated paperwork by scanning documents.
- Raised standards, reduced processing errors, and coached employees to achieve or exceed goals.
- Consistently achieved 100% of quality goals when the company standard is 95%.
- Contributed to the development of process improvements and procedures that impacted the organization at all levels.
- Authored a new quality assurance checklist that streamlined the records review process and dramatically improved the overall accuracy of documentation.
- Consistently arrived early and/or stayed late to ensure work was completed on time.
- Created multiple quick reference guides and job aids to improve work flow.
- Improved access to treatment options by developing a resource information sheet for drug treatment centers, respite options, and other resources in Colorado Springs and Denver, which was adopted by multiple centers statewide.
- Recognized as the "go-to" person in the division for questions about administrative processes.
- Identified and removed roadblocks to efficient processes. Allocated appropriate resources. Streamlined and improved operations.
- Handled details of setting up a new employee—cubicle assignment, phone, computers, equipment, start day/time, and payroll processes. Developed and presented orientation programs. Created processes that reduced new employee integration from six days to six hours.
- Given the power to manage credit cards, coordinate purchase orders, and track a $1.3 million overhead budget for nonproject billables.
- Instrumental in upgrading procedures from pen-and-ink to electronic documentation and processing.
- Identified the need for and created documents to clarify policies and procedures that are still used throughout the division today.
- Selected to serve on the Records Management Team charged with moving manual archiving processes to an electronic medium compatible with the National Archives. Set up nomenclature that was consistent across the organization. Facilitated changeover details behind the scenes.
- Received two Superstar Awards in recognition of exceptional effort and total commitment. Earned the Outstanding Effort Award. Recognized for largest dollar increase in gross margin.

BAKERY MANAGEMENT

- Evaluated and changed the production schedule of the bakery department to introduce new products, which increased profits and better met customer needs.

BANKING

- Implemented the training rollout for the automated profiling system, a computer-based contact management system that allows bankers to add value to their customer relationships and sell additional business lines.
- Created an inspection process to drive usage of the profiling system by bankers, achieving 45% system use for all customers purchasing product in the first year of implementation.
- Successfully managed a targeted census tract location with high burden ratios and processing costs (ranked second in transaction volume compared to size).

116

- Recommended, implemented, and managed an alternative delivery strategy known as dedicated bankers, which increased the percentage of mortgage customers buying additional products from 20% to 40% in only one year.
- Increased assets from $60 million to $99.5 million in five years; led the city in annuity sales.
- Determined that small-business customers were being underserved and developed a strategic plan to bring commercial banking back to the branch.

COMMUNICATION
- Established the division's quarterly newsletter for distribution to the staff and volunteers of the Olympic sports organizations, which significantly improved communication and compliance with grant guidelines.
- Facilitated communication between developers and users; improved relationships by prioritizing IT changes and setting realistic user expectations.

COMPUTERS
- As a system administrator, improved SMU's computer network efficiency by identifying areas requiring change and developing, testing, and implementing new practices and procedures.
- Streamlined an automated network-based database that maintained records in excess of $1.3 million within the External Relations Office.
- Created and maintained Web pages to improve executive relationships for the Dean's Council.
- Championed the first-generation informational website linked to major vendors and industry trade associations. Instrumental in the creation of the second-generation website offering an e-commerce component—the first in the textile converting industry *(www.tapetex.com)*.
- Maintained computer network support levels despite a $1.2 million budget cut.
- Decreased paperwork 50% by completely reviewing the circuit provisioning program.
- Opened an interactive CAD-CAM design studio used by customers to develop custom patterns and designs—the only one of its kind in the industry.

CONSTRUCTION
- Executed take-offs from blueprints, estimated costs, and bid jobs to ensure profitability.

CUSTOMER SERVICE
- Boosted customer retention rates from 85% to 99% by developing a Customer First program that was implemented in the field as well as in the call center.
- Interviewed all company departments and created a process flow map for service delivery that eliminated redundancies and improved overall efficiency.
- Provided a high level of customer service to patients and their families.
- Proactively maintained client relationships with 300+ corporate accounts.
- Created a quick response customer service team equipped with contact management software.
- Developed a new specialist concept for providing customer technical service and provisioning of Verizon's services that increased revenue by 40%.

EDUCATION ADMINISTRATION
- Selected to turn around a high school with declining enrollment, low teacher morale, a high dropout rate, deteriorating building, and poor academic reputation.
- Succeeded in revitalizing the staff and building consensus among teachers, the community, and students.
- Created a safe, productive, caring, and positive school climate through effective leadership that included modeling, rewards, communication, increased visibility, and appreciation for diversity.

- Developed and implemented innovative programs that have made Mitchell High School a magnet in the district.
- Implemented a variety of intervention programs to promote student achievement and retention.
- Improved attendance three percentage points by increasing the visibility of security personnel and creating an Attendance Committee that revised policies and improved parental involvement.
- Established an emphasis on instruction and ensured that all students were academically challenged and individually successful.
- Developed better programs and course offerings that resulted in the highest ACT improvement of any large high school on the Front Range.
- Improved writing scores on the DWA state assessments by an entire grade level.
- Achieved the highest scholarship dollar amount per graduate of any school in the district for 2011–2012.
- Recognized twice by the Chamber of Commerce for excellence in community partnerships.
- Partnered with Booz-Allen Hamilton, ARINC, Verizon, and the Citadel Mall to adopt classes. Employees followed the students through all four years of high school, providing mentoring, career exploration, and training opportunities. Received the Colorado CAPE Award for the Booz-Allen Hamilton partnership.
- Developed a unique partnership with Peterson Air Force Base to enhance the Career Technology Center.
- Created an award-winning mentorship program with the Colorado Springs Firefighters Association that involves local firefighters mentoring at-risk students.
- Developed community partnerships to rehabilitate the physical plant using volunteer help and donated materials, which has generated a new sense of pride among students.
- Led the development of a courtroom building that provides classroom space for pre-law courses, mock trial competitions, and simulations of actual court cases.
- Implemented a pilot mentorship program called "Choices" to teach junior and senior student leaders how to mentor freshmen classmates toward improved performance.
- Developed a partnership with the El Paso County building and construction industry to provide hands-on experience for students interested in the trade.
- Approached the El Paso County Contractors Association for grants and sponsorships for the Wheels of Learning program, which prepares students for careers in the building trades.

EVENT PLANNING
- Developed a wide network of vendors, facilities, speakers, and caterers to meet specific needs.
- Revitalized underperforming programs and achieved significant profitability.
- As an Executive Officer to an Army General, managed more than 35 worldwide trips in 12 months.
- Assisted the director of development with special events, notably the 25th Anniversary Gala, which was the single most profitable event in the organization's history.

FIELD ENGINEER
- Technical expert called in to resolve the most difficult problems.
- Improved efficiency and lowered labor/job costs, significantly improving profitability.
- Implemented an engineering approach to problem identification and achieved a defect density rating of 1.9 when the industry standard is 1.4 and perfection is 2.0.

FINANCE
- Represented the company during the preparation of the first registered Internet public venture capital offering as well as several private placements.

- Successfully guided the company through a lengthy period of extreme financial distress.
- Conceived a stabilization plan to reduce deficits inherited from previous management and negotiated forgiveness of significant vendor debt.

FUND-RAISING
- Raised $45,000 in three weeks for a heart transplant patient through newspaper, television, and radio promotion; set up bank accounts and coordinated special events.
- Provided information that helped one client reduce fund-raising costs by 65%.
- Founded a successful consulting business that provided fund-raising and development services to high-profile nonprofit organizations in New York and Colorado for more than 12 years.
- Developed a results-oriented reputation that ensured frequent referrals and repeat business from satisfied clients.
- One of three founders of a nonprofit theater venture that produced a three-week Equity showcase on Theatre Row, a premier Off-Broadway venue.
- Wrote and negotiated an umbrella agreement with an existing nonprofit organization to facilitate fund-raising.
- Succeeded in raising enough funds to meet budget requirements when the norm in the industry is a loss.
- Solicited government, foundation, corporate, and individual contributions accounting for 32% of the $1.2 million operating budget.
- Formalized the fund-raising program that is still used today. This established a sound financial foundation and provided the means for the organization to redefine itself amongst its peers as a premier instrument for promoting new playwrights.
- Created an all-purpose appeal that articulated the organization's history, mission, and programs.
- Part of a development team that raised $670,000—an 11% increase over the previous year—and exceeded corporate, foundation, and individual contribution goals.
- Researched and wrote grant proposals for foundation and corporate donors, generating an average of 20 grants per month to identified prospects.

GREENSKEEPER
- Gained extensive experience in growing and managing cool-season grasses, including knowledge of bentgrass greens, microclimatic conditions, and winterization.
- Enhanced turf grass quality and course playability using both current and innovative methods and technologies.

HEALTH CARE
- Part of the team responsible for the preparations that earned a score of 94 on the September 2007 JCAHO survey.
- Expanded the client base to include other Mercy subsidiaries, other hospitals, and various physician practices.

HOSPITALITY/TOURISM
- Built the hotel into a strong competitor for the city's business market and ranked in the top 10% for customer service out of 1,140 Hampton hotels.
- Developed housekeeping policies and procedures that resulted in a hotel cleanliness yield that exceeded corporate averages by as much as 23 points.
- Analyzed sales trends, developed forecasts and budgets, and set up rate structures that increased the average daily rate by $2.00 and occupancy by 1.7%.

- Promoted through the ranks from busboy to head waiter; developed a reputation for reliability and hard work; worked 35–40 hours per week while in college full-time.
- Inherited mother's restaurant specializing in casual lunch and catering; succeeded in growing the corporate client base and sold the business at a profit two years later.
- Maintained expenses below budget through accurate planning, purchasing, and waste reduction controls.
- Implemented operating efficiencies that kept the business profitable in spite of tight margins.
- Managed a restaurant and lounge recognized as first out of 54 in a five-state region.

HUMAN RESOURCES

- Designed and managed the company's self-funded hospitalization program, with resulting per-employee costs significantly below national averages.
- Created and implemented a progressive operations manual that significantly improved operating efficiency and, ultimately, profitability.
- Studied problematic behavioral trends, developed crisis intervention strategies and emergency responses, and made recommendations for changes to senior management.
- Conceptualized, developed, and co-facilitated The Silent Retreat, an award-winning experiential weekend for students and staff.
- Transformed the organizational culture and improved operating efficiency through cross-functional coaching/training and tactical restructuring that decentralized operations and brought the employees closer to their tasks and clients.
- Instituted a sales group compensation program that was completely performance based, motivating a 10% increase in sales.
- Developed a measurement process to analyze on-time and complete delivery performance, which permitted rapid corrective actions and improved response rates.
- Provided behavioral feedback as an executive coach to the group leaders and regional presidents.
- Created an atmosphere that valued continual learning, risk taking, and personal accountability among employees.
- Improved productivity and morale by initiating systems for accountability, formalizing job duties, and instituting training programs.
- Decreased recruiting costs 25% by implementing an employee referral system and using websites more effectively.

INVENTORY MANAGEMENT AND LOGISTICS

- Achieved a 98.8% service goal with 17.9 inventory turns in the grocery warehouse, where the corporate benchmark is 97% with 18 turns.
- Collaborated with category managers, marketing department, 113 vendors, and transportation providers to create supply and logistics cost-saving opportunities and to coordinate direct store deliveries.
- Helped save the Lane & Edson account by providing support for a critical shipping problem.
- Authored new interim and year-end physical inventory procedures for increased efficiency in the annual external audit.
- Improved warehouse requisition and receipt processing to less than one day, location accuracy to 98%, inventory accuracy to 97%, demand satisfaction rates to 90%, and zero balance rates to 3.6% (reduced from 36%).
- Re-engineered existing supply processes to save limited resources, recovering $26 million.
- Honored with two Meritorious Service Medals for innovations in logistical support.

- Received the Joint Service Commendation Award for improving inventory stock levels, accountability, consumption tracking, restocking, and customs procedures for the joint U.S. task force of Army, Navy, Air Force, and Marines.

JOINT VENTURES
- Approached a Belgian mill and formed a partnership that permits CTM to serve as their agent in the U.S., generating $2 million in new annual revenue.
- Created a strategic alliance with a major distributor of raw materials to the footwear industry, opening new Asian markets for the company and creating significant additional profit centers.
- Established a strategic distribution partnership in Latin America with Glen Raven Mexicana that expanded the market globally.
- Negotiated exclusive North American distribution agreements with two European mills, resulting in an annual sales increase of approximately $3 million.
- Developed a strategic partnership with Milliken, Inc., and Duro Industries to better serve one of the company's largest customers, W. L. Gore, resulting in a 350% increase in revenue over three years.

LAW
- Successfully negotiated individual product liability settlements of up to $250,000.
- Member of a three-attorney panel appointed by the New Mexico Court of Appeals to issue advisory decisions in pending civil appeals.
- Wrote the advisory decision in the appeal of *Miller v. NM Dept. of Transportation,* the essence of which was adopted by the New Mexico Supreme Court.
- Selected twice in fifteen months as an arbitrator for the New Mexico trial-level court to arbitrate cases with damage claims less than $15,000, using procedures similar to those governing American Arbitration Association proceedings.
- Lead counsel or sole counsel for the injured plaintiff / worker in at least 30 jury trials with a minimum trial length of three days, plus another 50 nonjury trials of at least two days.
- Since 1990, have prepared and prosecuted to conclusion, either by trial or settlement, more than 650 workers' compensation cases involving both physical and economic injuries.
- Met deadlines for pretrial procedures, trials, and appellate briefings by effectively using attorney associates and support staff.
- Designed a complete set of recurring forms to manage a typical workers' compensation claim from initial client interview through requested findings and conclusions.

MARKETING
- Developed a vital network of business and industry contacts instrumental to the rapid growth of the company.
- Successfully gained new customers through effective marketing, sales presentations, and follow-up.
- As marketing director for a retirement home, increased occupancy rates from 20% to 90%.
- Changed the company's perception in the marketplace by creating innovative marketing materials and making it more visible.
- Managed the company's transition to a global marketing focus through targeted sales planning, re-engineering of operations, and sound financial management, leading to sales diversification and enhanced opportunities for future growth in a shrinking market.
- Developed proprietary products for customers that strengthened their brand name equity and increased the company's profit margins.

- Enhanced domestic representation and diversified the product lines, increasing sales by 40% to $36 million.
- Developed and conducted quarterly focus groups with up to 150 management users; provided executive management with formal feedback that included solution-driven results.
- Developed effective sales and marketing programs that included direct mail campaigns, print advertising, promotions, and free delivery services.
- Wrote a strategic operating plan to improve profitability by more effectively allocating resources to key market segments and deploying technology to increase efficiency.

MANUFACTURING
- Increased equipment availability from 78% to 94% within the first month by reducing downtime through the implementation of a quality improvement strategy.
- Reduced maintenance work-in-process to less than 90 days with a production index of >1.0.
- Designed and implemented new floor layout to improve efficiencies and work flow.
- Reduced labor standards by an average of 25% on all product lines.
- Reduced rework rate by 50% by detailed in-process inspection.
- Reduced monthly failure rate from 2.5 units to .30 units.
- Implemented quick responses to assembly line accidents and other emergencies.

MERGERS & ACQUISITIONS
- Member of the Wells Fargo corporate steering committee responsible for merging the operations of the two banks (Norwest and Wells Fargo) into a functional sales tracking system.
- Coordinated the merger of a bank into one location and assumed the management of a new bank gained in the acquisition.

MILITARY
- Consistently promoted ahead of peers; selected for Technical Sergeant under the Stripes for Exceptional Performers (STEP) program.
- Selected for the 2006 Noncommissioned Officer of the Year Award at the command level for service above and beyond the expected.
- Successfully managed the maintenance of automotive equipment returning from Desert Storm, taking on twice the normal workload with no additional assets.

NURSING
- Member of the Access collaborative department team; helped to coordinate changes that improved patient satisfaction by allowing patients immediate access to the provider of their choice at times convenient for them.
- Ensured laboratory protocol was in compliance with Clinical Laboratory Improvement Amendment (CLIA).
- Coordinated a full 80-victim disaster drill and then rewrote the entire disaster plan in collaboration with the staff development RN.
- Furnished high-quality nursing care in the emergency room of a regional hospital seeing 4,000 patients per month, 600 requiring pediatric care.
- Instituted a Braslowe Tape System of acute pediatric assessment and treatment, as well as a geriatric fall prevention and risk assessment program.
- Designed and implemented a tool to identify victims of domestic violence who presented to the ER, which ensured proper care and follow-up.
- Ensured optimum patient care in spite of often adversarial relationships between private and public emergency services.

- Initiated and participated in staff and interdisciplinary team conferences to improve the quality of care delivered to residents.
- Served as a role model for county public health nurses and other providers.
- Acted as a resource person to new nursing staff and facilitated team cohesion.

QUALITY ASSURANCE
- Investigated and resolved quality and service complaints, promoting repeat business and improving profitability.
- Honored for a commitment to 100% customer satisfaction and zero defects.
- Improved response to system outages by streamlining procedures and keeping leadership informed.

SALES
- Referred more than $15 million in new placements annually.
- Recognized by Lanier's Atlanta headquarters for generating the highest yearly sales volume in the Western Region during the first six months on the job; eight-time recipient of the monthly top production award.
- Hired geographically dispersed sales executives and developed a team-based environment that communicates horizontally and not just vertically.
- Researched and implemented a Web-based software tool (salesforce.com) to enhance sales reporting from the field.
- Expanded the sales force to facilitate the development of high-profile key accounts, growing sales from $35 to $54 million.
- Designed sales management processes to promote sales effectiveness and achieve long-term revenue growth and increase customer loyalty across multiple channels.
- Created solid working relationships with internal and external partners to improve opportunity identification and sales closings.
- Selected for several corporate task forces, including retail job descriptions, retail incentives, and go-forward sales training curriculum initiatives.
- Selected as a statewide sales trainer to introduce and implement an innovative sales process long before the industry moved in that direction.
- Increased gross sales from $1,500 to $80,000 per month in one year.
- Interfaced with vendors, customer service representatives, and medical personnel to streamline product delivery and maintained effective working relationships.
- Used negotiation and persuasion skills to gain a continually higher percentage of sales per account.
- Influenced the group's senior leadership to support and participate in a defined sales management accountability matrix that promoted active supervision of operations that drive results.
- Completed monthlong corporate training program in Manhattan and succeeded in developing 200 clients in the first year with $4.3 million in assets.

TEACHER
- Selected to assist in the evaluation, modification, and organization of Cheraw Elementary School's math, science, reading, and writing curriculum.
- Developed a successful classroom motivational tool that included special shirts for students.
- Wrote multiple grants and received funding for special programs.
- Received Outstanding American History Teacher of the Year award for southeast Colorado by the Daughters of the American Revolution (2012).
- Appointed to the Master Teacher Advisory Group for the U.S. Space Foundation (2012).

- Selected for the national Time Magazine Award for developing and implementing a mock presidential election for all of the schools in the Cheraw District (2010).
- Recipient of a Colorado Endowment for the Humanities (2010).

TELECOMMUNICATION
- Identified 180 leased communication circuits for removal, saving $2.1 million in annual leased line costs.
- Researched and developed a communications network strategy for U.S. locations in the Netherlands, saving $480,000 in international leased line costs and ensuring survivability of communications services.

TRAINING
- Coached training staff to improve the quality of seminar presentations.
- Taught six weeks of initial management training and three weeks of continued management training at The Management Training Center; personally responsible for launching the careers of 400 management employees.
- Redesigned and implemented a new training model based on the Mager Method for the annual ten-day resident adviser training program, which is still in use today.
- Introduced a sales training program that included 18 months of in-house experience before being assigned to a designated territory.
- Developed cross-training programs that improved the morale and the efficiency of operations and lowered turnover rates.

Awards and Honors

In a study of corporate hiring practices, the researcher found that decision makers weren't much interested in awards even if they applied to the job they were trying to fill.

The study concluded, "Hiring managers don't know how to judge the value of awards. For example, a résumé that just mentions the name of the award might not provide enough information. However, readers would learn more if they knew this award went only to the top five performers in a sales force numbering more than five hundred."

The key, then, is to focus on the accomplishment more than the award itself. Naming the honor or award is secondary to the return on investment the hiring manager perceives from the sentence. For example:

- Received the National Sales Excellence Award in 2012 by becoming one of the top five producers of mutual fund sales within the peer group.

- Selected by United Technologies Sikorsky Aircraft Company to receive their Igor I. Sikorsky Helicopter Rescue Award for a successful high-risk mountain rescue.

- Won two quarterly superior customer service awards in two years by competing with 18 bakeries in the district.

- Selected for the Service Excellence Award (fourth quarter of 2012) for personal customer service excellence.

- Received a monetary award for improving the working relationship between couriers and service agents.

- Achieved Best-in-Class customer service scores based on quarterly client surveys.

- Recipient of the Gold Level Reward for exceptional performance during 2012.

- Received Gold Star award for exceptional performance during a crisis call.

Remember the rule that there is an exception to every rule in the résumé business? Well, here's another one. If the award is so self-explanatory in your industry that explaining it would be insulting to your reader, then list those awards or honors in a separate section at the bottom of your résumé, like this for a teacher:

- High Plains Educator Award (2012)
- Who's Who Among America's Teachers (2011, 2012)
- Outstanding Young Woman of America (2011)

… or like this for an Olympic medalist in Taekwondo:

- Awarded the USOC Developmental Coach of the Year, Taekwondo (2012)
- Olympic Games, Bronze Medal (2012), selected as captain of the team
- Taekwondo Times Hall of Fame (2012)
- Pan American Games, Bronze Medal (2011)
- Pan Am Taekwondo championships, Gold Medal (2010)
- U.S. Olympic Festival, Gold Medal (2010)
- World Games, Silver Medal (2009), U.S. World Team Member (8 times)
- World Championships, Bronze Medal (2007, 2009, 2011)
- Selected as an International Referee by the World Taekwondo Federation
- Captain, U.S. National Team (2007–2012)
- President's Best Player Award (2007)

Step 7
Delete

10

When you have the words on paper, go back to each list and think about which items are relevant to your current job target. Cross out those things that don't relate, including entire jobs (like flipping hamburgers back in high school if you are now an electrical engineer with ten years of experience).

Remember, your résumé is just an enticer, a way to get your foot in the door. It isn't intended to be all-inclusive. You can choose to go back only as far as your jobs relate to your present objective. Be careful not to delete sentences that contain the most important keywords you identified in Step 4 (Chapter 7).

Change Is Inevitable

You know the old saying "The only constant is change." Perhaps you should make a copy of the pages you have already completed before you begin marking them up. They are a great record of your work history, and you never know when you might want to change careers, which means you would need some of that information.

According to the U.S. Department of Labor, the average worker today will change jobs 20 times in his or her career and hold 9.2 jobs between the ages of 18 and 34. Today, workers are much more free to change not just jobs but careers, which they can change from three to five times in their work life.

I have been writing résumés since 1980, and the biggest change I've seen since the early 1990s is the number of clients who have decided to, for example, leave computer programming for acting or to change from nursing to pharmaceutical sales.

Part of the reason for this transition is social and part is the result of the modern workplace. According to William Hine, dean of the School of Adult and Continuing Education at Eastern Illinois University, "The half-life of a college degree is three to five years." There was a time when you could graduate from college

> *The average worker today will change jobs 15 times and careers 3–5 times.*

and stay in the same job for 30 years and then retire with a gold watch. Not so today. You must be committed to lifelong learning or your career will leave you behind.

That means you can also make the choice to retool, get a new degree, and start a new career in midlife. It's perfectly acceptable.

It also means that being a pack rat can pay off when you decide to change careers! So, store the original sheets in the same file you created for your performance evaluations and job descriptions, and use the copies for this step.

Take the copies and decide which jobs are relevant to today's job search. You need to use only about 10 to 15 years of those jobs, unless there is something very powerful in your early career that will help you get a job. Now, set aside the jobs that are too old or irrelevant. Try to limit your list of final jobs to no more than six, although you can list more if they are truly relevant or contain valuable experience.

Focus on the sentences in the relevant experience summaries.

- Which ones are the most powerful?
- Which ones summarize your experience the best?
- Which ones contain the keywords of your industry?
- Which ones highlight your accomplishments the best?

Delete Education

Next, do the same for your education and training worksheets. Copy them, file the originals, and cross out anything that doesn't relate to your current job goal.

That does not apply to your formal education, however. Even if you have a graduate degree in your career field and your undergraduate degree is unrelated, leave them both on your résumé. Your reader will need to see the progression of your formal education.

If you have a bachelor's degree and an associate's degree, you don't need to list them both unless there is something about the major of your associate's degree that you don't have in your bachelor's degree. Remember, it is okay to list almost anything on your résumé as long as it is relevant to your job search.

Step 8
Dynamic
Sentences

11

It's time to do some serious writing now. You must make dynamic, attention-getting sentences of the duties and accomplishments you have listed under each job, combining related items to avoid short, choppy phrases. Here are the secrets to great résumé sentences:

- In résumés, you never use personal pronouns *(I, my, me)*. Instead of saying, "*I planned, organized, and directed the timely and accurate production of code products with estimated annual revenues of $1.0 million,*" you should say, "*Planned, organized, and directed....*" Writing in the first person makes your sentences more powerful and attention grabbing, but using personal pronouns throughout a résumé is awkward. Your reader will assume that you are referring to yourself, so the personal pronouns can be avoided.

- Make your sentences positive, brief, and accurate. Since your ultimate goal is to get a human being to read your résumé, remember to structure the sentences so they are interesting to read.

- Use verbs at the beginning of each sentence *(designed, supervised, managed, developed, formulated,* and so on) to make them more powerful (see the list at the end of this chapter).

- Incorporate keywords from the list you made in Step 4 (Chapter 7).

- Make certain each word means something and contributes to the quality of the sentence.

Finding Help

If it is difficult for you to write clear, concise sentences, take the information you have just listed to a professional writer who can help you turn it into a winning résumé. Choose someone who is a

> *Make certain each word means something and contributes to the quality of the sentence.*

Nationally Certified Résumé Writer (NCRW), Master Résumé Writer (MRW), Certified Professional Résumé Writer (CPRW), or Certified Master Résumé Writer (CMRW). That way you can be assured that the person has passed the strictest tests of résumé writing and design in the country, including peer review, administered by the National Résumé Writers' Association (NRWA), Career Thought Leaders (CTL), Professional Association of Résumé Writers and Career Coaches (PARW/CC), and Career Directors International (CDI), respectively. The expense of a professional written résumé is a small investment when compared to the advantages it provides for your career.

To find certified résumé writers, visit these websites:

- National Résumé Writers' Association, *www.thenrwa.com*
- Career Management Alliance, *www.careerthoughtleaders.com/credentials*
- Professional Association of Résumé Writers and Career Coaches, *www.parw.com*
- Career Directors International, *www.careerdirectors.com*

What are the benefits of partnering with a professional résumé writer? According to the NRWA, you will gain access to the following:

- Expert résumé writing, editing, and design skills.

- Needed objectivity and expertise to play up your strengths, downplay your weaknesses, and position yourself for interview success.

- The precise know-how to target your career and industry correctly.

- Winning résumé, job search, interviewing, and salary negotiation strategies from recognized experts.

- Experienced professionals who have passed rigorous résumé industry exams and demonstrated their commitment to the profession by obtaining ongoing training.

- Writers who are dedicated to providing the highest quality service and a superior finished product.

Résumé writers work in one of three ways: (1) they gather all of the information they need from you in a personal interview, (2) they require that you complete a long questionnaire before they begin working on your résumé, or (3) they use a combination of both methods. In any case, you have already done most of the data collection if you have followed Steps 1 through 6 and Steps 10 and 11 in this book. This preparation sometimes makes the résumé easier to write, and many professional résumé writers will pass on that savings to you in the form of lower fees.

If you are going to proceed from here and finish the résumé on your own, let me show you how to rewrite sentences so they are more powerful. The original sentences in these examples were on real résumés. The rewrites are my fine-tuning based on interviews with each client, which gathered more information and clarified the original intent of the writer.

Original Sentence: Responsible for leading team of application engineers, delivery consultants, and technical trainers in pre-sales and post-sales activities.

Rewrite: Led a team of 20 application engineers, delivery consultants, and technical trainers in the development of customized enterprise software solutions.

Original Sentence: Generation of accurate and meaningful client proposals based on initial client needs and assessment.

Rewrite: Generated effective client proposals based on a comprehensive assessment of client requirements.

Original Sentence: Telecommunication sales associate who achieved quota each month after training phase.

Rewrite: Successfully sold telecommunication services, achieving sales goals each month and generating more than $1 million in annual revenue.

Original Sentence: Responsible to ensure that time is spent on being proactive about the future financial needs of the district.

Rewrite: Proactive in ensuring that the future financial needs of the district were met.

Original Sentence: Helped the district make assessment and accountability that accompanies data not an event but rather a practice that we seek and value.

Rewrite: Assured that assessment and accountability became part of the district's culture and not a simple event.

Original Sentence: Marketing Coordinator; for all internal and external marketing for Club Sports six upscale fitness clubs and a hotel and fitness resort.

Rewrite: Coordinated all of the internal and external marketing for six upscale fitness clubs and the Renaissance ClubSport hotel and fitness resort.

Original Sentence: Inside sale support responsible for aftermarket parts and equipment sales for over 200 municipalities as well as expediting and tracking purchase orders, sales generated yearly were approximately $100,000.

Rewrite: Provided inside sales support for aftermarket parts and equipment sales to 200+ municipalities, personally generating annual sales of more than $100,000.

Original Sentence: Processed and reviewed applications for residency.

Rewrite: Reviewed applications for residency, checked credit and personal references, and approved new occupants.

Original Sentence: Sold and achieved sales goals.

Rewrite: Integral member of the teller team responsible for exceeding sales goals for credit card accounts, ATM cards, instant cash cards, and new account referrals.

Original Sentence: Coordinating with the local printer, all collateral for the club.

Rewrite: Developed collateral materials and ensured that all clubs had the most recent sales aids.

Power Verbs

Now that you have some samples of good writing, let's look at the words that made it possible. Power verbs at the beginning of sentences make them more interesting and, well, "powerful." Try to use a variety of these words. It's easy to choose the same one to begin every sentence, but there are synonyms buried within this list that will make your writing better.

A

abated
abbreviated
abolished
abridged
absolved
absorbed
accelerated
accentuated
accommodated
accompanied
accomplished
accounted for
accrued
accumulated
achieved
acquired
acted
activated
actuated
adapted
added
addressed
adhered to
adjusted
administered
adopted
advanced
advertised

advised
advocated
affirmed
aided
alerted
aligned
allayed
alleviated
allocated
allotted
altered
amassed
amended
amplified
analyzed
answered
anticipated
appeased
applied
appointed
appraised
approached
appropriated
approved
arbitrated
aroused
arranged
articulated
ascertained
aspired
assembled

assessed
assigned
assimilated
assisted
assumed
assured
attained
attended
attracted
audited
augmented
authored
authorized
automated
averted
avoided
awarded

B

balanced
bargained
began
benchmarked
benefitted
bid
billed
blended
blocked
bolstered

boosted
bought
branded
bridged
broadened
brought
budgeted
built

C

calculated
calibrated
canvassed
capitalized
captured
cared for
carried
carried out
carved
catalogued
categorized
caught
cautioned
cemented
centralized
certified
chaired
challenged
championed

132

changed
channeled
charged
charted
checked
chose
chronicled
circulated
circumvented
cited
clarified
classified
cleaned
cleared
closed
coached
co-authored
coded
cold called
collaborated
collated
collected
combined
commanded
commenced
commended
commissioned
communicated
compared
competed
compiled
complemented
completed
complied
composed
compounded
computed
conceived
concentrated
conceptualized
concluded
condensed
conducted
conferred
configured
confirmed
confronted
connected

conserved
considered
consolidated
constructed
consulted
consummated
contacted
continued
contracted
contributed
controlled
converted
conveyed
convinced
cooperated
coordinated
copied
corrected
correlated
corresponded
counseled
counted
created
credited with
critiqued
cultivated
customized
cut

D

dealt
debated
debugged
decentralized
decided
decoded
decreased
dedicated
deferred
defined
delegated
deleted
delineated
delivered
demonstrated
deployed
depreciated

derived
described
designated
designed
detailed
detected
determined
developed
devised
devoted
diagnosed
diagrammed
differentiated
diffused
directed
disbursed
disclosed
discounted
discovered
discussed
dispatched
dispensed
dispersed
displayed
disposed
disproved
dissected
disseminated
dissolved
distinguished
distributed
diversified
diverted
divested
divided
documented
doubled
drafted
dramatized
drew up
drove

E

earned
eased
economized
edited

educated
effected
elaborated
elected
elevated
elicited
eliminated
embraced
emphasized
employed
empowered
enabled
encountered
encouraged
ended
endorsed
enforced
engaged
engineered
enhanced
enlarged
enlisted
enriched
enrolled
ensured
entered
entertained
enticed
equipped
established
estimated
evaluated
examined
exceeded
exchanged
executed
exercised
exhibited
expanded
expedited
experienced
experimented
explained
explored
exposed
expressed
extended
extracted
extrapolated

fabricated
facilitated
factored
familiarized
fashioned
fielded
filed
filled
finalized
financed
fine-tuned
finished
fixed
focused
followed
forecasted
forged
formalized
formatted
formed
formulated
fortified
forwarded
fostered
fought
found
founded
framed
fulfilled
functioned as
funded
furnished
furthered

gained
garnered
gathered
gauged
gave
generated
governed
graded
graduated

granted
graphed
grasped
greeted
grew
grouped
guaranteed
guided

H

halted
halved
handled
headed
heightened
held
helped
hired
honed
hosted
hypnotized
hypothesized

I

identified
ignited
illuminated
illustrated
implemented
imported
improved
improvised
inaugurated
incited
included
incorporated
increased
incurred
indicated
individualized
indoctrinated
induced
influenced
informed
infused

initialized
initiated
innovated
inspected
inspired
installed
instigated
instilled
instituted
instructed
insured
integrated
intensified
interacted
interceded
interfaced
interpreted
intervened
interviewed
introduced
invented
inventoried
invested
investigated
invigorated
invited
involved
isolated
issued
itemized

joined
judged
justified

L

launched
learned
leased
lectured
led
lessened
leveraged
licensed

lifted
lightened
limited
linked
liquidated
listened
litigated
loaded
lobbied
localized
located
logged

M

made
maintained
managed
mandated
maneuvered
manipulated
manufactured
mapped
marked
marketed
mastered
maximized
measured
mediated
memorized
mentored
merchandised
merged
merited
met
minimized
mobilized
modeled
moderated
modernized
modified
molded
monitored
monopolized
motivated
mounted
moved
multiplied

N

named
narrated
navigated
negotiated
netted
networked
neutralized
nominated
normalized
noticed
notified
nurtured

O

observed
obtained
offered
officiated
offset
opened
operated
optimized
orchestrated
ordered
organized
oriented
originated
outdistanced
outlined
outperformed
overcame
overhauled
oversaw
owned

paced
packaged
packed
paid

pared
participated
partnered
passed
patterned
penalized
penetrated
perceived
perfected
performed
permitted
persuaded
phased out
photographed
piloted
pinpointed
pioneered
placed
planned
played
polled
posted
praised
predicted
prepared
prescribed
presented
preserved
presided
prevailed
prevented
priced
printed
prioritized
probed
processed
procured
produced
profiled
programmed
progressed
projected
promoted
prompted
proofread
proposed
protected
proved
provided

pruned
publicized
published
purchased
pursued

Q

quadrupled
qualified
quantified
queried
questioned
quoted

R

raised
rallied
ranked
rated
reached
reacted
read
realigned
realized
rearranged
reasoned
rebuilt
received
reclaimed
recognized
recommended
reconciled
reconstructed
recorded
recovered
recruited
rectified
redesigned
redirected
reduced
re-engineered
referred
refined
refocused
regained
registered

regulated
rehabilitated
reinforced
reinstated
reiterated
rejected
related
released
relied
relieved
remained
remediated
remodeled
rendered
renegotiated
renewed
reorganized
repaired
replaced
replicated
replied
reported
represented
reproduced
requested
required
requisitioned
researched
reserved
reshaped
resolved
responded
restored
restructured
retained
retooled
retrieved
returned
revamped
revealed
reversed
reviewed
revised
revitalized
revolutionized
rewarded
risked
rotated
routed

S

safeguarded
salvaged
saved
scanned
scheduled
screened
sculptured
searched
secured
segmented
seized
selected
sent
separated
sequenced
served as
serviced
settled
set up
shaped
shared
sharpened
shipped
shortened
showed
shrank
signed
simplified
simulated
sketched
skilled
slashed
smoothed
sold
solicited
solidified
solved
sorted
sourced
sparked
spearheaded
specialized
specified
speculated

spent
spoke
sponsored
spread
spurred
stabilized
staffed
staged
standardized
started
steered
stimulated
strategized
streamlined
strengthened
stressed
stretched
structured
studied
subcontracted
submitted
substantiated
substituted
succeeded
suggested
summarized
superceded
supervised
supplied
supported
surpassed
surveyed
swayed
swept
symbolized
synchronized
synthesized
systemized

T

tabulated
tackled
tailored
talked
tallied

targeted
tasted
taught
teamed
tempered
tended
terminated
tested
testified
tied
tightened
took
topped
totaled
traced
tracked
traded
trained
transacted
transcribed
transferred
transformed
transitioned
translated
transmitted
transported
traveled
treated
trimmed
tripled
troubleshot
turned
tutored
typed

U

uncovered
underlined
underscored
undertook
underwrote
unearthed
unified
united
updated

upgraded
upheld
urged
used
utilized

V

validated
valued
vaulted
verbalized
verified
viewed
visited
visualized
voiced
volunteered

W

weathered
weighed
welcomed
widened
withstood
witnessed
won
worked
wove
wrote

Y

yielded

Step 9
Rearrange

12

You are almost finished! Now go back to the sentences you have written and think about their order of presentation. Put a number 1 by the most important description of what you did for each job. Then place a number 2 by the next most important duty or accomplishment, and so on until you have numbered each sentence.

Again, think logically and from the perspective of a potential employer. Keep related items together so the reader doesn't jump from one concept to another. Make the thoughts flow smoothly.

The first sentence in a job description is usually an overall statement of the position's major responsibilities. The rest of the sentences should begin with your most important duties and accomplishments and proceed to lesser ones.

Let me give you an example of a job description in rough draft format and one that has been rearranged, and I'm sure you will see what I mean.

JOHNSON UNIVERSITY HOSPITAL, New Brunswick, New Jersey (2009–2012)
Director, Pediatric Emergency Department
- Recently developed and implemented an expansion of the department into a new children's hospital.
- Hired and managed a staff of 40 employees, directed performance improvement initiatives, and implemented departmental standards of care.
- Analyzed trends for key indicators to improve subsequent code responses.
- Member of the Performance Improvement Committee.
- Analyzed 72-hour readmission trends to find problems with practice patterns.
- Selected for the Code Response Team: Developed a new performance improvement form.
- Redesigned resuscitation guidelines for residents and nursing staff.
- Directed clinical and administrative operations of a 12,000-visit-per-year pediatric emergency department.
- Developed and managed an operating budget of $1.3 million.
- Developed staffing standards and evaluated the qualifications/competence of department personnel to provide appropriate levels of patient care.

> *The first sentence in a job description is usually an overall statement of the job's major responsibilities.*

- Member of the Health Policy and Strategic Planning Committee responsible for preparing the hospital and staff for JCAHO accreditation reviews.
- Implemented a pain initiative.

After numbering and rearranging the sentences, the section reads much stronger and has a better flow. I like to use a paragraph format for duties and bullets for accomplishments, like in the sample below.

JOHNSON UNIVERSITY HOSPITAL, New Brunswick, New Jersey (2009–2012)
Director, Pediatric Emergency Department
Directed clinical and administrative operations of a 12,000-visit-per-year pediatric emergency department. Developed and managed an operating budget of $1.3 million. Hired and managed a staff of 40 employees, directed performance improvement initiatives, and implemented departmental standards of care. Developed staffing standards and evaluated the qualifications and competence of department personnel to provide appropriate levels of patient care. Served as a member of the Health Policy and Strategic Planning Committee responsible for preparing the hospital and staff for JCAHO accreditation reviews.

Key Accomplishments
- Recently developed and implemented an expansion of the department into a new children's hospital.
- Member of the Performance Improvement Committee: Analyzed 72-hour readmission trends to find problems with practice patterns. Implemented a pain initiative. Redesigned resuscitation guidelines for residents and nursing staff.
- Selected for the Code Response Team: Developed a new performance improvement form. Analyzed trends for key indicators to improve subsequent code responses.

Here is my reasoning for rearranging the sentences:

1. The first sentence was selected because it was a good overall statement of the job's major responsibility.

2. The second sentence added a further sense of scope by describing the size of the director's budget.

3. The third sentence also increased the scope by discussing the number of employees managed and other supervisory responsibilities.

4. The next two sentences are secondary job duties and special assignments.

5. In order to emphasize achievements, key accomplishments were pulled out into a separate section.

6. The first bullet was the most important accomplishment and the most recent.

7. All of the bullets that applied to the Performance Improvement Committee were listed together in a separate paragraph.

8. The last accomplishment was the least important.

Before and After Sample

Perhaps it would help to see a sample of a résumé before it was rewritten and rearranged. The résumé on the next two pages was a first attempt without following the instructions in this book. The final version is shown on the last two pages of this chapter.

Pay special attention to the way bullets were expanded and rearranged to make them more powerful and compelling. The computer skills and education sections were moved to the top of the résumé because they were Paul's strongest qualifications for his new job goal (website design).

PAUL O. JONES
1234 North Tejon Street
Denver, CO 80210

Before
Sample

303.123.4567
Jones1234@pcisys.net

Objective
A challenging technical position at an excelling high tech company.

Education
University of Colorado, Colorado Springs
Bachelor of Arts in Fine Arts Studio, December 2002
BOL183\f"Symbol"\s10 Primary Emphasis: Digital Imaging, Sculpture

Professional Courses
- Intermediate HTML
- Advanced HTML
- Windows NT 4.0 Administration
- UNIX Fundamentals

Qualifications
Very attentive to accuracy and detail, as well as efficiency and organization. Excellent written, verbal, and interpersonal skills.

- Programming Languages: HTML, exposure to JavaScript.
- OS Platforms: Windows (9x/NT/2000/XP), exposure to MacOS and UNIX.
- Software: Adobe Photoshop, Adobe Image Ready, Microsoft Internet Information Server, WebTrends Analysis Suite, and Microsoft Office.

Experience
Verizon, Inc.   **May 2008 – June 2012**
1234 Garden of the Gods Road • Colorado Springs, Colorado 80919

Software Development (Applications Developer II)
- Responsible for the design, development, and maintenance of several Verizon intranet and internet web sites.
- Redesigned existing intranet and internet web sites inherited from other groups/organizations within Verizon to provide users with a fresh browsing experience and enhanced organization of the web site content.

System Administrator (Software Systems Engineer I)
- Responsible for the implementation, monitoring, and maintenance of several Verizon intranet and internet web sites and web servers within both Windows and UNIX environments.
- Provided weekly web traffic and usage analysis reports for many of the sites hosted within the Windows and UNIX web server environments using WebTrends Analysis Suite.

Best Buy Stores, Inc.   **August 2000 – April 2008**
5678 North Academy Boulevard • Colorado Springs, Colorado 80909

Customer Service, Service Technician, and Sales
- Performed sales and return/exchange transactions, handled customer issues, and placed service orders.
- Performed testing/troubleshooting and minor repairs on consumer electronics, handled shipping, receiving, and inventory of repair units.
- Made sales in Media (software & music), Computer hardware and accessories, Cellular Phones, and Digital Satellite Systems.

140

Other Experience   **The Mercury Cougar Collector's Page**   **Sep 2005 – 2009**

Conception, design, and maintenance of an automotive web site, in which enthusiasts of the 1967-73 Mercury Cougar could display photos of their cars and obtain information.

Exhibitions and Awards

Student Art Exhibition

Gallery of Contemporary Art • University of Colorado, Colorado Springs

May 2008–Sculpture
May 2007–Sculpture
May 2006–Digital Image

Aardvark-Zymurgy: The works of the 2007-2008 UCCS Art Graduates
December 2007

The Warehouse Gallery, Colorado Springs, Colorado

Display of two sculptures and a digital image.

***Purchase Prize,* Student Art Exhibition**   **May 2006**

Gallery of Contemporary Art • University of Colorado, Colorado Springs

Digital image, *Message from the Gods*, was purchased by the university for display in the University Center.

PAUL O. JONES

QUALIFICATIONS

After Sample

- Creative Web Developer with a strong background in the design, development, and administration of large corporate Intranet and Internet websites.
- Detail-oriented professional who gains great satisfaction from knowing that a project was done right.
- Enthusiastic team player with an outgoing, friendly communication style.

COMPUTER SKILLS

Programming Languages: HTML, MS Visual InterDev, JavaScript

Operating Systems: Windows (9x/NT/2000/XP), Macintosh, and UNIX

Design Software: Adobe Photoshop, Adobe Image Ready, Adobe Live Motion, Lightwave 3-D

Business Applications: MS Word, Excel, Access, PowerPoint, Outlook, Internet Explorer, Microsoft Internet Information Server, WebTrends Analysis Suite

EDUCATION

BACHELOR OF ARTS (December 2012)
University of Colorado, Colorado Springs, Colorado
- Major in Fine Arts Studio with an emphasis on digital imaging and sculpture
- Computer course work: Electronic Imaging, Advanced Project in Electronic Imaging, Web Art, Advanced Computer Art, Introduction to Computer Art
- Design course work: Independent Study in Fine Arts, Photography, 20th Century Sculpture, Advanced Drawing, Art History, Color Drawing, Advanced Studio Problems, Studio 3-D, Beginning Studio 2-D
- 3-D Topics: Form, Wood, Wood Sculpture, Advanced Sculpture, Advanced Figure Sculpture
- Business course work: Conflict Management, Macroeconomics, Interpersonal Communications, Political Science, Quantitative and Qualitative Reasoning Skills

PROFESSIONAL DEVELOPMENT
- Intermediate and Advanced HTML, Verizon, Colorado Springs, Colorado
- Windows NT 4.0 Administration, Verizon, Colorado Springs, Colorado
- UNIX Fundamentals, Verizon, Colorado Springs, Colorado
- Lightwave 3-D Modeling Software, Washburn University, Denver, Colorado

EXPERIENCE

FREELANCE WEB DESIGNER (2005–present)
Paul White Consulting, Colorado Springs, Colorado
- Designed a website for High West Siding and Windows—*www.highwestsiding.com.* (2012)
- Conceived, designed, and maintained a website for enthusiasts of the 1967–1973 Mercury Cougar called The Mercury Cougar Collector's Page. The site allowed interested people to display photos of their classic cars and obtain information. (2005–2009)

APPLICATIONS DEVELOPER II (Software Developer) (2009–2012)
Verizon, Colorado Springs, Colorado
- Designed, developed, and maintained several Verizon Intranet and Internet websites.
- Met with internal customers to determine their requirements, brainstormed with the development team, and designed the look and feel of each site.
- Redesigned existing websites inherited from other groups and organizations within Verizon to provide users with a fresh browsing experience and enhanced organization of content.
- Recognized for reliability, initiative, customer service skills, and ability to meet tight deadlines.
- Discovered a virus attack on the servers and recovered data quickly to minimize downtime.

ADDRESS

1234 N. Tejon Street • Denver, Colorado 80210 • (303) 123-4567 • E-mail: jones1234@pcisys.net

**EXPERIENCE
(continued)**

SOFTWARE SYSTEMS ENGINEER I (System Administrator) (2008–2009)
Verizon, Colorado Springs, Colorado

- Served as primary systems administrator for 20 Windows NT servers and backup administrator for the UNIX servers, together hosting up to 150 websites.
- Backed up the systems weekly to ensure that data was available for recovery purposes.
- Configured and managed Web server software, including MS Internet Information Server and Netscape Enterprise Server.
- Monitored and maintained Intranet and Internet websites and provided weekly Web traffic and usage analysis reports using WebTrends Analysis Suite.
- Served as team leader on various server installation projects.
- Customized website configuration to provide user-friendly development environments and convenient access for content management.

CUSTOMER SERVICE REPRESENTATIVE, TECHNICAL SERVICE TECHNICIAN (2002–2008)
Best Buy Stores, Inc., Colorado Springs, Colorado

- Successfully sold computer hardware and accessories, cellular telephones, digital satellite systems, software, and music in a retail setting.
- Won numerous sales awards for consistently meeting or exceeding revenue goals and selling value-added services.
- Handled returns and exchanges, placed service orders, and ensured customer satisfaction.
- Performed testing, troubleshooting, and minor repairs on consumer electronics.
- Managed shipping, receiving, and inventory of repair units.

ART EXHIBITIONS

STUDENT ART EXHIBITION (2006–2008)
Gallery of Contemporary Art, University of Colorado, Colorado Springs, Colorado

- Displayed a digital image and two sculptures.
- Won a Purchase Prize for a digital image entitled *Message from the Gods.* The image was purchased by the University for display in the University Center.

AARDVARK–ZYMURGY: THE WORKS OF UCCS ART GRADUATES (2007–2008)
The Warehouse Gallery, Colorado Springs, Colorado

- Displayed two sculptures and a digital image.

Step 10
Related
Qualifications

13

At the bottom of your résumé (or sometimes toward the top), you can add anything else that might qualify you for your job objective. This includes licenses, certifications, special skills, publications, speeches, presentations, exhibits, grants, special projects, research, affiliations, and sometimes even interests if they truly relate. See the form at the end of this chapter to collect this information.

People often ask me what should NOT be included in a résumé. Well, there are very few times when photographs or personal information are appropriate on a résumé. Usually such facts only take up valuable white space, especially details such as age, sex, race, health, or marital status, and other information that potential employers are not allowed to ask anyway. If such information is included on a résumé, there is always the possibility a hiring manager will unintentionally discriminate against you during the hiring process.

As I said before, however, there are exceptions to every rule in the résumé business! Here are some of them:

- Submitting a résumé to a U.S. company doing business in certain foreign countries is one example. On such a résumé, an "Interests" section would show a prospective employer that your hobbies are compatible with the host country.

- Students, or those who have recently graduated, often have a difficult time coming up with enough paid experience to demonstrate their qualifications. But if they have held leadership positions in campus organizations or have supervised groups of people and organized activities on a volunteer basis, then an "Activities" section could strengthen those qualifications.

- A list of sporting interests would be helpful for a person looking for a sports marketing position.

Use your judgment. Only you know best what qualifications are important in your field.

- International résumés in almost all cases require date of birth, place of birth, citizenship, marital status, sex, and often a photograph.

And the list goes on. It is important to use your judgment, since only you know best what qualifications are important in your field. For instance, several of my clients are ministers. In their line of work, it is very important to list a great deal of personal information that most employers would not need to know or even be allowed by law to request. In their case, the information they provide relates directly to bona fide occupational qualifications for the jobs they are seeking.

Photographs

Photographs on a résumé are required by many foreign companies requesting a curriculum vitae. However, in the United States, photographs are discouraged in all but a few industries. For instance, if you are trying for a job as an actor, model, newscaster, or in some other field where your appearance is, again, a bona fide occupational qualification, then a photograph is appropriate.

Photographs are usually added to your LinkedIn and Facebook profiles and can become part of the design of your e-folio or visual CV. When these technologies first became popular, HR professionals became concerned about seeing these photographs and being accused of discrimination. Now, they are so commonplace that hiring managers don't think twice about seeing your photograph.

My only concern is if there is something about your appearance that might automatically invite discrimination based on Title VII protected classes—race, color, religion, sex, or national origin. In that case, avoid adding your photograph to your social networking profiles.

References

References are not usually presented on a résumé since most employers will not take the time to check references until after an interview. By then, they will have your completed application with a list of references. You also don't want to impose on your friends, associates, or former employers unnecessarily or too frequently. There is nothing wrong with taking a nicely printed list of professional (not personal) references with you to an interview, however. The form at the end of this chapter will help you prepare that list.

Here's one of those exceptions to the rule again. If an advertisement requests that a list of references be sent with the résumé and cover letter, then by all means supply the list. You don't want to be accused of not following directions!

Avoid that needless line at the bottom of the résumé that says, "References available upon request." It takes up valuable white space that you need to define the sections of your résumé in order to draw the reader's eyes logically down the page.

Pretend you are an interviewer. You ask, "Will you provide references?" The interviewee replies, "Sorry, no, I can't do that." Will you even think twice about continuing to consider this candidate? I think not. It is assumed that you will provide references when requested.

Samples

Here are some samples of additional information included in real résumés. Remember, each one had a bona fide reason for including this information. In other words, the information strengthened their qualifications in some way.

TECHNOLOGY SKILLS (when the goal is a network system administrator job in military telecom)

Networking
- Served as System Administrator for an AT&T UNIX-based mainframe computer system supporting national consumers on four workstations tied into a global network of 14 servers and 16 clients.
- Evaluated information management requirements and identified organizational IT needs.
- Maintained consistent, reliable, and secure information by establishing policies, procedures, methods, and standards for system access and disaster recovery.
- Performed systems analysis and programming tasks to maintain computers and control their use.
- Created new user accounts, logon scripts, network directory shares, and password resets.
- Installed and upgraded software and tested programs to ensure functionality.
- Maintained and troubleshot printer servers, configured printers, and created new printer shares.
- Proficient in real-time system integration and troubleshooting techniques, process flow, and equipment requirements.

Telecommunications
- Seventeen years of experience in the operation, installation, activation, and maintenance of telecommunications systems for the U.S. Navy, including HF, UHF, VHF, FDM, TDM, and satellite voice and data communications circuitry, call routing, and translations.
- Supported commands over a 3,000-mile area with telephony, digital/analog voice, data, and video systems.
- Coordinated with commercial carriers to restore high- and low-speed circuits: cross-connects, CODEX modems, troubleshooting using frequency and time division multiplexing, repairs, and basic maintenance of telecommunications equipment.
- Performed daily quality control checks on hundreds of voice, data, and video circuits, coordinating usage and outages with commercial carriers, global commands, and in-house users.
- Reported circuit outages to various local and national authorities, made restoration recommendations, and kept senior management informed of problems.
- Tested telecommunications systems, modems, PC hardware, and associated terminals, cabling, and switching equipment/facilities.

- Experienced in the operation and troubleshooting of FCC-100, Racal 9600, and SDD 1900 modems, CV-8448 and CV-2048 NRZ-CDI converters, multiplexers, key switching units, and Voxtel PBX.

Security
- Managed the operation, installation, maintenance, and troubleshooting of Communications Security (COMSEC) equipment, including KG-84A/C, KG-75 FASTLANE, KG-175 TACLANE, KG-96, KYV-5, KY-57/58, KIV-19, KYK-13, KOI-18, CZY-10, STU-III secure phone cryptography equipment.
- As Communications Security Material (CSM) System Controller, managed a COMSEC account with more than 1,000 highly classified, extremely sensitive items.
- Issued, destroyed, and documented COMSEC materials. Inventoried and tracked each piece of CMS using an automated tracking system. Issued receipts and destroyed CMS material, maintaining two-person integrity at all times

Hardware
- Mainframe Computer Systems and Architecture: Tellabs DAX, Alcatel 600E, MUSIC, Streamliner, Newsdealer, TACINTEL, VAX 6000, DECstations, DEC PDP-11/70, GTE IS-1000.
- Storage Devices: magnetic tape drives, optical disk drives.
- RF Equipment: antennas, satellites, transmitters, receivers.
- Imagery Systems: FIST, DVITS, JDISS.
- Test Equipment: Data Sentry 10, ADC Patch Panels, Firebird 6000, Logitech Test Generator, Halcyon Test Set, Sage 930 and 950, T-Com, T-Berd, oscilloscopes, multimeters, signal analyzers.

Business Applications
- Proficient in Microsoft Word, Excel, PowerPoint, Outlook, and Internet Explorer.
- Extensive experience working in Windows and SCO UNIX environments.
- Working knowledge of various Defense Information Systems Agency (DISA) circulars.
- Experienced in statistical analysis and data processing.

TECHNOLOGY SKILLS (for network/system administration)

CERTIFICATIONS
- Microsoft Certified Professional (MCP)
- Certified in Microsoft Windows 7 Pro
- Certified in Microsoft Windows 7 Server
- Certified in Active Directory Administration and Design

NETWORKING
- **Operating Systems:** Linux, Solaris 10.1, Windows XP/Vista.
- **Servers:** Dell PowerEdge 4400 Server, CNS 6200 Communications Network Server.
- **Cisco Network Map:** Cisco 7507/720D, Cisco 7200 VXR Service Delivery Point, Cisco 6509/6513, Cisco 4506/4507/4507R, Cisco 3845, Cisco 3560, Cisco 3750/3750G, Cisco 2800 Voice Bundle Router, Cisco 2960 Catalyst Switch.
- **Networks:** Juniper Router, NIPRnet, AMP Netconnect, CAT-5E Patch Panels, Digital Patch Panels, KIV-7 Line Encryption Device, TimePlex Promina 200, ADC Digital Patch Panel, DMPS Power Supply, Digital 186 Processors, AN/TSQ-209 Automated ASOC (Servers, Switches).

- **Communications Equipment:** Cryptographic Equipment Component-Level Repair (KY-3/57/58/65/68/75) (KG-13/30/84/94/94A), APC 1400 Smart UPS, SB-385/3614 Tactical Digital/Analog Telephone Switchboard, Optical Distribution Systems, Nortel Telephone System, TA-312/1038/1042 Analog/Digital Telephones, RMC-1210, TRC-170 Wideband, TSC-94A Satcom, S-530 Maintenance Shelter, GRC-206 Radio Pallet.
- **Software / Applications:** Microsoft Word, Excel, PowerPoint, Access, Outlook, Internet Explorer.

PRESENTATIONS (for nursing administration)

- *Pediatric Emergency Department Product Line Implementation,* Organization of Nurse Executives, New Jersey, March 2012.
- *Pediatric Education for Prehospital Professionals,* National Course Roll Out, Robert Wood Johnson University Hospital, New Brunswick, New Jersey, September 2011.
- *Financial Awareness of Hospital Nurses,* Robert Wood Johnson University Hospital, New Brunswick, New Jersey, May 2011.
- *Initiatives in Pediatric Emergency Services,* Board of Directors, Robert Wood Johnson University Hospital, New Brunswick, New Jersey, May 2011
- *Hypothermia: Emergency Care of the Complex Patient,* Nursing Grand Rounds, CentraState Medical Center, Freehold, New Jersey, September 2009.
- *Newborn Care: Basic Assessment to Resuscitation,* Paramedic Curriculum, Robert Wood Johnson University Hospital, Emergency Medical Services Program, New Brunswick, New Jersey, June 2009, 2010, 2011, 2012.
- *Introduction to Pediatric Emergency Care,* Robert Wood Johnson University Hospital, New Brunswick, New Jersey, October 2009.
- Course Instructor for the Neonatal Resuscitation Program, Robert Wood Johnson University Hospital, New Brunswick, New Jersey, quarterly since January 2009.
- Course Instructor for Pediatric Advanced Life Support classes, Robert Wood Johnson University Hospital, New Brunswick, New Jersey, quarterly since January 2009.

AFFILIATIONS (for nursing administration)

- Executive Board Member, Seton Hall University Nursing Alumni (2010–present)
- Member, American Nurses Association (ANA) (2011–present)
- Member, New Jersey State Nurses Association (NJSNA) (2011–present)
- Member, American Association of Nurse Executives (AONE) (2011–present)
- Member, Gamma Nu Chapter, Nursing Honor Society (2010–present)
- Member, Chair's Council of the College of Nursing (2008–2009)
- Peer Mentor, Sophomore and Junior Nursing Students (2008–2009)
- Member, Student Nurses Association, Seton Hall University (2006–2009)
  - President (2008–2009)
  - Delegate to the 2009 NSNA Convention, Pittsburgh, Pennsylvania
  - Delegate to the 2009 NJSNA Convention, Atlantic City, New Jersey
  - Publicity Chairperson (2007–2008)

AFFILIATIONS (for tourism management)

- Appointed to the Rules Committee of the Colorado Passenger Tramway Safety Board; created guidelines for funicular railway rules that were adopted nationwide (2008–2011).

- Member, Board of Directors, Pikes Peak Country Attractions Association (2005–present); Executive Board Member (2007–2009), Vice President (2010–2011), and President (2011–2012).
- Member, Trees Committee, Pikes Peak Hospice (1997–2010); coordinated the installation of lighting on all trees for an annual fund-raising event that generates $135,000 a year.

CERTIFICATIONS (for nursing)

- Instructor, Pediatric Advanced Life Support (PALS)
- Instructor, Neonatal Resuscitation Program
- Instructor, Pediatric Emergency for Prehospital Providers
- Provider, Basic Life Support (BLS)
- Licensed Registered Nurse in Illinois and New Jersey

KEY CONTACTS (for public relations)

Print Media
- Newspapers: Sports editors, national sports columnists, and NBA columnists from the top 40 major newspapers and wire services, including *USA Today, The New York Times, Chicago Tribune, Los Angeles Times, The Wall Street Journal,* Associated Press, Bloomberg, Reuters, among others. Beat writers covering NBA teams in all 29 NBA markets, representing 100 major newspapers.
- Magazines: Top NBA and sports columnists from leading sports publications (*Sports Illustrated, The Sporting News, ESPN Magazine,* etc.) and mainstream news and business writers from *Time, Newsweek, Fortune, Business Week,* and others.

Television
- Network sports executives and on-air announcers and correspondents for major network and cable stations, including NBC, ESPN, HBO, TNT, Fox Sports, CNN, MSG Network, and others.
- A variety of contacts among on-air correspondents and producers from network television news departments, including NBC's *Meet the Press,* the *CBS Evening News,* and ABC's *20/20,* among others.

Sports
- Comprehensive working relationships with executives in the legal, marketing, and communications departments of professional sports leagues, unions, and teams.
- Broad contacts with a significant number of influential sports agents and many other player representatives, concentrating in areas such as marketing, public relations, and financial planning.
- Extensive interaction with NBA players serving on the NBPA Executive and Negotiating Committees, and each NBA player serving as a team player representative over the past three years.

COMMUNITY SERVICE (for law enforcement)

- Member, Colorado Springs Workforce Management Council (2010–present); Chairperson of the Recruitment Subcommittee for all city employees
- Board of Directors, National Alliance of the Mentally Ill (NAMI)
- Member, El Paso County Justice Advisory Council responsible for allocating resources for the jail population and addressing issues affecting law enforcement in the community
- Member, National Organization for Black Law Enforcement Executives (NOBLE)

- Member, International Association of Chiefs of Police (IACP)
- Member, 4th Judicial District Domestic Violence Recertification Board for health care providers (2009–2012)
- Member, School District 20 Principal Selection Committee (2008–present)
- Served as liaison between the Police Department and the NAACP
- Worked with the Care Coalition Community Network to develop prevention programs for high-risk youth
- Member, Martin Luther King Jr. Holiday Committee
- Public Information Chairman for the Cinco de Mayo Committee
- Liaison to the Armed Forces Disciplinary Control Board
- Member, Consortium for the Developmentally Disabled
- Director and Past President of the Colorado Springs Police Athletic League
- Regional Chairman, National Police Athletic League

LEADERSHIP (for sports management)

U.S. Olympic Committee
- Member, Audit Committee (2011–2012)
- Appointed to the CEO Transition Team (2010–2011)
- Athletes Advisory Committee (1995–2003)

World Taekwondo Federation
- Vice Chair, Junior Committee (2011–present)
- Member, Collegiate Committee (2008–2010)

U.S. Taekwondo Union
- Member, Executive Committee (1995–2008)
- Member, Coaching Science Committee (2005–2008)
- Member, National Tournament Committee (1995–2008)
- Member, Board of Directors (1994–2007)
- Chairman, Athletes Advisory Council (1995–2006)

Taekwondo Associations
- President, Big Sky Taekwondo Academy (1990–2001)
- President, Montana State Taekwondo Association (1994–2001)
- Chief Instructor, Montana State University (1990–2001)

Community Organizations
- Board of Directors, Citrus Heights Chamber of Commerce (2008–2011)
- Director of Workforce San Juan, a guidance program for at-risk youth (2008–2011)

VOLUNTEER EXPERIENCE (for admission to law school)

- Volunteered more than 130 hours to the Peterson Outdoor Adventure Program; served as a guide for all-terrain vehicle, water skiing, sailing, and canoe trips (2010–2012).
- Organized numerous community activities as a member of Beta Sigma Phi; donated baked goods monthly for the Center for Domestic Violence; raised more than $500 for the Circle of Hope Foundation; delivered holiday baskets for needy families (2009–2010).
- Fed homeless and needy families during the holidays; organized the entire military unit to assist for two years, feeding 500+ homeless at each event (2007–2010).

- Led neighbors in developing a local Neighborhood Watch program; collaborated with local sheriff's deputies to provide signs and organize meetings to deter violence and crime (2009).
- Raised more than $500 in food, clothing, and toys for the needy at Christmas (2006–2009).
- Represented the military at the Colorado State Fair to provide the public with information about Cheyenne Mountain Air Force Base (2008).
- Organized a class at the Airman Leadership School to refurbish the Colorado Springs Ronald McDonald House (2008).
- Coordinated two very successful base-wide cookie drives to provide treats for military members stationed in the Middle East during the holiday season (2007–2008).
- Organized two holiday parties for residents of Laurel Manor Nursing Home (2006, 2008).
- Raised hundreds of dollars for local charities by organizing the 21st Operation Group's annual "Slip-n-Slide" charity softball tournament (2007).
- Volunteered with Special Olympics; motivated participants during relay activities (2001).

CERTIFICATIONS (for quality assurance)

Certified Quality Manager, American Society for Quality (2010–present)
Certified RAB Quality System Auditor, RAB 16-hour Lead Auditor Course (2006)
Certified Quality Auditor, American Society for Quality (2005–present)
Certificate of Quality Auditing, Pennsylvania State University (2005)
Certificate of Environmental Management System, Pennsylvania State University (2004)

LANGUAGES (for international jobs)

Spanish: Native tongue
English: Highly proficient, writing and speaking (PET, FIST Certificate, TOEFL, TSE, TWE)
Portuguese: Fluent speaking, proficient writing
French: Working knowledge (5 years Alliance Française)

CREDENTIALS FILE (for a recent graduate)

A credentials file is available from the University of Kansas upon request.

CREDENTIALS (for a teacher)

Colorado Professional Principal License (2005–2010)
Colorado Professional Administrator License (2005–2006)
- K–12 Director of Special Education Endorsement
Colorado Professional Teacher License (2005–2010)
- K–12 Aurally Handicapped Endorsement

LICENSES AND CERTIFICATIONS (for a nurse)

- Registered Nurse, State of Connecticut, E-20143
- Registered Nurse, State of Florida, RN-2382391
- Certified, Advanced Cardiac Life Support (ACLS)
- Certified, Basic Life Support (BLS)

RELATED QUALIFICATIONS

AFFILIATIONS (professional associations, chambers of commerce, Toastmasters, etc.) _____

_____

_____

_____

_____

_____

LANGUAGES (with levels of proficiency*) _____

_____

_____

*Fluent (absolute ability, native), Highly Proficient (three to five years of usage in the country), Proficient (able to understand the subtleties of the language), Working Knowledge (can conduct everyday business), Knowledge (exposure to the language, courtesy phrases)

LICENSES _____

_____

_____

_____

CERTIFICATIONS _____

_____

_____

_____

CREDENTIALS _____

_____

_____

_____

PRESENTATIONS/SPEECHES (title, meeting, sponsoring organization, city, state, date) _____

_____

_____

_____

EXHIBITS _____

_____

_____

_____

PUBLICATIONS (authors, article title, publication title, volume, issue, page numbers, date) _____

_____

_____

_____

GRANTS _____

_____

_____

_____

RELATED QUALIFICATIONS

SPECIAL PROJECTS _____
_____
_____
_____

RESEARCH _____
_____
_____
_____

UNIQUE SKILLS _____
_____
_____
_____

VOLUNTEER ACTIVITIES, CIVIC CONTRIBUTIONS _____
_____
_____
_____
_____
_____
_____

HONORS, AWARDS, DISTINCTIONS, PROFESSIONAL RECOGNITION _____
_____
_____
_____

COMPUTERS _____
_____
Applications (MS Word, Excel, PowerPoint, etc.) _____
Operating Systems (Windows, Macintosh, UNIX, etc.) _____
Databases (Access, Oracle, etc.) _____
Programming Languages _____
Networking _____
Communications _____
Hardware _____

OTHER RELEVANT SKILLS _____
_____
Actors (singing, musical instruments, martial arts, etc.) _____
Secretaries (typing speed, shorthand, etc.) _____
Welders (TIG, MIG, ARC, etc.) _____

INTERNATIONAL (travel, living, cross-cultural skills, etc.) _____
_____
_____
_____

OTHER RELATED QUALIFICATIONS

REFERENCES

Unless an advertisement specifically requests references, don't send them with your résumé. Type a nice list of three to six references on the same letterhead as your résumé to take with you to the interview. Use this form to collect the information for your reference list. Choose people who know how you work and are not just personal friends or family members.

NAME _____

RELATIONSHIP TO YOU _____ NUMBER OF YEARS KNOWN _____

COMPANY _____

MAILING ADDRESS _____

CITY, STATE, ZIP _____

WORK PHONE _____ CELL PHONE _____

HOME PHONE _____ E-MAIL _____

NAME _____

RELATIONSHIP TO YOU _____ NUMBER OF YEARS KNOWN _____

COMPANY _____

MAILING ADDRESS _____

CITY, STATE, ZIP _____

WORK PHONE _____ CELL PHONE _____

HOME PHONE _____ E-MAIL _____

NAME _____

RELATIONSHIP TO YOU _____ NUMBER OF YEARS KNOWN _____

COMPANY _____

MAILING ADDRESS _____

CITY, STATE, ZIP _____

WORK PHONE _____ CELL PHONE _____

HOME PHONE _____ E-MAIL _____

NAME _____

RELATIONSHIP TO YOU _____ NUMBER OF YEARS KNOWN _____

COMPANY _____

MAILING ADDRESS _____

CITY, STATE, ZIP _____

WORK PHONE _____ CELL PHONE _____

HOME PHONE _____ E-MAIL _____

NAME _____

RELATIONSHIP TO YOU _____ NUMBER OF YEARS KNOWN _____

COMPANY _____

MAILING ADDRESS _____

CITY, STATE, ZIP _____

WORK PHONE _____ CELL PHONE _____

HOME PHONE _____ E-MAIL _____

NAME _____

RELATIONSHIP TO YOU _____ NUMBER OF YEARS KNOWN _____

COMPANY _____

MAILING ADDRESS _____

CITY, STATE, ZIP _____

WORK PHONE _____ CELL PHONE _____

HOME PHONE _____ E-MAIL _____

Step 11
Personal Branding Statement

14

We really are almost finished! One last thing before you put it all together. Think about the objective (or focus) that you determined in Step 1 (Chapter 4). Rewrite this objective on the form at the end of this chapter, then write four or five sentences that give an overview of your qualifications.

This profile, or personal branding statement, should be placed at the beginning of your résumé. This is the first thing that the recruiter reads, so it is extremely important. You need to communicate what makes you special—your unique value proposition—and how that unique combination of knowledge, skills, abilities, and track record of accomplishments can meet the needs of your potential employer.

That means you need to know your industry very well and the "players" in your field, in addition to knowing yourself. Only then can you put the pieces together into a dynamic personal branding statement that convinces your reader that you are the ideal fit for their opening.

Here is an example of a true personal branding statement. You will find many more at the end of this chapter. They are real profiles from a variety of résumés with diverse goals. You can list each sentence as a separate bullet or use a single paragraph, depending on how you plan to format the résumé.

FOR AN ATTORNEY WHO SPECIALIZES IN HIGHER EDUCATION:

Experienced attorney, management consultant, change agent, and regulatory expert with a proven track record of adding value to stable companies and turning around struggling organizations, bringing them into compliance with strict government and industry regulations. One of only a few generalist lawyers left in the country. Able to bring to any industry a diverse background in litigation, mergers and acquisitions, due diligence, regulatory compliance, education as a business, higher education instruction, and academic program development.

Avoid using laundry lists of keywords in place of the sentences of a profile section. First of all, they aren't very interesting for a human being to read, and second, keywords used out of context do

> *Communicate what makes you special—your unique value proposition.*

not have the same impact when processed by electronic résumé processing software. Newer applications use artificial intelligence to determine a keyword's credibility based on the surrounding text.

For human readers, however, it is okay to pull out a few key bullets that highlight your areas of expertise (see sample below). Just make sure you use the same words somewhere within the body of your résumé.

- Dedicated accountant with thirteen years of diverse experience that includes
  - Public accounting
  - Internal auditing
  - Nonprofit accounting
  - Compliance auditing
  - Tax preparation
  - Reporting
- Certified Public Accountant in California and Colorado; Certified Internal Auditor.
- Analytical and thorough professional with a track record of success managing the toughest assignments.
- Effective team player with exceptional communication, writing, and interpersonal skills.

A new trend in résumé writing allows us to incorporate philosophy statements or a favorite quote into the profile of a résumé. The "Executive Summary" is more accomplishment driven and uses fewer soft-skill keywords.

AREAS OF EXPERTISE

P&I Management • Strategic Planning
Transportation/Logistics • Budgeting
Sales/Marketing • Business Development
Supply Chain Management • Outsourcing
Technology Enhancements
Quality Management • Regulatory Affairs
Customer Satisfaction • Vendor Relations

"It's all about the people. The greatest reward of leadership is helping to develop people, which, when handled properly, leads to exceptional organizational results."

EXECUTIVE SUMMARY

- Strong record of streamlining operations, reducing costs, and increasing profitability while facilitating quality and operations improvements for both large and small organizations.

- Definitive success in start-up and turnaround situations, as well as stable business environments.

- Domestic and international experience in a broad range of industries.

- Recent Executive MBA with a concentration in Finance, International Business, and Corporate Strategy.

A similar idea creates a section for quotes from performance evaluations, letters of reference, customer comments, and other positive comments that provide external validation of your knowledge, skills, and abilities. These are the same quotes you will use on your LinkedIn profile. You can put the quotes in the margins of the résumé, in pull-out boxes, in a separate section, or worked individually at the end of a list of accomplishments. Here is a sample of customer comments in a separate section:

CUSTOMER COMMENTS

"As a representative for Adelphia Cable, Allan was one of the few who understood the true meaning of the word 'service.'" — Robert Smith, Adams Advertising Agency

"Allan has proven to be extremely knowledgeable and professional in executing my local cable TV media campaigns. Having worked in cable advertising sales myself for six years, I can appreciate when a media salesperson does a great job from the initial schedule planning stage to the final invoice." — Mike Smith, Champion

"His thorough knowledge of the product and the sales process are evidence of his many years of success in media sales. I enthusiastically recommend Allen for any sales position and am confident that his competency and positive attitude would make him a valuable asset." — Christin Jones, Academy Agency & Advisors

"Allan has the four traits that make him a great sales rep: friendly, responsible, efficient, and fun. If Allan is applying for a job with your company, I suggest hiring him immediately!" — Brian Jones, Hanson Marketing & Advertising

Now, back to the profile section and your personal branding statement. It must reflect your unique value proposition, but it must also be relevant to the type of job for which you are applying, so customize it for each application if possible. It might be true that you are "compassionate," but will it help you get a job as a high-pressure salesperson? Write this profile from the perspective of a potential employer. What will persuade this person to call you instead of someone else?

Busy recruiters spend as little as ten seconds deciding whether to read a résumé from top to bottom. You will be lucky if the first third of your résumé gets read, so make sure the information at the top entices the reader to read it all.

Profile Samples

Let's look at some sample profiles for various industries. You will notice some significantly different styles of presenting the information. Choose the style that best presents your information.

ARTIST

Creative graphic artist with experience in pen-and-ink illustration, watercolor, and oil mediums. Background in magazine/book, children's book, graphic novel, and comic book illustration. Hardworking, loyal artist with definitive leadership and sales abilities. Self-starter; able to motivate others to perform to their maximum potential.

ATTORNEY

- Licensed attorney in private practice since 1990 (Colorado and New Mexico).
- Board Certified Civil Trial Specialist, National Board of Trial Advocacy, with extensive litigation experience (initially certified 1995, recertified 2000, 2005, and 2010).
- Recognized specialist in workers' compensation law by the New Mexico Legal Specialization Board.
- Extensive experience in the preparation and trial of injury claims resulting from both workers' compensation and off-the-job injuries.

- Admitted to practice before the U.S. Court of Appeals, 10th Circuit; U.S. District Court for the District of New Mexico; U.S. District Court for the Western District of Texas; District Courts of the State of Colorado; and all courts in the State of New Mexico.
- Successful Federal Administrative Law Judge applicant (awaiting placement).
- Exceptional knowledge of administrative procedures, rules of evidence, and trial practices.
- Able to communicate in a clear, concise manner with people of diverse backgrounds and levels of authority.

BOOKKEEPER

- Experienced bookkeeper and administrator with twenty years of diverse experience.
- Background in management, general ledger, financial statements, accounts payable, accounts receivable, and payroll.
- Computer literate in Windows, QuickBooks Pro, One-Write, MS Word, Excel, and Business Works.
- Dependable, accurate, and well organized; able to handle multiple tasks simultaneously.

BUYER

Dependable, efficient procurement professional with thirteen years of experience in the grocery business. Quick learner who is able to troubleshoot complex problems and multitask effectively. Self-motivated team player with exceptional communication and interpersonal skills. Proven leader who enjoys finding better ways of doing things and making value-added improvements.

CERTIFIED PUBLIC ACCOUNTANT, FINANCIAL EXECUTIVE

- Experienced Financial Executive and Certified Public Accountant with a strong background in the following:

– Accounting	– MIS	– Acquisitions
– Budgeting	– Administration	– Banking Relationships
– Credit Management	– HR Management	– Environmental Compliance
– Reporting	– Benefits	– Legal Issues

- CFO at the time of an initial public offering; supervised SEC reporting and investor relations.
- Managed preparation of the first registered Internet public venture capital offering and several private placements to accredited investors.
- Negotiated a variety of long-term and short-term loan syndications and developed cash management functions.
- Licensed CPA in Arizona and Ohio (inactive); won the Silver Award for the second-highest exam grade in Ohio.

CHILD CARE PROVIDER

Dedicated child care provider with more than 11 years of experience. Fair and just with a commitment to setting a good example. Patient instructor who enjoys working with children. Effective team player with strong interpersonal and communication skills.

COMPUTER NETWORK TECHNICIAN WITH A MILITARY CONTRACTOR

- Experienced systems/network technician with significant communications and technical control experience in the military sector.
- Focused and hardworking; willing to go the extra mile for the customer.
- Skilled in troubleshooting complex problems by thinking outside the box.
- Possess a high degree of professionalism and dedication to exceptional quality.
- Current Top Secret security clearance with access to Sensitive Compartmentalized Information.

CONSTRUCTION PROFESSIONAL

Experienced construction professional with a background in residential and commercial roofing and general contracting. Quality oriented with a dedication to getting the job done right the first time. Well organized with a natural aptitude for math; skilled in analyzing tasks and breaking them down into manageable pieces.

CONSULTANT

- Detail-oriented consultant with a strong entrepreneurial spirit and a background in consultative selling and MIS.
- Experience with e-business, competitive strategy development, strategic business planning, re-engineering, custom development, data-driven models, process assessment/improvement, and information technology.
- Extensive background in international marketing, importing, advertising design, and new business development.
- Proven history of building new business by identifying, calling on, and driving business decisions at the executive level.
- High-energy team player with exceptional leadership, analytical, problem-solving, communication, and presentation skills.

CRIMINAL INVESTIGATOR

Experienced criminal investigator with eighteen years as a Deputy U.S. Marshal with full law enforcement authority and a background in management, investigative, and supervisory positions. Dedicated manager who welcomes a challenge. Team player who is willing to work long hours to get the job done. Proven reputation for working well with others and serving as a role model/mentor.

EDITOR, BOOK PUBLISHING

- Experienced editor with a strong book publishing background, including the following topics:

– Math	– Medical	– Business	– Juvenile
– Science	– Nursing	– Art	– Parenting
– Test Preparation	– Allied Health	– Gardening	– Child Care

- Skilled wordsmith with the ability to transform a rough draft into a marketable finished product.
- Effective team player with outstanding communication and interpersonal skills.
- Knowledge of Windows, MS Word, Excel, Internet browsers, and e-mail.

EMT/FIREFIGHTER

- Experienced EMT and registered firefighter with a strong desire to help people.
- Quick thinker who enjoys a fast pace and the challenge of a job's physical demands.
- Adept at working under pressure and managing multiple tasks simultaneously.
- Effective team player with a positive attitude and strong interpersonal skills.
- Proven problem solver who enjoys getting to the root of a challenge.

ELECTRONICS TECHNICIAN

Experienced electronics technician with a strong background in test and engineering. Detail oriented and analytical; able to manage the details while seeing the whole picture. Respected for the ability to solve problems and get things done when others give up. Effective team player with exceptional communication and interpersonal skills.

ENGINEER

- Experienced engineering professional with a strong background in the following:
  - Quality control/quality assurance
  - Electrical/mechanical systems
  - Precision-process maintenance
  - Analysis and problem solving
  - Equipment fabrication
  - Test equipment operation
  - Electronic principles and theories
  - Computer-controlled devices
- Proven expertise in engineering enhancements to fabrication tools, chemical mechanical polishing, vacuum systems, pneumatic systems, diffusion, and gas delivery systems.
- Skilled in reading and interpreting blueprints, engineering prints, and other schematic drawings.

EXECUTIVE ASSISTANT

Experienced executive assistant with a strong work ethic and proven customer service skills. Quick learner who enjoys the challenge of new responsibilities. Effective team player who is dependable, cooperative, and able to work under tight deadlines. Strong communication and interpersonal skills; tactful when working with difficult people.

FACILITY MAINTENANCE

- Experienced technician with a diverse background in industrial and commercial facility maintenance.
- Nationally Certified Apartment Maintenance Technician (CAMT) since 2010.
- HVAC Certified (Universal), Esco Institute since 2003; EPA Certified since 2006.
- Dependable, loyal worker who can fix just about anything and learns quickly.
- Personable and courteous; proven track record of exceptional customer service.
- Good listener with a quick sense of humor and the ability to work well with all types of people.
- Exceptional attendance record; never missed a page call in eight years of 24-hour-a-day availability.

FASHION DESIGN DIRECTOR

Innovative, high-performing designer who approaches creative work with excellence while maintaining commercial appeal. Able to act as a "telescope" to spot trends and then to tie those trends back to growth categories. Proven ability to bring fresh ideas to the table and to create designs that protect core brand concepts while delivering on fashion and innovation.

FIELD ENGINEER, TELECOM

- Experienced field engineer, cable splicer, communications technician, and supervisor.
- Background in the installation, testing, and maintenance of analog/digital telephone and central office equipment.
- Self-motivated team player who works well independently and manages time efficiently.
- Long track record of perfect attendance with no on-the-job accidents.
- Flexible worker with the ability to analyze and prioritize project assignments.
- Proven reputation for providing exceptional customer service.

FINANCIAL PLANNER

- Experienced financial planner with proven expertise in retirement planning, investments, insurance, and asset management.
- Hold current Series 7, 63, 65, 31, life, health, and accident insurance licenses.
- Committed to the highest levels of integrity and professional ethics.
- Team leader with exceptional communication skills and an engaging interpersonal style.
- Able to work effectively with people from diverse backgrounds and levels of authority.
- Knowledge of Windows, MS Word, Outlook, and the Internet.

FINANCE PROFESSIONAL

- Seasoned finance professional with extensive experience in the following areas:
  - Venture capital
  - Mergers/acquisitions
  - Business plan analysis
  - Business valuation
  - Due diligence
  - Financial modeling
  - Operations management
  - Strategic planning
  - New business development
- Multidisciplinary executive with a diverse background in marketing/sales, finance, accounting loan origination and servicing, and public accounting.
- Able to effectively motivate both management and operating personnel to achieve maximum results.
- Skilled in applying logical but creative approaches to problem resolution.

HIGH-TECH or CORPORATE TRAINING

Eight years of experience as an **Instruction Designer** and **Trainer** in both the corporate and public sectors. Strong background in developing company training programs, computer-based instruction, and corporate university programs. Skilled in organization, leadership, project management, team building, and problem solving. Effective team player with proven interpersonal, communication, presentation, and writing skills.

INFORMATION ANALYST

- Dedicated information analyst with more than 18 years of programming/data processing experience in the telecommunications, banking, and government sectors.
- Certified Xenix Systems Administrator.
- Skilled in analysis, construction, implementation, troubleshooting, production support, operations support, help desk, testing (unit, regression, integration, and systems), training, and maintenance.
- Detail oriented and organized; comfortable taking the initiative and working independently.

LAW ENFORCEMENT

Proven leader with more than 20 years of law enforcement experience and expertise in program development, project management, team motivation, and public relations. Service-oriented professional with the ability to promote positive organizational values. Personally dedicated to ensuring the delivery of quality service. Experienced public speaker with strong communication and presentation skills.

LOGISTICIAN, MATERIALS MANAGER

HIGHLIGHTS OF QUALIFICATIONS
Experienced materials manager and gifted logistician with a proven background in these areas:
Administration • Operations • Contract Negotiations • Cost Control • Budgeting
Forecasting • Purchasing • Automated Inventory Tracking Systems • Transportation • Distribution
Self-motivated leader with strong interpersonal, communication, and motivation skills.
Able to organize and prioritize multiple projects with divergent needs.
Hold a current secret security clearance.

MANAGER, GENERAL

- Forward-thinking manager with diverse experience in the following areas:
  - Business development
  - Change management
  - Process re-engineering
  - Strategic planning
  - Consultative selling
  - Marketing
  - Employee development
  - Training and facilitation
  - Supervision
- Skilled in applying logical but creative approaches to problem resolution.
- Self-motivated; comfortable working independently and taking the initiative.
- Effective team player with exceptional communication and presentation skills.

MANAGER, GENERAL

- Experienced manager with a proven track record of improving productivity and profitability.
- Resourceful at finding innovative solutions to complex problems.
- Able to work outside the job description and to manage crises with ease.
- Personable team player with strong communication and interpersonal skills.

MANAGER, HEALTH CARE

Self-motivated health care manager with a passion for taking on new responsibilities. Proven supervisor with the ability to motivate workers and lead by example. Skilled in applying logical but creative approaches to problem resolution. Open to re-evaluating traditional methods and finding better ways to get the job done. Personable team player with strong communication and presentation skills.

MANAGER, HUMAN RESOURCES

Well-rounded human resource management professional offering
more than five years of experience in these areas:
Recruiting • Interviewing • Employee Selection • Placement • Job Descriptions
Compensation • Position Evaluation • Training • Discipline • Workers' Compensation
EEOC Compliance • Labor Relations • ADA • FMLA

MANAGER, TOURISM/HOSPITALITY

- Adaptable manager with nine years of experience in the tourism/hospitality industry.
  - Strategic planning
  - Multi-property management
  - Budgeting and operations
  - Marketing and promotion
  - Personnel development
  - Public/guest relations
  - Reservation sales
  - Revenue maximization
  - New property construction
- Confident leader who is able to motivate employees to excel in customer service.
- Effective team player with excellent communication and interpersonal skills.
- Self-motivated professional with a strong work ethic and proven problem-solving skills.

MANUFACTURING

Sixteen years of manufacturing experience from research and development phase to high-volume production requirements. Skilled in the development of documentation and procedures to meet regulatory requirements. Able to work equally well on an independent basis or as a cooperative team member. Excellent leadership and organizational skills; strong oral and written communication abilities.

MEDICAL ASSISTANT

- Registered Medical Assistant with an associate's degree in medical assisting.
- Experienced in record keeping, filing, typing (55 wpm), scheduling, phone etiquette, dictation, and most office machines.
- Knowledge of computers; experienced with MS Word and MEDISOFT; familiar with many other Windows and MS-DOS applications.
- Responsible and dependable professional with a strong medical ethic.
- Excellent organizer who is able to work independently and as part of a team.

MENTAL HEALTH PROFESSIONAL

- Experienced mental health professional with a diverse background in inpatient and medical psychiatric assessment and therapy, including the following:
  - Social work
  - Individual therapy
  - Group therapy
  - Evaluation
  - Disposition
  - Domestic violence
  - Crisis intervention
  - Suicide prevention
  - Chemical dependency
- Certified Alcohol Counselor I (CACI) in the state of Colorado.
- Innovative, highly energetic worker with demonstrated organizational and social skills.
- Able to accept and appreciate differences in others; nonjudgmental and impartial.
- Sensitive and empathetic team player with finely tuned communication and interpersonal abilities.

MORTGAGE SALES MANAGER

Ambitious sales leader with more than 15 years of experience as a renovation specialist. Driven professional who combines business savvy with a passion for the product to create win-win experiences for both the company and the customer. Able to quickly build trust and rapport with the customer, handle objections, and close the sale. Proven track record of demonstrating professional ethics, leading with integrity, and adhering to a core set of values in a challenging economic climate. Recognized for the ability to take on new responsibilities and quickly produce positive results.

NURSE

- Dedicated Interventional Cardiology Nurse with a reputation for astute clinical judgment.
- Respected professional with a strong background in critical care nursing and pharmacology.
- Compassionate caregiver who quickly establishes and maintains rapport with patients.
- Detail oriented and precise; dedicated to providing excellence in patient care.
- Adept at managing multiple tasks simultaneously and working under pressure.
- Knowledge of Windows, computerized charting, and electronic cardiac systems.

NURSE ADMINISTRATOR

- Dedicated nurse administrator who enjoys new challenges and works well in high-pressure environments demanding hard work and self-motivation.
- Licensed Registered Nurse (New Jersey 120960) with graduate education in health systems administration and business management.
- Effective team leader with proven communication, interpersonal, and presentation skills.
- Detail-oriented professional with strong problem-solving abilities.
- Compassionate caregiver who is able to quickly establish and maintain rapport with patients and other health care providers.

OCCUPATIONAL THERAPIST

Compassionate occupational therapist with an enthusiasm for helping others. Persuasive motivator with an inherent understanding of people and a genuine caring attitude. Effective team player who works well with others and strives to create win-win relationships. Able to collaborate with other health care professionals to develop productive treatment plans.

OFFICE WORKER

- Dependable office worker with more than five years of hands-on experience.
- Able to thrive in a fast-paced environment, managing multiple tasks simultaneously.
- Versatile, quick learner who loves challenge and adapts well to new situations.
- Self-motivated; works well with little or no supervision.
- Knowledge of Windows, MS Word, Excel, Access, and SQL computer software.
- Skills: typing, ten-key, fax, copiers, laser printers, and multiple phone lines.

PILOT

Experienced leader with a proven track record in aviation operations and safety management. Diverse background as a pilot with strong technical and training skills. Current FAA Commercial Pilot License with rotorcraft and instrument ratings. Ambitious professional who adapts quickly to changing conditions.

PROJECT MANAGER

- Experienced project manager with a proven background in the development and implementation of complex computer and communication networks.
- Dedicated professional who is skilled at identifying process improvements and developing quality solutions that are faster, cheaper, and better.
- Effective team leader with strong communication and interpersonal skills

PUBLIC RELATIONS

Creative public relations expert with a vast range of industry and media contacts. Nationally recognized spokesman, commentator, and expert on the business and law of sports. Strong background in sports journalism with major newspapers, radio stations, and television networks. Quick thinker who is skilled at applying logical but creative approaches to challenges

RETAIL MANAGER

- Experienced Retail Manager with the proven ability to streamline operations, improve productivity, and enhance market share.
- Consistently made significant contributions to meet or exceed goals and ensure maximum profitability by improving inventory management and merchandising.
- Customer-driven focus—worked as an advocate to build a strong partnership between the customer and workers to improve loyalty.
- Able to inspire a shared vision that ensures team members meet and exceed sales performance targets and deliver exceptional customer service.

SALES AND MARKETING POSITION

- Demonstrated success in sales and management positions for more than seventeen years.
- Proven ability to develop new markets and maintain profitable client relationships.
- Consistent high achiever recognized for exceptional sales accomplishments with fiercely competitive products in a shrinking marketplace.
- Respected for powerful negotiating and closing abilities.
- Self-motivated and focused; comfortable working independently with little supervision.

SCHOOL SUPERINTENDENT

Visionary leader with a collaborative management style and proven record of achievement. High-energy administrator with a personal commitment to excellence in education and extensive experience with diverse quality systems. Effective team player who values the freedom of the human spirit and makes every effort to protect that spirit from control. Accomplished public speaker who knows how to work a crowd.

SENIOR EXECUTIVE

- High-energy senior executive with a demonstrated track record of success in these areas:
  - – Sales/marketing
  - – Technical innovations
  - – Operations management
  - – Finance
  - – Business development
  - – International business
  - – Strategic planning
  - – Negotiations
  - – Staff development
- Proven ability to combine high-caliber analytical and strategic planning skills with outstanding business development and marketing expertise in both domestic and global business arenas.
- Fast-track professional who thrives on challenges and takes a hands-on leadership role to position the company for growth in a changing environment.
- Recognized for ingenuity, integrity, and the ability to negotiate win/win scenarios.

SOCIAL WORKER / THERAPIST

Empowering counselor who is able to integrate theoretical and practical ideas and apply them to real-world counseling situations. Dedicated to maximizing the potential of others through careful assessment and acknowledgment of their personal strengths and weaknesses. Experienced operations manager and team leader with the proven ability to maximize efficiencies.

SUPERINTENDENT, GOLF COURSE

- Experienced golf course superintendent focused on efficient operations, exceptional attention to detail, and the highest level of course conditioning and playability for the perfect golf experience.
- Ten years of experience in greenskeeping and golf course management.
- Skilled administrator who leads by example and promotes a strong team work ethic.
- Extensive knowledge of horticulture, including an undergraduate degree in landscape horticulture and turf management.

TEACHER

Dedicated teacher with the desire to instill in children the passion to be lifelong learners. Able to set and maintain high expectations with the belief that children will rise to them and be reliable, respectful, responsible, and ready to learn. Outgoing and patient instructor who enjoys working with children. Effective team player with strong communication and interpersonal skills.

TECHNICIAN, TELECOMMUNICATIONS

- Self-motivated telecommunications technician with 14 years of diverse experience.
- Expertise in the installation, troubleshooting, and repair of digital and analog communications, teleconferencing, video, and computer network equipment.
- Respected for the ability to solve complex problems and to get things done when others give up.
- Thrives in fast-paced, challenging environments; holds a current secret security clearance.

TRAINER, INSTRUCTIONAL DESIGNER

- Experienced trainer, instructional designer, manager, and change agent with a background in both corporate and academic environments.
- **Training:** Creative presenter, facilitator, and coach with strong communication and interpersonal skills. Proven ability to use innovative delivery methods and group dynamics to improve the quality of the training experience.
- **Problem Solving:** Conceptual thinker who enjoys the challenge of analyzing systems and making them more effective. Experienced organizational developer who has conducted focus groups and sensing interviews to design departmental improvements.
- **Teamwork:** Collaborative team player with the ability to motivate others and build strong teams that can work together to accomplish an organization's goals.
- **Certifications:** Ropes Course Trainer. Mager Criterion Referenced Instructor. Train the Trainer. Myers-Briggs Type Indicator, FIRO-B, Strong, and Campbell instruments.

CONTACT INFORMATION

This final stage of information gathering will provide you with all the information you need to begin your résumé. For the contact information, you can use your full name, first and last name only, or shortened names (Pat Criscito instead of Patricia K. Criscito). If you will be relocating yourself to another city and/or state, then get a post office box or another type of address in the city where you will be living. Most companies won't pay to relocate you, so you need to appear "local."

Do not use work telephone numbers or a work e-mail address on your résumé. Potential employers tend to consider that an abuse of company resources, which implies you might do the same if you are working for them. Listing a cellular telephone number on your résumé gives a hiring manager a way to reach you during working hours. Today, people often have only a cell phone, which is fine. It is also okay to keep a cell phone with an area code that is different from the area code where you live. That is becoming so common that hiring managers don't even question it anymore.

Avoid the use of "cutesy" e-mail addresses on a résumé. If you use *babycakes@aol.com* for your personal e-mail, create a second e-mail address under your account that will be more professional. If you have an e-mail address that you love, create a different one for your job searches. Why? Because the e-mail address you use for your job search will end up with lots of spam and junk mail within a month of posting your résumé online. If your only access to the Internet is at work, then create a free-mail account at *hotmail.com, aol.com, msn.com, juno.com, about.com, yahoo.com, excite.com, gmail.com, mail.com, gawab.com, inbox.com, fastmail.com, bigstream.com,* or any other free e-mail service. For a list of even more free e-mail services, put "list of free e-mail services" in any search engine.

If you have accounts with social networking sites, make sure they are "safe" for your career before listing them on your résumé. You don't want a potential employer to see photos of you at a drunken toga party. Even if you don't list your site addresses on your résumé, a potential employer could Google you and find them anyway.

NAME _____

ADDRESS _____

CITY/STATE/ZIP _____

COUNTRY (if applying outside the country where you live) _____

HOME PHONE _____ CELL PHONE _____

E-MAIL ADDRESS _____

WEBSITE OR E-FOLIO URL _____

LINKEDIN _____ FACEBOOK _____

TWITTER _____ MYSPACE _____

BLOG _____ OTHER _____

PERSONAL BRANDING PROFILE

Keep the profile short, sweet, and to the point. I tend to limit them to five or six sentences or bullets, although there are exceptions to this rule when creating a curriculum vitae or other types of professional résumés. I'll give you a few extra places to list that information if you need a longer profile, but try to use no more than six.

You can title this section with any of the following headlines: Profile, Qualifications, Highlights of Qualifications, Expertise, Strengths, Summary, Synopsis, Background, Professional Background, Executive Summary, Highlights, Overview, Professional Overview, Capsule, or Keyword Profile. Even though this section is a personal branding statement, you don't name it that.

OBJECTIVE/FOCUS (This can become the first sentence of your profile or stand alone.) _____
_____
_____
_____

SECOND SENTENCE (areas of expertise) _____
_____
_____
_____

STRENGTH / UNIQUE VALUE PROPOSITION / ACCOMPLISHMENT_____
_____
_____
_____

STRENGTH / UNIQUE VALUE PROPOSITION / ACCOMPLISHMENT _____
_____
_____
_____

STRENGTH / UNIQUE VALUE PROPOSITION / ACCOMPLISHMENT _____
_____
_____
_____

STRENGTH / UNIQUE VALUE PROPOSITION / ACCOMPLISHMENT _____
_____
_____
_____

STRENGTH / UNIQUE VALUE PROPOSITION / ACCOMPLISHMENT _____
_____
_____
_____

STRENGTH / UNIQUE VALUE PROPOSITION / ACCOMPLISHMENT _____
_____
_____
_____

Step 12
Putting It
All Together

15

Now it's time to put this all together into the perfect résumé. You have a personal branding profile, your education, experience, and other relevant information. How do you decide which section goes first, second, third, and last? That depends … everything in the résumé business depends!

Start with the section that contains your strongest qualifications for your target job. If you have had little experience in your prospective field but have a degree that qualifies you for a starting position in the industry, then by all means list your education first. Most people eventually move their education below their experience as they get further from their school days. If you change your career and go back to school, then the education will move to the top again and begin to gravitate to the bottom as you gain relevant experience.

The same idea goes for information within each section. For instance, if your job title is more impressive than where you worked, then list it first.

VICE PRESIDENT OF MARKETING
Little Known Company, Seattle, Washington

MICROSOFT CORPORATION, Redmond, Washington
Assistant Sales Coordinator

Functional or Chronological

There are three basic types of résumés—reverse chronological, functional, and a combination of the two. There are fad styles that come and go, but the three I've just mentioned are the classics.

A reverse-chronological résumé arranges your experience and education in chronological order with the most recent dates first. This style is the most popular résumé with recruiters and hiring managers. It showcases your jobs one at a time and shows a clear chronology of your work history. Use it under these circumstances:

1. When your last job is a strong foundation for your current objective.

Everything in the résumé business depends.

2. When you are staying in the same field as your past job(s).

3. When you have a strong history of promotion or development in your career.

4. When your prior titles or company names are an asset to your current job search.

5. When you are in a highly traditional field (education, banking, government, etc.).

6. When you are working with an executive recruiter.

Most of the résumés I write are reverse-chronological, but that doesn't mean a different type of résumé might not fit your needs better. A functional résumé organizes your work experience by the functions you performed regardless of date. The functional résumé highlights your skills and potential instead of your work history. Use it in these situations:

1. When you want to play down gaps in your experience, like in recession economies when jobs are scarce.

2. When you have changed jobs too many times or have lots of jobs to show because you have been doing consulting, freelance, or temporary work.

3. When you are entering the job market for the first time.

4. When you are reentering the job market, for example after raising children.

5. When you want to change careers.

6. When you have done the same things in every job and don't want to use the same descriptions over and over again.

7. When you need to de-emphasize your age but exploit older experience.

8. When you need to list volunteer experience and community or school activities to strengthen your qualifications.

List your functional paragraphs in their order of importance, with the items listed first that will help you get the particular job you are targeting. Refer to Step 9 (Chapter 12) of this book for ideas on how to rearrange your résumé sentences to better capture your reader's attention.

You should know that there are very rare instances when I would recommend a purely functional résumé, however. In the 1980s, true functional résumés developed a bad reputation because applicants were not listing where they gained their experience. It made recruiters suspicious that the applicant was trying to hide something. A combination functional/chronological résumé will avoid this problem. Always list a brief synopsis of your actual work experience at the bottom of your functional résumé with each title, employer, and the dates worked.

Here are some sample functional/chronological combination résumés that might help you decide if this style is right for you.

Leesa A. Murphy

PROFILE

- Dedicated administrative assistant with 7+ years experience in the judicial court system.
- Self-starter with strong problem-solving and organizational abilities.
- Demonstrated ability to handle difficult situations with tact.
- Skilled in analyzing a task and breaking it down into manageable pieces.
- Team player with exceptional communication and interpersonal skills.
- Knowledge of MS Word, Windows, Excel, and proprietary software.

EXPERIENCE

LEGAL EXPERIENCE

- Coordinated and set court dockets and dates, prepared juries for trial, and assisted *pro se* individuals.
- Created new files, maintained filing system, and typed judge's directives, orders, and letters.
- Collected traffic fines, managed collections registry for criminal/juvenile cases, and assisted in the collections process by turning cases over to State Collections.
- Worked closely with the Department of Labor in the investigation of employment status and wage garnishments; met with 20 to 30 people per day.
- Maintained the personnel expense reimbursement program (COFORS).
- Set appointments for 30 probation officers.
- Performed intake and input new cases in the computer system.
- Routed mail and copied files for the District Attorney's office.
- Entered data for child support and domestic cases.

ADMINISTRATION/MANAGEMENT

- Developed and implemented all office procedures for the Recovery Center.
- Accountable for the establishment and preparation of financial statements, insurance billings, monthly and daily accounting reports.
- Reviewed all deposits, accounts receivable, and insurance payments.
- Analyzed, negotiated, and resolved problem accounts.
- Supervised and evaluated office personnel.
- Issued demand letters, negotiated repayments/settlements, developed payment plans, and processed collection paperwork.
- Improved monthly accounts receivable status ratings from below standard (a $40,000 deficit) to 98% in less than a year.
- Developed systems for work flow and record keeping that significantly improved efficiency.

OTHER EXPERIENCE

- Extensive public relations and customer service background.
- Excel in dealing with difficult people and situations.
- Provided secretarial support and front desk reception services.
- Processed military personnel paperwork for transitions, issued passports, and maintained records.

WORK HISTORY

Municipal Court Clerk, Municipal Court, Colorado Springs, Colorado	2010–present
Collections Investigator, 4th Judicial District Court, Colorado Springs, Colorado	2009–2010
Assistant Division Clerk, 4th Judicial District Court, Colorado Springs, Colorado	2007–2009
Court Clerk II, 4th Judicial District Court, Colorado Springs, Colorado	2005–2007
Secretary I, 4th Judicial District Court, Colorado Springs, Colorado	2004–2005
Office Manager, Lakeside Recovery Center, Tacoma, Washington	2002–2003
Administrative Assistant, United States Army, various locations	1996–2002

EDUCATION

Pikes Peak Community College, 3-hour course in psychology
Kansas State University, 12 hours of liberal arts studies
Central Texas College, 6 hours of liberal arts studies

ADDRESS

12345 Anywhere Street • Newtown, CO 80907 • (719) 555-1234 • lamurphy@protypeltd.com

MICHAEL D. NEWMAN

Phone: (781) 555-1245 ▪ 20 Anywhere Street ▪ Newtown, Massachusetts 02368
www.linkedin.com/in/mdnewman ▪ mnewman@protypeltd.com

PROFILE
- Experienced Advertising Director with demonstrated success in the following:
  - Major accounts
  - Classified advertising
  - Retail accounts
  - Research
  - New product development
  - Sales and training
  - Budgeting
  - Graphic arts and production
  - Planning and scheduling
- Practical problem solver with exceptional analytical, creative, and communication skills.
- Strong background in building new territories and using creative marketing approaches.
- Demonstrated ability to create client loyalty above and beyond the relationship.
- Proficient in Windows 95, MS Word, Excel, PowerPoint, Access, Quark, AIM billing system, and ATEX classified front-end software.

EXPERIENCE
Major Accounts
- Managed the major accounts sales team for *The Gazette*, a Freedom Corporation newspaper with a circulation of 121,000.
- Made sales presentations to senior management of major accounts in cities nationwide.
- Developed a new client base and expanded existing accounts to achieve $17 million in annual sales.

Research and New Product Development
- Directed the development of new products for *The Gazette*, including demographic and psychographic market research, feasibility studies, product design and packaging, budgeting, scheduling, implementation, sales, and P&L.
- Analyzed statistical and other market data and used the results to create sales presentations to advertisers; researched and analyzed competitive information.
- Instrumental in building the online division of the newspaper (coloradosprings.com).
- Developed the *Home in Colorado* magazine that won the 1999 Addy Award for best in-home publication with more than four colors.
- Created a sales and marketing product manual to delineate newspaper sections, ancillary products, and the demographics of the newspaper's core readership.
- Implemented the weekly *Peak Computing Magazine* from the ground up, including product development and design, placement, distribution, setting advertising rates, sales, and creation of a companion website.
- Collaborated with sister properties to develop "Living Well," a health tab special feature of the *Patriot Ledger*.
- Created an innovative research program for the *Times Advocate* (Team: Research) that provided the sales team with comprehensive and accurate demographic information to increase the effectiveness of client advertising.

Classified and Retail
- Directed retail sales to major, national, local, and automotive accounts of the *Patriot Ledger*, a daily newspaper with a circulation of 82,000.
- Directly supervised all commercial advertising sales functions for the *News-Chronicle* (a community newspaper with a circulation of 30,000), increasing revenues by 22%.
- Sold *Pennysaver* classified advertisements to commercial account advertisers.
- Increased gross sales by 131%, decreased new territory delinquencies by 40%, and achieved the top 10% of all sales executives.

Management and Supervision
- Developed and managed sales budgets of up to $17 million; accountable for print bids, production costs, and full profit and loss.
- Negotiated dollar volume contracts averaging $400,000, with highest being $1 million.
- Hired, trained, supervised, and mentored up to 5 managers and 45 staff members.
- Developed and negotiated a new commission plan for the *Patriot Ledger* retail department with union leaders.
- Managed production functions for the *Patriot Ledger* through prepress, including graphic design, copy input, page layout, and dispatch.

EXPERIENCE   *Management and Supervision (continued)*
- Contributed to the design and installation of an integrated advertising computer system that provides fully automated order entry, advertisement tracking, production, and pagination.
- Increased revenues for *Peak Computing* by 870% in 13 months and display advertisers by 400%, ultimately achieving $750,000 in annual sales.
- Managed the Porch Plus alternative delivery program for the *Times Advocate*, increasing revenues from $130,000 to $1.5 million.
- Collaborated with *The Orange County Register* to increase the market for Porch Plus.
- Served as co-chair of the San Diego North County Golf Expo, generating significant goodwill and $70,000 in new revenue.

Training
- Developed curriculum for and implemented a complete sales training program for all advertising associates of *The Gazette.*
- Wrote the company training manual for all departments.
- Conducted sales training seminars and created incentive programs.

HISTORY   **PATRIOT LEDGER**, Quincy, Massachusetts   2010–present
                    Retail Advertising Director

                    THE GAZETTE, Colorado Springs, Colorado   2006–2010
                    Manager of Research and New Products   2010
                    Major Accounts / New Products Development Manager / Trainer   2008–2010
                    Sales Manager for Peak Computing Magazine   2006–2008

                    TIMES ADVOCATE, Escondido, California   2005–2006
                    Marketing / Research Coordinator
                    Retail Sales Manager for Porch Plus (Alternative Delivery Service)

                    NEWS-CHRONICLE, Encinitas, California   2004–2005
                    Sales Manager (Retail and Classified)

                    PENNYSAVER, San Diego, California   2001–2004
                    Classified Account Executive and Line Supervisor

EDUCATION   **BACHELOR OF ARTS, Material and Logistics Management**   1994
                    Michigan State University, East Lansing, Michigan

                    CONTINUING EDUCATION
                    Numerous leadership development training programs, including Legal Issues for Supervisors, Tactical Leadership (Hiring the Best, Performance Management, Documentation and Discipline, and Sexual Harassment), Train the Trainer, among others.

PUBLICATION   Wrote and published an article in *Retail Insights* titled "Customer Service" directed toward media advertising managers and directors.

TONY PACHECO

12 Anywhere Trail
Newtown, Colorado 81005

Phone: (719) 555-1234
E-mail: pacheco@protypeltd.com

PROFILE

- Experienced human resources manager with a diverse background in both manufacturing and high-tech services industries.
- Self-motivated professional with a strong work ethic and the ability to get the job done.
- Flexible, quick learner who enjoys taking on new challenges and learning new processes.
- Known for the ability to bridge philosophies, build mutual trust, and create consensus.
- Bilingual—native English speaker, working knowledge of Spanish.
- Knowledge of Windows, MS Word, Excel, PowerPoint, Access, Outlook, Internet Explorer.

AREAS OF EXPERTISE

Human Resource Regulations
- Safety Management/OSHA
- Wage and Hour/Wage Determinations
- State Laws/Federal Laws
- Service Contract/Davis-Bacon
- Employment/Labor Law/NLRB

Salary Administration
- Job Descriptions
- Standard Operating Procedures
- Position Evaluation
- Exempt/Nonexempt Pay
- Rate Ranges and Progression

Recruitment/Selection
- Executive/Administrative
- Nonexempt Hourly Sourcing
- Temporary Employment
- Outside Contractors
- Examination/Placement

Employee Relations
- EEOC/ADA/EEO-1 Reporting
- Affirmative Action Program Report
- Human Resources Auditor
- Corporate Advisor to the VP Services Dept.
- Federal Mediation and Conciliation
- Management Training of Contractual Intent
- Employee Relations Committee
- Negotiations Observer/Advisor
- Chief Contract Negotiator
- Grievance Handling/Steps I-II-III Arbitration
- Mutual Gains Bargaining Negotiations
- Arbitrator Selection
- Collective Bargaining Agreement (CBA)
- Arbitration Hearings (opening statement to end)

Benefits/Compensation
- 401k/Pensions/COBRA/WARN
- Workers' Compensation
- Loss Control

EXPERIENCE

HUMAN RESOURCES/LABOR RELATIONS MANAGER (2010–present)
Mason and Hanger Corporation, Colorado Springs, Colorado
Provide advice and counsel to managers and supervisors relating to human resource policies, procedures, and employee benefits for this military contractor with 400 employees in three sites. Listen to employee problems and provide feedback to functional managers to ensure that corrective action is taken. Discuss employee morale with site and program managers, indicating remedial action to resolve problem areas. Motivate and educate supervisors and manager to ensure consistent, equal, and fair treatment of all employees. Administer compensation and benefit programs, including insurance and 401k pension plans. Audit personnel records and maintain their security and confidentiality. Serve as a liaison between management and three unions.

- Developed policies and procedures for exit interviews and ensured compliance with federal and state laws and regulations.
- Implemented an affirmative action program to meet federal requirements.
- Negotiate and administer three collective bargaining agreements.
- Successfully increased trust between the union and the company, resulting in fewer filed grievances; saved more than half a million dollars by settling disputes without arbitration.
- Selected to diffuse a stalled bargaining agreement that had been referred for mediation with the Federal Mediation and Conciliation Board.
- Brought negotiations back on track and succeeded in negotiating a three-year contract in only four hours.

176

EXPERIENCE
(continued)

BUSINESS PROCESS TEAM MEMBER AND BUYER (2009–2010)
Colorado Fuel and Iron Corporation, Pueblo, Colorado
Made recommendations to hiring managers for staffing levels to meet production needs. Conducted performance evaluations of department managers and counseled them on areas needing improvement. Screened résumés, interviewed hundreds of workers, and made hiring recommendations to restaff the mill with non-union workers during an extended strike. As a buyer, sourced vendors and purchased more than $12 million in raw materials per month. Inventoried products received by rail and ensured that raw materials were received in time for production.
- Re-engineered departments and implemented process efficiencies.
- Rewrote job descriptions, combined jobs, and downsized operations of the tube mill, which saved $1 million a year in salaries, benefits, and production costs.
- Reorganized the Human Resources Department by outsourcing benefits administration to contractors, eliminating a vice president position and downsizing the department by two-thirds.
- Conducted task analyses, combined responsibilities for salespeople, eliminated outside sales positions with extravagant perquisites, and instituted accountability measures to save more than $1 million per year.
- Lowered the rejection rate of the rail mill by 7% through re-engineering of the dock to reduce damaged finished goods.
- Negotiated an across-the-board 10% decrease in prices from all vendors.

HUMAN RESOURCES/SAFETY COORDINATOR (2008)
Colorado Fuel and Iron Corporation, Pueblo, Colorado
Conducted training classes on safety issues; developed drug and alcohol policies and procedures for the Human Resources Department.
- Implemented a $500,000 fall protection program for the steel mill that saved $4 million in non-compliance fines from OSHA.

PRODUCTION WORKER (2005–2008)
Colorado Fuel and Iron Corporation, Pueblo, Colorado
Financed a full undergraduate and graduate education as a laborer in this steel mill. Worked up the ladder to supervisor on the production floor of the Steel Making Department.

EDUCATION

MASTER OF BUSINESS ADMINISTRATION (2006)
Regis University, Denver, Colorado
- Emphasis on international business.
- Graduated in the top 15% of the graduating class.

BACHELOR OF ARTS DEGREE (1999)
Antioch University, George Meany Center for Labor Studies (AFL–CIO), Yellow Springs, Ohio
- Major in labor studies/labor relations.
- Completed 180 credit hours to graduate first in the class.
- Served as class president for two years.

LABOR CERTIFICATE (1997)
University of Colorado, Boulder
- Completed two six-week programs per year for a total of four years.

AFFILIATIONS

Member, Human Resources Association, Pueblo, Colorado
Member, Human Resources Association, Colorado Springs, Colorado
Member, National Society for Human Resource Management

COMMUNITY
SERVICE

Volunteer to teach and tutor adult students at the community college level in adult basic education, reading, literacy, and international business.

LORETTA SCHWARTZ

PROFILE
- Focused retail manager with 20 years of experience.
- Background in marketing, sales, staff development, merchandising, and customer service.
- Effective team player with strong interpersonal and communication skills.
- Skilled in creating staff loyalty and empowering employees to excel.

EXPERIENCE

MANAGEMENT/ADMINISTRATION
- Directed the operations of 22 retail stores in three states with combined sales volume of $17.1 million.
- Served as a liaison between store management and home office merchandisers and senior managers.
- Approved sales goals and provided direction for floor sets (merchandising).
- Managed the daily operations of a high-volume retail clothing store, including visual merchandising, floor supervision, and resolution of customer complaints and adjustments.
- Promoted from supervisor to manager of a $750,000 volume store and then to manager of a Casual Corner with more than $1 million in annual sales volume.
- Conceptualized and coordinated innovative fashion shows, breakfast clubs, and other promotions to increase sales volume and create customer loyalty.
- Developed new business through community involvement, seminars, and monthly training of sales staff to enhance customer service through the merchandise sales approach.

SUPERVISION/STAFF DEVELOPMENT
- Developed ten staff members for promotion to store manager or assistant store manager positions.
- Recruited, hired, trained, supervised, and evaluated sales associates, store supervisors, assistant managers, and store managers.
- Scheduled staff, ensuring adequate floor coverage, and oversaw payroll.

ACHIEVEMENTS
- Assumed responsibility for a failing district, closed unprofitable stores, and turned around declining units until all stores were profitable.
- Honored with membership in the Champions Club (2006–2007) for achieving #26 out of 860 stores in the country; Champions Club (2008–2009) achieving #48 out of 860 stores.
- Won numerous suit, dress, and pantyhose promotions by increasing sales over plan.
- Built sales volume through focused productivity training, visual merchandise presentation, and exceptional customer service.
- Voted President (2001–2006) and Vice President (2000) of the Towne Square Merchants Association.
- President (2000–2004) and Vice President (2007) of Citadel Merchants Association.
- Selected as City Fashion Coordinator for Colorado Springs (1999–2000).
- Miss America Pageant Official (1999); First Runner-Up, Miss Colorado Springs (2000).

WORK HISTORY

DISTRICT SALES MANAGER, Casual Corner, Denver, CO	2011–present
MANAGER, Casual Corner, Citadel Mall, Colorado Springs, CO	2005–2011
MANAGER, Casual Corner, Towne East, Wichita, KS	2003–2005
MANAGER, Casual Corner, Towne West, Wichita, KS	2000–2003

TRAINING   **CASUAL CORNER CORPORATE TRAINING**: TRAC I-III (Personal Selling, Beyond Customer Service, Driving the Business), MOHR Management Training

---

1445 Anywhere Court • Newtown, Colorado 80906 • (719) 555-1234 • Email: lschwartz@protypeltd.com

Sylvia Valley

4605 Anywhere Drive • Newtown, Colorado 80915 • Home (719) 555-1234 • Cell (719) 123-4567

PROFILE
- Versatile lyric soprano singer with more than twenty years of experience.
- Proven ability to sing in both solo and chorus performances.
- Background in classical, opera, sacred, and popular music.

EXPERIENCE

SOLO
- Solo vocal recitals with a wide variety of music, including Broadway, opera arias, and classical
- Rehearsal soprano soloist with the CS Chorale for Mendelssohn's *Elijah,* Verdi's *Requiem,* and Beethoven's *Missa Solemnis,* 2007–2012
- Handel's *Israel in Egypt,* soprano I in duet for two sopranos, Colorado Springs Chorale, Donald Jenkins, Director, 2010
- Brahms' *Requiem,* soprano solo, Colorado Springs Chorale and Colorado Springs Philharmonic, Lawrence Leighton Smith, Director, 2009
- Beethoven's *Choral Fantasy,* second soprano solo, Colorado Springs Chorale and Philharmonic, Lawrence Leighton Smith, Director, 2009
- Robert Ward's *The Crucible,* Sara Goode, Opera Theater of the Rockies, 2008
- Douglas Moore's *Ballad of Baby Doe,* Samantha, Opera Theater of the Rockies, 2006
- Orff's *Carmina Burana,* soprano solos, Colorado Springs Children's Chorale and Youth Symphony, Dr. Anton Armstrong, Director, 2006
- Poulenc's *Gloria,* soprano solos, Soli Deo Gloria choir, Bob Crowder, Director, 2005
- Brahms' *Requiem,* soprano solo, Soli Deo Gloria choir, Edmund Ladouceur, Director, 2004
- Bach's *Magnificat,* "Quia Respexit" and Vivaldi's *Gloria,* "Domine Deus," soprano solo, Soli Deo Gloria choir, Edmund Ladouceur, Director, 2003
- Sang the part of the youth from Mendelssohn's *Elijah* with the Soli Deo Gloria choir, Anna Hamre, Director, 1993
- Handel's *Messiah,* "He Shall Feed His Flock," Chapel Choir, Spangdahlem AFB, Germany, 1991

OPERA CHORUS
- *Puccini Spectacular,* soprano, Opera Theater of the Rockies, 2012
- *Le Nozze di Figaro,* soprano, Opera Theater of the Rockies, 2010
- *Daughter of the Regiment,* soprano, Opera Theater of the Rockies, 2009
- *Trial by Jury* and *The Crucible,* soprano, Opera Theater of the Rockies, 2008
- *Pagliacci,* soprano, Opera Theater of the Rockies, 2007
- *La Boheme,* soprano, Colorado Opera Festival, 2004
- *Carmen,* soprano, Colorado Opera Festival, 2003
- *Lucia de Lammermoor,* second soprano, Colorado Opera Festival, 2002

CHORAL
- Soprano with the Colorado Springs Chorale, Donald Jenkins, Director, 2007–present
- Soprano with Soli Deo Gloria choir, Colorado Springs, 1993–2007
- Soprano with the Abbey Singers, Colorado Springs, Judy Wescott, Director, 2002–2006

VOICE TRAINING
- Pat Staubo, Colorado Springs, Colorado, 2003–present
- Connie Heidenreich, Colorado Springs, Colorado, 1995–2003

179

LARRY D. SISK

3480 Hoofprint Road
Peyton, Colorado 80831

Mobile: (719) 555-1234
Email: ldsisk@protypeltd.com

PROFILE

- Seasoned construction superintendent with a comprehensive knowledge of the business and more than 30 years of experience in the following:
  - Commercial and residential building
  - New construction and renovations
  - Bid preparation and contract negotiations
  - Surveying
  - Job scheduling
  - Blueprint specifications
- Effective leader who is able to motivate employees and subcontractors to complete jobs on time and under budget. Skilled at evaluating margins to ensure profitability at project completion.

SUMMARY

- Supervised large commercial construction projects from bid through final walk-through.
- Skilled at project takeoffs, estimating, and development of project schedules and milestones.
- Sourced vendors, purchased supplies and equipment, and ensured timely delivery of materials.
- Evaluated blueprints and schematics; ensured compliance with regulations and specifications.
- Consulted with clients regarding design modifications and change orders; ensured customer satisfaction throughout the project life cycle.
- Interviewed, hired, scheduled, and supervised employees and subcontractors.
- Evaluated bids from subcontractors, ensured the quality of their work, and resolved problems.
- Implemented safety and quality control programs and regulations.
- As a business owner, was accountable for long-range planning, profit and loss, controlling costs, invoicing, record keeping, collecting accounts receivable, and monitoring financial performance.

SIGNIFICANT PROJECTS

- Biggs Kofford, CPA, Office Addition, $1.2 million (2011)
- Lake Point Medical Center, Design/Build Medical Office Building, $4.5 million (2009–2010)
- Falcon School District, Classroom Remodels, Gymnasium Additions, $1.9 million (2007–2009)
- Summit County Jail, New Detention Facility, Breckenridge, $7.5 million (2008)
- Santa Fe County Jail, New Detention Facility, Santa Fe, New Mexico, $8 million (2006)
- Evans Army Hospital, New Facility, Fort Carson, $95 million (2005)
- ADAL Computer Center, New Computer Facility, USAF Academy, $2.5 million (2004)
- Nixon Power and Sewage Disposal Plant, City Utility Project, $20 million (2000)
- American Numismatic Building, New Corporate Headquarters Building, $1.5 million (1998)
- Doherty High School, New Facility, $14 million (1985–1998)
- First Bank, New Building, $12 million (1994)

EXPERIENCE

Superintendent, Classic General Contractors, Colorado Springs, Colorado (2010–present)
Estimator, BMC West, Colorado Springs, Colorado (2010)
Owner/Manager, Bulldog Construction, Peyton, Colorado (2009–2010)
Journeyman Carpenter, AA Construction, Colorado Springs, Colorado (2008–2009)
Journeyman Carpenter, Robert E. McKee Construction Company, Denver, Colorado (2007–2008)
Journeyman Carpenter, Desman Corporation (Chapman), Colorado Springs, Colorado (2007–2008)
Cement Finisher, Transco Pacific Company, Fort Carson, Colorado (2007)
Superintendent, Hibbitts Construction Company, Colorado Springs, Colorado (2007)
Carpenter Foreman, Sommers Building Company, Colorado Springs, Colorado (2007)
Journeyman Carpenter, Alvarado Construction Company, Denver, Colorado (2006–2007)
Ironworker, Bates Construction Company, Colorado Springs, Colorado (2006)
Superintendent, H. W. Houston Construction Company, Pueblo, Colorado (2005–2006)

EDUCATION

JOURNEYMAN CARPENTER, Southern Colorado State College, Pueblo, Colorado (2001–2005)
Completed a four-year carpenter apprenticeship program under the Carpenters and Joiners of America Local 515, Pueblo, Colorado

MILD STEEL ARC WELDER, Pikes Peak Community College, Colorado Springs, Colorado (2005)

Paragraph Style or Bullets

Good advertisements are designed in such a way that the reader's eye is immediately drawn to important pieces of information using type and graphic elements, including bold, italics, headline fonts, and so forth. Then the design must guide the reader's eye down the page from one piece of information to the next with the judicious use of white space or graphic lines.

In this science of typography, very long lines of text (longer than six or seven inches, depending on the font) and large blocks of text (more than seven typeset lines) are considered to be tiring to the reader's eye. If you look closely at textbooks, magazines, and newspapers, you will notice that the information is usually typeset in columns to reduce line lengths, and journalists intentionally write in short paragraphs because they are more reader-friendly.

How does this science translate into a résumé? As a general rule, you should keep your lines of text no longer than seven inches—five to six inches is even better—and your paragraphs shorter than seven lines of text each. Many people find it difficult to cram the description of a job and its accomplishments into a single paragraph while following this rule. Therefore, you will often see a brief description of the job and your duties in paragraph format, followed by bulleted sentences for accomplishments like the following:

Provost and Dean of Faculties, Hofstra University 2010–present
Interim Provost and Dean of Faculties, Hofstra University 2008–2009
In a position second only to the President of the University, the Provost is responsible for the entire academic area of the University, including all of the Colleges and Schools, Libraries, Honors Program, Center for Teaching Excellence, Computer Center, Scott Skodnek Business Development Center, and the Joan and Arnold Saltzman Community Services Center. Accountable for developing and managing an annual budget of $80+ million.

- *Successfully negotiated two five-year contracts with the University faculty* (1991–1996, 1996–2001) as the chief negotiator. Completed negotiations three months before the expiration of the existing contracts. The first five-year contract resulted in a nine-hour teaching load for faculty at a manageable economic cost to the University. The present contract has a unique incentive plan to promote early retirement, and the contract also provides compensation increases that are tied, in part, to the well-being of the University.

- *Currently leading the efforts to establish the Honors College,* which is a key aspect of our strategy for the future and an important factor in tailoring the profile of the entire class. The Honors College builds on the existing Honors Program and will be open to all qualified undergraduate students regardless of their major.

If you need more than seven lines to describe your job, divide your experience into related information and use several shorter paragraphs under each job description.

EXPERIENCE	**EXECUTIVE DIRECTOR OF ASSESSMENT** (May 2012–present)

EXECUTIVE DIRECTOR OF ASSESSMENT (May 2012–present)
Colorado Springs School District 11, Colorado Springs, Colorado
Direct all operations related to research, planning, assessment, evaluation, technology integration, and technology support for every school in the district (elementary, middle/senior high, and charter schools). Participate in the development of long-range strategic plans for the district and the department. Develop assessment methodology, reporting systems, and related utilization of technology.

Serve as a liaison between the Research Center of the University of Colorado at Colorado Springs and District 11's Board of Education. Develop and lead the Coordination Committee responsible for bringing IT and Instruction together on a district level. Oversee the Evaluation Unit that monitors district programs, task forces, and initiatives. Meet weekly with instructional services to align technology integration and assessment with the needs of literacy resource teachers and instructional specialists.

Accomplishments
- Significantly revitalized the Assessment Unit by improving communication and implementing changes based on feedback from performance measurements.
- Personally conducted teacher telephone surveys throughout the year to evaluate service delivery.
- Piloted the concept of Building Assessment Teams to promote better utilization of assessment data. Improved service delivery by aligning the work of technical support, network administration, and the call center.

Fiscal Responsibility
- Set budget priorities for two units; accountable for a total of $2.5 million in district funds. Actively campaigned for the 2002 bond issue.

You can use left headings instead of centered headings to make the line lengths shorter (like in the sample above). This won't work, however, when the shorter line length forces your information into very long paragraphs. It is better to have longer line lengths and shorter paragraphs, like in the example on the previous page.

Bullets are a good way of presenting information on a résumé. Bullets are special characters (• ✦ ■) used at the beginning of indented short sentences to call attention to individual items on a résumé. Short, bulleted sentences are easier to read than long paragraphs of text, and they highlight the information you want the reader to see quickly. Bullets also add some variety to a résumé and make it just a touch more creative.

In both MS Word and Corel WordPerfect for Windows or Macintosh, clicking on "Insert" gives you access to a myriad of special characters that are not found on your keyboard, most of which can be used to create bullets.

On the following pages are sample résumés designed using paragraph formats, bulleted styles, and combinations thereof.

REGINA A. WILLIAMS

1400 Lascassas Park #H45
Murfreesboro, Tennessee 37132

Email: regina.thomas14@gmail.com

Mobile: (303) 587-0892

ASPIRING CHEF AND RESTAURANT MANAGER

Creative cook with a passion for Italian cuisine and a desire to bring an entrepreneurial spirit to the hospitality industry. Effective team player who collaborates well with others and motivates team members toward a common goal. Self-motivated, hardworking professional with proven strengths in these areas:

- Recipe development
- Production management
- Plating design
- Nutrition
- Team work
- Quality control
- Cost control
- Customer service
- Communication

EDUCATION

BACHELOR OF BUSINESS MANAGEMENT (May 2012)
Middle Tennessee State University, Murfreesboro, Tennessee
- Concentration in Entrepreneurship
- Minor in Business Administration
- GPA in major: 3.00

UNDERGRADUATE LIBERAL ARTS/PSYCHOLOGY STUDIES (2008–2009)
Adam State College, Alamosa, Colorado

RELEVANT EXPERIENCE

- Developed a passion for cooking early in life. Assumed responsibility for cooking family suppers with both parents working full-time outside the home. Learned the fundamentals of cooking, nutrition, diverse menus, and ethnic cuisines.

- Focused on nutrition and cooking with ProStart vocational classes while a sophomore in high school. Learned all aspects of the food industry with field trips to chain restaurants and a local five-star, five-diamond resort hotel (The Broadmoor). Participated in culinary competitions. Catered school events. Raised money for school organizations by developing ethnic meals cooked at a contest winner's home. Developed an eye for plating design.

- Currently cooking full time for a student apartment complex. Create new recipes and ensure that each meal fulfills nutritional requirements. Focus on impeccable food appearance and the highest quality ingredients and preparation. Estimate consumption, purchase foodstuffs, and inspect them upon delivery to ensure that only the highest quality products are used. Maintain expenses at or below budget through accurate planning, purchasing, and waste reduction.

- Spend school breaks cooking in a hospital and chain restaurant. Prepare food for hospital patients and families, assemble and deliver trays, assist with catering, and accept payments as a cashier. Ensure the delivery of exquisite customer service, and optimize patient quality of life. Investigate and resolve food/beverage quality and service complaints, ensuring customer satisfaction.

WORK HISTORY

PRESBYTERIAN/ST. LUKE'S HOSPITAL, Denver, Colorado
Head Housekeeper (2009–present)
Lead Food Service Worker (2008–2009)

BLACK-EYED PEA RESTAURANT, Parker, Colorado
Fry Cook, To-Go Curbside Takeaway (2006–2008)

COMPUTER SKILLS

- Proficient in Windows, MS Word, Excel, PowerPoint, Outlook, and Internet Explorer.

Jennifer Steel
EXPERIENCED FASHION DESIGN DIRECTOR

CORE COMPETENCIES

Management • Team Development
Strategic Planning • Concept Creation
Branding • Rebranding • Launches • Sales
International Vendor / Factory Relations
Trend Research • Themes • Original Designs
Production • Samples • Cost Engineering

EXECUTIVE SUMMARY

Innovative, high-performing designer who approaches creative work with excellence while maintaining commercial appeal. Able to act as a "telescope" to spot trends and then to tie those trends back to growth categories. Proven ability to bring fresh ideas to the table and to create designs that protect core brand concepts while delivering on fashion and innovation.

SUMMARY OF EXPERIENCE

- Developed, implemented, and managed the design strategy, aesthetic, and concepts for diverse fashion lines.
- Created and grew highly profitable fashion categories with annual values up to $300 million.
- Managed the entire product design process from concept to final bulk approval and merchandising. Developed new collections, seasonal themes, original designs, silhouette directions, color palettes, and print stories.
- Researched trends and produced concept boards for innovative seasonal themes, and used other tools to help rebrand and relaunch core fabric-based collections.
- Formed collaborative interdepartmental groups to ensure a cohesive brand image and seasonal look.
- Traveled extensively throughout Europe, Asia, and Southeast Asia to source new production facilities.
- Built and maintained trusting relationships with vendors that facilitated delivery of products on time.
- Met target margins for multiple programs by strategic selection of raw materials and cost engineering of styles.
- Sourced all varieties of custom trims, artwork, embroidery techniques, and fabrications.
- Used line plans to meet assigned style allowances; evenly distributed and placed fabrics and colors to meet fabric mill minimums.
- Hired, trained, supervised, and mentored teams of designers, assistant designers, and associates.

PROFESSIONAL EXPERIENCE

VICTORIA'S SECRET DIRECT, New York, New York
Design Director, International Full Collection (2011–present)
Senior Designer, Knit Dressing/Active, Knit Tops, Knit Dresses (2009–2011)
Designer, Knit Dressing/Active (2007–2009)
Led the design team in the creation of the Victoria Secret Beach Sexy line and the full collection of MODA International knits. Created and grew profitable categories accounting for $300 million in annual sales. Started the Beach Sexy apparel division, which has been positioned to become the largest lifestyle collection in the business. Traveled extensively to oversee production in Hong Kong, Korea, Sri Lanka, India, and Peru.

- Selected to direct the merger and maintenance of the VSD and MODA collections with combined volume of $750 million in annual business.
- Created and launched three unique knit collections over two years, resulting in combined incremental sales of $60 million per year.
- Rebranded the knit dressing division, which resulted in a 58% growth rate for 2011 and $90.7 million in sales.
- Created and launched the daily separates program, resulting in $20.1 million in incremental volume.
- Relaunched collections to successfully replace outdated programs. Established core slopers and managed refits for carryover styles, which ensured consistency and relevancy to customers.
- Traveled to India to create white-space opportunities for the brand, resulting in millions of dollars in new sales.
- Initiated best practices for the team and established consistencies across all areas of the design business.
- *"Jessica's design talent is clearly a strength and an incredible asset. She can ideate against strategy and concepts; she understands the customer and brand positioning. She executes the creative process with excellence. Jessica has brought great new design innovation into some of our most important classifications. Her keen eye for product that aligns with the strategy and appeals to the customer has been validated by sales."* –Daniela M., Sr. VP of Design

1234 Greenwich Avenue, 4C
New York, New York 10001
Mobile: (347) 555-1234
Email: jsteel@protypeltd.com

PROFESSIONAL EXPERIENCE

VICTORIA'S SECRET DIRECT (continued)
- *"Jessica lives the culture of the brand. She is diligent about delivery on deadlines, has a keen sense of urgency, an astute ability to prioritize, and embraces change openly. Her energy is infectious and she sets an amazing example to the team through her leadership. Jessica mentors her assistants as she guides them with best practices and pushes them to be their best."* –Krista B., Assistant VP of Design

EKCO RED DIVISION / PDI, New York, New York
Senior Knit Designer / Merchandising (2006–2007)
Developed and implemented branding and merchandising strategies for $30 million in annual production. Created innovative concepts, designed cohesive collections, and delivered to the brand filter. Managed the entire product design process for knit tops from concept to final bulk approval.
- Chosen as the sole designer to transition the company when the license expired.
- Worked exclusively with the Vice President of Design to create the proper exit strategy for the entire collection.
- Entered the job with no knowledge of working with overseas vendors and developed a broad range of experience with Korean production facilities.

THE VANITY ROOM, FOUR STARS, New York, New York
Senior Designer, Product Development and Sourcing (2002–2006)
First (and only) designer hired to create private-label collections for this start-up company. Managed all aspects of design, design operations, domestic production, and costing while remaining historically understaffed. Produced 40 to 70 samples and 20 to 30 styles per month. Conducted in-house fittings. Collaborated with the sales team to merchandise the line for market week presentation.
- Doubled revenue from the company's largest account, Forever 21.
- Developed and/or managed such accounts as Venus Catalogue, Nordstrom TBD, Macy's, White House Black Market, Belk, Urban Outfitters, Wet Seal, and Alloy, among others.
- Played a vital role in securing the Urban Outfitters account, which ultimately led to full in-store buys and featured mannequin looks.

ICON STUDIO, New York, New York
Freelance Designer (2002–2003)
Specialized in the design and production of contemporary-cut and sew-knit tops and dresses. Set seasonal themes, colors, and silhouette directions. Managed a pattern-maker and sample room.

EDUCATION

PARSONS SCHOOL OF DESIGN, New York, New York
Bachelor of Fine Arts, Fashion Design (2001)

INTERLOCHEN ARTS ACADEMY, Interlochen, Michigan
Graduate, Fine Arts Diploma (1997)

1234 Greenwich Avenue, 4C
New York, New York 10001
Mobile: (347) 555-1234
Email: jsteel@protypeltd.com

Executive Résumés

Webster defines an executive as "a person whose function is to administer or manage affairs of a corporation, division, department, group of companies, etc." This can be the president, director, any C-level executive (chief executive officer, chief financial officer, chief information officer, chief marketing officer), controller, executive director, vice president, general manager, treasurer, principal, owner, and the list goes on.

Generally, a person in such a position has strategically worked his or her way to the top echelons of management over a period of at least ten years. Executives tend to have many relevant past positions, credentials, achievements, published articles, speaking engagements, community service activities, or other important qualifications.

In order to reflect this experience, an executive résumé is almost always more than one page. In fact, an executive résumé can be as long as it needs to be in order to convince the reader that the candidate has what it takes to manage an organization effectively. The first page is the most important and persuades the reader to continue onto page two. If your résumé extends to a third page, it should contain only backup information that isn't critical if it doesn't get read.

Just because an executive résumé is long doesn't mean it should be wordy. The same good writing described in Step 8 (Chapter 11) is even more important in an executive résumé. Because the number of applicants for an executive position is generally not as large as for lower-level positions, every word of an executive's résumé will be read many times before a decision is made. Make sure every word you write serves a purpose!

There are some alternative styles that can help an executive manage a résumé that is getting too long. You can create a one-page summary that highlights your entire career and can stand alone. It is generally in a functional style with a simple listing of work experience.

Follow that one-page summary with a couple of pages that describe each job in detail, focusing on accomplishments using the CAR format (Challenge, Action, Result). Or, create a separate document listing critical leadership initiatives (success stories) or technology case studies. A brief narrative biography can be used instead of a résumé for networking purposes where a three-page résumé would be overkill.

On the next four pages are two examples of executive résumés. The first is a two-page résumé with standard formatting, and the second is an executive résumé with a more succinct, result-oriented style in a functional/chronological combination format.

DAVID A. SMITH, JD, LL.M., CPA

5797 South Anywhere Street • Newtown, Colorado 80111
Cellular: (720) 123-4567 • E-mail: dsmith@protypeltd.com • www.linkedin.com/in/dasmith

---

EXECUTIVE SUMMARY

Chief Financial Officer and Strategic Business Executive with 15+ years of proven achievement driving solid revenue and bottom-line gains through expert financial, legal, and operational contributions to merger and acquisition transactions, new business development, turnaround operations, and high-growth ventures. Quantifiable results in these areas:

Negotiations • Board/Investor Relations • Effective Communications
Cost Containment • Integration Planning • Results Analysis • System Conversions/Upgrades
Public/Private Infusions • Equity/Debt Financing • Financial Reporting

Aggressive, results-focused, strategic leader offering a unique blend of operations, financial, and legal expertise producing significant financial gains and meeting operational objectives. Led dynamic growth and expansion efforts for investments of Goldman Sachs and other investment firms. Championed bankruptcy workouts and business turnarounds. Full P&L responsibility for multiple divisions in multi-million-dollar organizations. Intrinsic leadership skills fostering top performance and efficiency through team-focused strategies.

PROFESSIONAL EXPERIENCE AND ACHIEVEMENTS

VICE PRESIDENT, LEGAL AND BUSINESS SERVICES (2010–present)
Coram Healthcare Corporation, Denver, Colorado

Spearheaded aggressive financial, legal, and operational turnaround for the nation's second largest supplier of infusion therapies. Streamlined and maximized budgetary accountability for $75 million in legal affairs, merger and acquisition activities, business development, SEC reporting, human resources, compliance, risk management, and administrative departments.

- Achieved and surpassed investor EBITDA and capital/debt restructuring goals.
- Initiated, negotiated, and closed $230+ million of capital restructurings at critical stages of the bankruptcy workout.
- Delivered a 23% EBITDA increase through combined M&A revenue enhancements and cost reductions.
- Enhanced cash flow 13% and contribution margins 9% by restructuring multiple departments for improved efficiencies.
- Infused business with $41.5 million cash by leading divestiture of non-accretive divisions.
- Negotiated a successful $18+ million resolution of $28+ million in tax liens.
- Produced 7% shift in core business and revenue quality through trend analysis and deployment of a benchmarking financial model to branch operations.

SVP BUSINESS AND LEGAL AFFAIRS / CHIEF FINANCIAL OFFICER (2008–2010)
ExchangeBridge.com, Atlanta, Georgia

Achieved financial, legal, and operational goals for this telecommunications e-business start-up. Raised venture capital and implemented core business strategies focusing on cash flow, M&A activities, return on investments, business line mix, and same-store EBITDA levels. Led business development initiatives for an aggressive marketing strategy that created new distribution channels for product lines.

- Strengthened cash position by leading $75+ million in business development efforts and divestiture of multiple websites and by transferring intellectual property for publishing and pharmacy-based businesses.
- Accelerated return on investment from 3.6% to more than 28%, dramatically exceeding investor goals and building momentum for the eventual sale of the company to a strategic partner with full payout to investors.
- Brought the company from the brink of bankruptcy by structuring the workout of payroll tax liens, realigning staff functions, and negotiating favorable arrangements with vendors.

- Raised financing for senior and subordinated mezzanine debt restructuring required for merger of an insurance-based business using discounted cash flow variable analysis.
- Championed fivefold increase in EBITDA, 20% improvement in receivable collections, and 33% enhancement of inventory turns, achieving business turnaround despite rapidly decreasing cash flows (high growth, low margins) and culminating in a profitable exit event for investors.
- Ensured SEC compliance and registration of an IPO offering. Minimized operational challenges associated with post-closing integrations by consolidating all due diligence efforts.

SENIOR VICE PRESIDENT, FINANCIAL AND LEGAL AFFAIRS / GENERAL COUNSEL (2002–2008)
Meridian Corporation, Memphis, Tennessee

Led team efforts for expansion and integration planning, including consolidation of financial, operational, and administrative functions for the nation's largest home health care company with 12,000+ employees and $500+ million in revenues. Negotiated and closed 75+ M&A transactions for management services divisions, producing debt/equity infusions. Consolidated $50+ million budgetary responsibility for financial services, marketing, legal, back office, and administrative departments.

- Spearheaded strategic three-year expansion for 350+ locations in 34 states and three countries by developing effective M&A growth strategies, leading due diligence, and reducing integration time lines to less than 150 days.
- Orchestrated $500+ million industry consolidation/merger through negotiations with industry leaders and alignment of investor and shareholder objectives.
- Reduced costs 15% by introducing stringent resource management and budgeting policies, reorganizing the sales force, and eliminating unproductive administrative support functions.
- Negotiated and closed $250 million syndicated debt restructuring and $85 million equity capitalizations.
- Decreased Medicare denials 13+% as chair of the Compliance and Risk Management Committees with rollout of improved financial reporting guidelines to all branch operations.
- Led successful integration of financial and telecommunications arrangements across more than 200 locations.

--- **EDUCATION** ---

LL.M. IN TAXATION (1998)
Washington University School of Law, St. Louis, Missouri

JURIS DOCTOR (1995)
University of Memphis School of Law, Memphis, Tennessee

BACHELOR OF ARTS, PSYCHOLOGY AND ACCOUNTING (1992)
Christian Brothers University, Memphis, Tennessee

--- **AFFILIATIONS AND PUBLICATIONS** ---

Certified Public Accountant	1989, 250+ hours Continuing Education Units (CEU)
Tennessee Bar Association	1985–2001, Young Lawyers Division, Chairman of Child Waiting Room Project, Chairman of Oversight Committee, ADR Section
Author	"Keeping the Secret in Trade Secrets," (April 1997), *ACCA Magazine*
Speaker	Financial Statements for Nonfinancial Attorneys, Trade Secret Protection, M&A Planning, Integration Activities and Time Lines: Application Service Provider Issues and Practical Solutions

DARIN R. SMITH

1234 Deer Creek Drive
Falcon, Colorado 80831

Cellular: (719) 555-1234
Email: darinsmith@protypeltd.com

FOOD AND BEVERAGE EXECUTIVE

"It's all about the food. A good manager will get out of the chef's way and let the food shine." — Darin Smith

EXECUTIVE QUALIFICATIONS

Experienced General Manager with a passion for combining quality food and diverse menus with exceptional customer service. Confident leader who has served in every facet of the business, from the front to the back of the house. Self-motivated and focused with a powerful drive to succeed—at ease when working collectively with executive management. Highly focused, results-oriented professional with expertise in managing complex, chef-driven operations.

AREAS OF EXPERTISE

- Food and Beverage Management
- Hiring, Supervision, and Training
- Purchasing and Inventory Management
- Budgeting and Effective Cost Control

SUMMARY OF EXPERIENCE

KEY ACCOMPLISHMENTS

- History of successfully managing multi-unit, upscale, and volume restaurants with buffet operations generating millions of dollars in annual revenue.
- Turned around unprofitable operations by developing and implementing new processes, upgrading food service, and improving customer service.
- Built operations from scratch, including staffing, training, and operating policies and procedures.

OPERATIONS MANAGEMENT

- Accountable for strategic planning, profit and loss, cost control, budgeting, cash handling, and general record keeping.
- Maintained expenses at or below budget through accurate planning, purchasing, waste reduction, and cost-effective operating procedures.
- Recruited, hired, supervised, and motivated assistant managers, chefs, and 200+ staff members.
- Mentored and trained managers and chefs. Instituted high standards for the service staff.
- Developed innovative training programs that emphasized safety, organization, and the importance of exceptional customer service.
- Initiated systems of accountability, and perpetuated a firm, fair, and consistent management style that improved productivity and lowered turnover.

PURCHASING

- Estimated food and beverage costs, sourced suppliers, and purchased inventory, kitchen equipment, china, glass, and silver.
- Set product standards and ingredient specifications; structured purchasing and receiving processes and procedures.
- Solicited competitive bids and negotiated cost-effective contracts with major wholesale suppliers and boutique vendors.

WINE, SPIRITS, AND NONALCOHOLIC BEVERAGES

- Set standards, controls, and procedures for efficient beverage operations that consistently reduced liquor costs and excess inventory.
- Implemented a liquor pouring system that improved pouring accuracy and controlled costs.
- Served beverages in glassware that was appealing to customers while at the same time allowing cost-effective portion control.

CULINARY EXPERIENCE

- Managed the kitchens of fine-dining restaurants, including menu and recipe development, food preparation, and presentation.
- Planned and coordinated banquets, private/corporate parties, and off-site catering.
- Focused on highest quality ingredients and preparation, impeccable food appearance, and exquisite service.

EDUCATION   **CULINARY INSTITUTE OF AMERICA (CIA),** Hyde Park, New York
                      Associate of Science (1993)

PROFESSIONAL   **GENERAL MANAGER / OPERATING PARTNER, Outback Steakhouse,** Denver, CO (2007–2013)
EXPERIENCE   Took over a declining operation and turned it around, implementing standards that were higher than
                      corporate expectations. Improved service and food quality, replaced service staff, and created new training
                      programs. Expedited the food, checking every plate to ensure consistent products from the first customer
                      to the last. Marketed this casual/family-style steakhouse by participating in community charity events,
                      including golf tournaments, bike races, school career days, and athletic award banquets. Selected as
                      Proprietor of the Year in 2011. Sold interest in the business at the end of the contract period when the
                      company went private.

                      EXECUTIVE CHEF, The Peaks at Telluride, Telluride, Colorado (2006–2007)
                      Opened the culinary operations for this 181-room luxury alpine resort serving Rocky Mountain cuisine—
                      staffed and furnished a kitchen serving two restaurants, purchased equipment, developed the menus and
                      kitchen flow, set timing standards for cooks and servers, and created relationships with new vendors.

                      EXECUTIVE CHEF, The Lodge at Koele, Lanai City, Hawaii (2003–2006)
                      Recruited away from The Ritz Carlton and back to Rockresorts to manage the kitchen of a 102-room,
                      world-class resort (#3 on the Zagat Survey of Top 50 Resorts). Rapidly promoted from Chef de Cuisine
                      to Executive Chef after the departure of John Farnsworth. Oversaw the production of three sous chefs,
                      an executive steward, and 40 employees. Prepared three meals a day in the formal dining room, in
                      addition to private dining and banquets. Created a Guest Chef Program to promote the hotel with nation-
                      ally known chefs such as Dean Fearing and George Marrone. Developed a Community Farm Project that
                      contracted with local growers for garden-fresh, organic produce.

                      *"At the time of our visit and until recently, the kitchen was run by John Farnsworth, one of the most gifted
                      chefs of his generation. His talent for using an amazing range of fresh ingredients, all local or homegrown,
                      lives on in chef Darin Smith, who is creating the same deeply flavored, beautifully presented dishes."*
                      — Suzanne Hamlin, Hawaii: Catch the Next Food Wave, ***Food & Wine,*** March 2005

                      *"Since guests in both places have nowhere else to eat, the food at The Lodge and Manele Bay had better
                      be good. And it is. Chef Darin Smith is intense. 'In The Lodge's fine dining room, I call my style Up Coun-
                      try Cooking. Continental on the terrace.' Smith makes the most of culled Lanai venison, smokes his own
                      salmon, pheasant, turkey, and marlin that's startling. He raises his own pigs, keeps chickens for eggs, and
                      grows papayas. Vegetables and herbs come from the hotel's private gardens, goat cheese from a nearby
                      island."* — Kit Snedaker, ***New York Post,*** July 28, 2005

                      *"All this serves as food for thought for Chef de Cuisine Darin Smith, whose extraordinary menus have
                      been inspired by frequent visits to the fields. . . . Chef Smith manages to perk up even the mundane."*
                      — Cheryl Chee Tsutsami, The Great Escape, ***Aloha,*** March/April 2005

                      RESTAURANT CHEF, The Ritz Carlton Mauna Lani, Kawaihae, Hawaii (2002–2003)
                      Member of the opening team responsible for hiring, training, setting up, and organizing the culinary
                      department and complete kitchen operations for the American Grill Restaurant (Zagat #16).

                      EXECUTIVE SOUS CHEF, Carambola Beach Resort and Golf Club, St. Croix, USVI (2002–2003)
                      SOUS CHEF, The Greenbrier Resort, White Sulphur Springs, West Virginia (1998–2000)
                      SOUS CHEF, Keystone Ski Resort and Lodge, Keystone, Colorado (1996–1998)
                      Managed the kitchen operations of these Rockresorts, Inc., properties during alternating winter and
                      summer seasons. The Greenbrier was a Mobil Five-Star Resort (Zagat #18) with banquets and dining
                      rooms that accommodated 1,500 guests. Worked under Hartmut Handke, a Certified Master Chef.

Curriculum Vitae

Remember when I said there is an exception to every rule in the résumé business? Well, here's another one. In most cases, résumés should be concise and limited to one or two pages at the most. You will carefully select your information to provide a synopsis. In some professions, however, a much longer résumé is expected and the longer the résumé, the better your chances of getting an interview.

Those industries generally include medicine, law, education, and the sciences. If you are applying for a job in a foreign country, long résumés with more detail and a considerable amount of personal information are the norm.

Such a professional résumé is called a *curriculum vitae* (CV) from the Latin meaning "course of one's life" (literally like running a race—and you just *thought* your life was a rat race!).

A successful CV will include not only education and experience but also some of the following categories:

- Publications (books, magazines, journals, and other media)

- Certifications and Licenses

- Grants and Research

- Professional Affiliations

- Awards and Honors

- Presentations and/or Courses Taught

Anything relevant to your industry is appropriate to use on a CV, and the résumé can be as long as it needs to be to present the "course of your life."

A CV—or any résumé with multiple pages, for that matter—must contain a header with your name and page number on each successive page. Should the pages become separated, the reader should be able to easily put your subsequent pages in their proper order and with *your* résumé!

Let's take a look at a sample CV, beginning on the next page.

CAROL S. KLEINMAN, PhD, RN

PROFILE

- Experienced university professor and academic administrator.
- Able to bring real-world nursing and health care administration experience to the classroom.
- Effective team player with strong communication and interpersonal skills.
- Known for dynamic presentation style and the ability to reach any student.

TEACHING EXPERIENCE

ASSOCIATE PROFESSOR (2009–present)
College of Nursing, Seton Hall University, South Orange, New Jersey
- Developed and delivered the first completely online College of Nursing course in multimedia format—Theoretical Basis of Advanced Practice Nursing.
- Teach graduate courses in nursing and health services administration.

ADJUNCT CLINICAL PROFESSOR (2009–present)
Department of Nursing, Essex County College, Newark, New Jersey
- Guide undergraduate students through clinical rotations in psychiatry.

PROFESSOR OF GRADUATE NURSING (2007–2009)
Clarkson College, Omaha, Nebraska
- Taught selected courses in health services administration, all courses in the nursing administration major, and core courses in graduate nursing curricula.
- Consistently received among the highest student reviews of all the faculty in the college.

ADJUNCT PROFESSOR (2003–2007)
School of Nursing, Barry University, Miami, Florida
- Taught core courses in the graduate nursing curriculum.

ASSISTANT PROFESSOR AND COURSE COORDINATOR (1995–2003)
School of Nursing, City College of New York
- Coordinated teaching team in upper junior-level integrated nursing course.
- Taught all psychiatric content throughout the undergraduate nursing curriculum, including clinical teaching in psychiatric inpatient settings.
- Member of the Course and Standing Committee; Chair of the Evaluation Committee; Member of the Community Mental Health Liaison Committee.

COURSES TAUGHT

GRADUATE NURSING COURSES:
- Nursing Theories and Concept Development
- Theories and Concepts of Advanced Nursing Practice
- Nursing Research
- Social Context of Healthcare
- Theories and Concepts of Nursing Administration
- Psychosocial Assessment and Intervention in Primary Care
- Thesis Development

GRADUATE HEALTH SERVICES ADMINISTRATION COURSES:
- Operations Management
- Organizational Theory and Behavior
- Human Resources Management
- Reimbursement and Managed Care
- Forces in Healthcare
- Thesis Development

GRANTS AND RESEARCH

- Health and Human Services, Division of Nursing, Online MSN/MBA, December 2011.
- Health and Human Services, Division of Nursing, Online MSN, Health Systems Administration, December 2011.
- Developed research proposal for "Leadership styles and staff nurse retention" approved for implementation at Clara Maass Medical Center.

ADDRESS

18 Anywhere Court, Anytown, NJ 07747, Phone: (732) 555-1234, E-mail: drcsk@protypeltd.com

192

EDUCATION	**CERTIFICATES**

CERTIFICATES
Imago Relationship Therapy, Institute for Imago Relationship Therapy (2001)
Clinical Fellowship in Hypnotherapy, Morton Prince Center for Hypnosis (1989)

PhD, BEHAVIORAL SCIENCE, Specialization in Psychotherapy (1993)
Florida Institute of Technology, School of Professional Psychology
- Dissertation: "Attitudes Toward Mental Illness by Student Nurses from Various Ethnic Groups"
- Honors: Graduate Assistantship (2 years)

MASTER OF SCIENCE, Psychiatric-Mental Health Nursing (1985)
Adelphi University, School of Nursing
- Thesis: "A Conceptual Model of Female Homosexuality from the Perspective of Analytical Psychology"
- Honors: NIMH Traineeship for Graduate Study, Sigma Theta Tau

BACHELOR OF SCIENCE IN NURSING, Major in Psychiatric Nursing (1983)
State University of New York at Stony Brook
- Honors: Graduated cum laude

ASSOCIATE OF APPLIED SCIENCE IN NURSING (1981)
Kingsborough Community College, City University of New York
- Honors: Salutatorian (third in a class of 1,000), Phi Theta Kappa, Dean's List, President's Award, Department of Nursing Award

---

ADMINISTRATIVE EXPERIENCE

DIRECTOR, NURSING ADMINISTRATION PROGRAM (2009–present)
Seton Hall University, South Orange, New Jersey
- Developed a dual degree program with the Stillman School of Business offering an MSN/MBA as a collaborative degree program.
- Created a Master of Nursing Education program offered completely online through SetonWorld-Wide, the virtual university branch of Seton Hall.
- Completed a comprehensive revision of the Master of Science in Nursing Case Management program.
- Developed a grant proposal to obtain funding for the Nursing Administration graduate program.

DIRECTOR, HEALTH SERVICES ADMINISTRATION (2007–2009)
Nebraska Health Services, Omaha, Nebraska
- Directed the graduate program in Health Services Administration; responsible for operations management, budgeting, curriculum design, faculty supervision, and student recruitment initiatives.
- Developed and implemented a complete redesign of the curriculum based on market analysis.
- Involved in developing innovative new Internet-based distance learning programs.
- Created a program that allowed students to obtain dual graduate degrees.
- Developed incentives and interfaces between the undergraduate and graduate programs of the college to prevent loss of graduate students to competitive schools.
- Member of the Heartland Healthcare Executive Group; revitalized this regional chapter of the American College of Healthcare Executives, developed relationships with health care leaders in the community, and served as faculty adviser.

DIRECTOR, BEHAVIORAL HEALTH SERVICES (2003–2006)
Broward General Medical Center, Ft. Lauderdale, Florida
- Responsible for the administrative and clinical management of the behavioral health department of the fourth largest integrated health care delivery system in the nation.
- Directed the 98-bed inpatient service, crisis stabilization unit, psychiatric emergency services, specialty treatment unit, and mental health initiatives within primary health centers.
- Developed a consultation and liaison service to trauma and other hospital departments.
- Managed an expense budget of more than $7 million and a staff of 135 FTEs.
- Developed a re-engineering plan that modernized the care delivery model and restaffed the department, saving $400,000 a year in salary and benefit expenses.
- Absorbed all of the county mental health services valued at $4 million.
- Rewrote the department's policy and procedure manual; implemented a new quality assurance program.

EXPERIENCE (continued)	**EXECUTIVE DIRECTOR** (2002–2003)

EXECUTIVE DIRECTOR (2002–2003)
American Day Treatment Centers of Miami, Florida
- Directed all administrative and clinical operations of a freestanding, for-profit center that provided adult, adolescent, and geriatric partial hospitalization programs.
- Developed this new program from the ground up, including definition and marketing of products, programs, and services.
- Responsible for managing the construction project, purchasing capital equipment, and staffing.
- Administered a $2 million budget, achieving profitability within twelve months.

DIRECTOR, OUTPATIENT SERVICES (1996–2002)
Green Oaks Psychiatric Hospital, Dallas, Texas
- Created and directed the outpatient department of a 106-bed psychiatric hospital, including adult, adolescent, and chemical dependency partial hospitalization programs.
- Developed and implemented programs and services, making them profitable in less than a year.
- Grew the program to 25 staff members in a dedicated 10,000 sq. ft. office space with a $2 million budget and 50 patients per day.
- Responsible for strategic planning, marketing, referral development, and regulatory compliance.
- Elected to the national Board of Directors of the Association for Ambulatory Behavioral Healthcare.

SELECTED PRESENTATIONS
- Business and Health Administration Association Conference, Chicago, Illinois, February 28, 2012.
- "Education for future nurse leaders." Keynote presentation for the Council of School Presidents, New Jersey Nursing Students, Inc., November 2012.
- "Education for nurse leaders of the future." New Jersey State Nurses Association, Atlantic City, New Jersey, April 2011.
- "Roles, power, and opportunities for men in nursing." American Assembly of Men in Nursing, Seattle, Washington, December 2010.
- "Graduate education for the 21st century nurse." Poster presentation for the Fourth State of the Art of Nursing Conference, University of Nebraska Medical Center, April 4, 2009.
- "Psychological aspects of menopause." Grand Rounds, Department of Psychiatry, Broward General Medical Center, January 16, 2007.
- "Enhancing and expanding established partial hospitalization programs." American Association for Ambulatory Behavioral Healthcare Seminar; March 17–18, 2004; August 16–17, 2004; February 18–19, 2003; August 24–25, 2003; March 4–5, 2002, August 10–11, 2002.
- "Setting up partial hospital programs for accreditation and other key aspects of program success." Texas Association of Partial Hospitalization Annual Meeting, April 26, 2001.
- Kleinman, C., and Halperin, D. "Cults: Fact or fiction?" Southwestern Conference on Cult Issues, Dallas, Texas, April 10, 2000.

SELECTED PUBLICATIONS
- Kleinman, C. (Manuscript under review). "Understanding men's advantages in nursing." *Nursing Leadership Forum.*
- Kleinman, C. (In press). "Nurse executives." *Journal of Health Administration Education.*
- Kleinman, C. (1992). State Board Review Examination: Grant-funded development of 240 test items for New York State nursing examination, City College of New York.

AFFILIATIONS
- Council on Graduate Education for Administration in Nursing, National Treasurer
- Institute for Nursing of New Jersey, Member, Board of Trustees
- Organization of Nurse Executives of New Jersey, Membership and Fund-Raising Committees
- Bureau of Health Professions, Division of Nursing, Health and Human Services, Peer Reviewer
- New Jersey Student Nurses, Inc., Faculty Adviser
- East Orange School District, Member, Health Advisory Committee
- Healthcare Foundation of New Jersey, Clinical Fellowship Grant, Project Director
- American Organization of Nurse Executives
- American Nurses Association
- American Psychiatric Nurses Association
- Association of University Professors of Health Administration

Designing the Perfect Résumé

Even though content is important, many times well-qualified people aren't considered for positions because a poorly designed résumé didn't grab the reader's attention long enough to make sure the words were read. Just the opposite can be true as well. Even if your qualifications aren't the greatest, a well-designed résumé improves your chances of getting an interview because it stands out in a crowd of poorly designed ones.

The choice of overall style, font, graphics, and even paper color says something about your personality. In this chapter, you have already seen some résumé designs to help you find ways to express your unique personality on paper. Now I will show you a few more examples.

If you want additional design ideas, then you should read the fourth edition of *Résumés That Pop!* (Barron's, 2010), with more than 200 sample layouts. It also covers in great detail the various elements of design.

Suzanne Davis

210 Anywhere Drive ✦ Newtown, Colorado 80906
Home: (719) 555-1234 ✦ Cell: (719) 123-4567 ✦ E-mail: sdavis@protypeltd.com

PROFILE

- ✦ Experienced multimedia sales director with demonstrated success in these areas:
  - – Brand definition
  - – Market penetration
  - – Product positioning
  - – New product development
  - – Online advertising
  - – Franchise building
  - – Marketing plan creation
  - – Strategic market research
  - – Sales management
- ✦ Innovative thinker who is willing to step outside the box and take a risk.
- ✦ Proven sales leader with a strong background in building new territories and using creative marketing approaches to increase revenue.

EXPERIENCE

METRO NEWSPAPERS, FREEDOM COMMUNICATIONS, Colorado Springs, Colorado
Director, Major Accounts and Motion Pictures/Entertainment (May 2010–present)
Recruited by the publisher of *The Orange County Register* to join the new Metro Newspaper Division, Freedom Media Enterprises (FME). FME is an integrated information and media company designed to service marketing and advertising needs in new and exciting ways offering one central account contact for three markets—*The Orange County Register* (Santa Ana), *The Gazette* (Colorado Springs), and *The Tribune* (Phoenix).

- ✦ Developed the business plan, sales plan, policies and procedures, execution, and implementation of the new organization.
- ✦ Developed and managed a revenue budget of more than $30 million.
- ✦ Grew incremental revenues to $3.1 million in the first five months of operation.

FREEDOM COMMUNICATIONS, Newspaper Division, Colorado Springs, Colorado
Vice President, Corporate Sales (June 2008–April 2010)
Recruited by *The Gazette*'s parent company to develop a new business venture to generate advertising for 28 newspapers (1.1 million total circulation), 6 Internet portals, 12 Hispanic publications, and 10 military newspapers nationwide. Wrote the business plan, policies and procedures, sales plan, and job descriptions. Hired, trained, and managed four account managers and an office manager.

- ✦ Created strategic and tactical marketing plans for the branding of Freedom Communications and generated more than $1.7 million in new revenue in the first year.
- ✦ Sourced contacts, developed sales presentations, made sales calls, and captured significant market share.

THE GAZETTE, Colorado Springs, Colorado
Director, Display Advertising (January 2002–May 2008)
Built a national advertising division from the ground up and managed major accounts, generating $24 million in annual advertising revenue. Hired and managed a team of sales managers responsible for 40 account executives. Instrumental in securing advertising for the interactive division of the newspaper *(Coloradosprings.com)*.

- ✦ Developed the *Home in Colorado* magazine that won the 2007 Addy Award for best in-house publication with more than four colors.
- ✦ Partnered with The Broadmoor (a Mobil five-star, five-diamond resort) to deliver *The Gazette* to guests every day; created a four-color, in-room *Broadmoor Magazine* for guests that generated significant income for the paper.
- ✦ Created partnerships with cruise lines and travel agencies to give the newspaper travel section a more national feel and to offer new opportunities to readers.

EXPERIENCE
(continued)

LOS ANGELES TIMES, Los Angeles, California
Advertising Sales Manager, Entertainment Category (May 2002–December 2003)
Recruited from *The Orange County Register* because of the phenomenal success of its news entertainment section. Developed strategic plans for future growth and franchise protection. Created and promoted unique online advertising programs that were ahead of their time.
- Managed a team of six sales associates responsible for selling advertising space in the entertainment *Calendar* section that generated $150 million in annual revenue.
- Implemented performance management and team-building strategies that improved morale, reduced turnover, and increased individual sales revenue.

THE ORANGE COUNTY REGISTER, Santa Ana, California
Sales Manager, Major Accounts Division (June 2000–May 2002)
Recruited, hired, and supervised a staff of 14 account executives.
- Succeeded in growing revenue to more than $50 million a year from department, grocery, electronics, and small/medium specialty stores (Target, Macy's, Homestead House, etc.).

Retail Territorial Manager (June 1998–May 2002)
Managed six regional sales managers responsible for generating local advertisements from retailers throughout Orange County.

Sales Manager, Entertainment Division (January 1994–May 2002)
Developed and launched the Show Section, an entertainment tab that competed directly with the *Los Angeles Times Calendar* section.
- Grew the insert from 80 to 124 pages through aggressive advertising sales.
- Created significant advertising revenue with innovative partnerships, promotions, and special events.

EDUCATION

SAN FRANCISCO STATE UNIVERSITY, San Francisco, California (1992–1996)
- Completed three years of full-time undergraduate studies.

PROFESSIONAL DEVELOPMENT
- **Landmark Forum Education** (2010)
- **Community Leadership Forum**: Better Business Bureau (2009, 2010)
- **Associated Press Institute**: Publishing Your Own Newspaper (2007)
- **Center for Creative Leadership**: Leadership Development Program (1 week, 2006)
- **University of Southern California**: Management Institute (2003)
- **Aubrey Daniels**: Performance Management Training (2003)

AFFILIATIONS
- NAA Advertising Committee Board
- Better Business Bureau Board of Directors
- CASA Fund-Raising Committee
- Denver Ad Federation

Melissa Hardy

STRENGTHS
- Experienced loan processor and investigator with exceptional customer service skills.
- Responsible and dedicated worker who learns quickly.
- Effective team player with strong interpersonal/communication skills; highly proficient in Spanish.
- Proficient in WordPerfect, Windows, MS Word, Excel, PowerPoint, Outlook, and proprietary database and contact management software.

EXPERIENCE

DEALER SERVICE REPRESENTATIVE   2012–present
AmeriCredit Financial, Colorado Springs, Colorado
- Serve as a loan officer, working directly with car dealerships to sell loans to their customers.
- Call on 4 to 5 dealers per day in the Colorado Springs and Pueblo territory, generating sales of as much as $4 million per month.
- Supervise the branch during the absence of the manager.
- Rapidly promoted from customer service representative responsible for loan processing and verification of employment, credit history, and other loan data.

LOAN PROCESSOR/ADMINISTRATIVE ASSISTANT   2012
World Class Homes and Mortgage, Colorado Springs, Colorado
- Entered data for loan applications and Loan Handler computer files.
- Made weekly customer courtesy calls to update customers on the status of their loans.
- Answered phones and customer inquiries; set appointments with prospective customers.
- In charge of coordinating subordinations and preparing associated paperwork.
- Ordered titles, payoffs, mortgage ratings, appraisals, and evidence of insurance.
- Designed and updated database of all clients; organized paperwork in stacking order.
- Helped start the business from the ground up; ordered office furniture and supplies.

LOAN PROCESSOR AND INVESTIGATOR   2011–2012
Champion Financial Services, Colorado Springs, Colorado
- Processed vehicle loans, verified calculations on buyer orders, gathered stipulations from customers, and prepared paperwork.
- Verified employment and residency, checked credit ratings, requested proofs of income, and investigated incoming applications for completeness and accuracy.
- Communicated with dealerships regarding stipulations and rollbacks.
- Determined Blue Book and NADA values of vehicles.
- Made ten-day calls to remind customers of first payments and processed requests for deferred payments.
- Answered questions from customers, resolved complaints, and communicated with Spanish-speaking customers.
- Designed an improved filing system for home office loans.

SALES REPRESENTATIVE   2011
MCI Telecommunications Corporation, Colorado Springs, Colorado
- Sold long-distance services and Continental Airlines frequent flyer programs.
- Set goals in a highly competitive environment.
- Received Player of the Month award for highest sales.
- Won a trip to Orlando, Florida, and other incentives for sales achievements.

CUSTOMER SERVICE REPRESENTATIVE   2009–2010
Maxserve, Inc. (for Sears), Tucson, Arizona
- Provided customer service and telephone sales of appliance parts.
- Entered data into the computer and researched part numbers.
- Used communication skills to determine correct parts from customer descriptions.

ADDRESS   5390 Anywhere Drive, Newtown, Colorado 80918, (719) 534-0570, mhardy@mail.com

Lisa Schenck

PROFILE

- Self-motivated sales professional with more than 15 years of proven experience.
- Top performer with a strong background in building new territories and using creative marketing approaches.
- Respected for the ability to get to the decision maker and close the sale.
- Demonstrated ability to create client loyalty beyond the sales relationship.
- Entrepreneurial thinker who works well independently or as part of a team.

EXPERIENCE

SALES REPRESENTATIVE, Waxie Sanitary Supply, Denver, Colorado (2011–present)
Sell paper products, chemicals, equipment, and cleaning supplies to large corporate clients, including The Pepsi Center, Coors Field, Invesco, Coors Brewery, casinos, hospital, and various other market segments. Made sales presentations to upper-level management based on comprehensive needs analyses.

- Formulated a two-year strategic sales plan for territory growth and built the territory from zero to $1.2 million.
- Created and conducted on-site training programs for end users, focusing on the safe use of chemicals and equipment

SALES REPRESENTATIVE, Unisource, Denver, Colorado (2003–2011)
Sold paper products, chemicals, and cleaning supplies to large corporate and government clients, including hospitals, hotels, casinos, City of Denver, and Coors. Created and conducted sales presentations to upper-level management, assessed their needs, and developed unique customer applications. Designed and executed training programs for key clients.

- Formulated a strategic plan for the territory and grew the account base by 350% through effective cold calling and account development.
- Successfully regained former customers through effective marketing and follow-up.
- Achieved the President's Club through exceptional sales performance; ranked the number one salesperson in the Denver metropolitan territory.

SALES REPRESENTATIVE, Moore Business Forms, Denver, Colorado (2001–2003)
Sold customized business forms to companies in the Denver territory. Designed special forms to fit proprietary computer systems.

- Increased sales to existing customers and developed the territory by 178%.
- Created a forms management program for the Poudre Valley Hospital.

SALES REPRESENTATIVE, Pitney Bowes, Denver, Colorado (1998–2001)
Developed markets for Pitney Bowes copiers throughout 20 zip codes in the Denver metropolitan area. Completed a comprehensive Pitney Bowes professional sales training program.

- Consistently exceeded production quotas by as much as 250%, producing nearly half a million dollars a year in sales.
- Honored as one of the top five Pitney Bowes salespeople in the state of Colorado.

EDUCATION

BACHELOR OF ARTS IN BUSINESS MARKETING
Colorado State University, Fort Collins, Colorado

8641 Anywhere Lane • Newtown, Colorado 80124
Phone: (303) 555-1234 • Cellular: (303) 123-4567 • E-mail: lisor@protypeltd.com

199

Howard E. Hyde

1223 Anywhere Drive, Suite A • Newtown, CO 80906
Home: (719) 555-1234 • Cellular: (719) 123-4567
E-mail: hehyde@protypeltd.com

PROFILE

- Results-oriented senior executive with expertise in the following areas:
  - Organizational development
  - Strategic planning
  - Change management
  - Marketing/sales
  - Problem solving
  - Customer service
  - Line management
  - Staffing
  - Training and development
- Conceptual thinker who can see the whole picture, create a vision for the enterprise, and generate commitment from employees.
- Respected for the ability to lead business units through dramatic turnarounds and periods of high growth.

EXPERIENCE

PRESIDENT (2010–present)
The Center for Customer Focus, Colorado Springs, Colorado
Developed a successful business that provides consulting and training services to organizations desiring to become more customer focused. Create and present workshops and seminars that help client organizations dramatically improve their competitive advantage by creating more value for their customers. Analyze client needs, develop innovative solutions, and serve as a change agent. Recruited, hired, and supervised a staff of four employees in addition to independent contractors. Accountable for operations management, business planning, profit and loss, accounting, marketing, and customer service functions.

- Developed measurement technologies that provided a systems approach to the measurement of a company's values and beliefs, its perceptions of service and quality, and the employees' perception of the organization's customer orientation.
- Successfully marketed services to clients such as Del Webb, NorthStar Print Group, Madison Fireplace and Lighting, and Long Island Pipe, among others.
- Exceeded revenue and profit goals by setting high goals and mobilizing a strong work ethic.

GENERAL MANAGER, MARKETING STRATEGY AND CORPORATE MARKETING (2008–2010)
Control Data Corporation, Minneapolis, Minnesota
Selected to develop a complete plan for transforming the culture of the company from a product-driven organization to a customer-driven one. Conducted extensive secondary research at Harvard, Stanford, and the Kellogg Graduate Schools of Business, and visited numerous customer-driven companies to broaden the knowledge base.

- Designed a measurement instrument to define discrete customer-driven factors and implemented a survey to measure the current culture of the company.
- Consulted with internal business units to strengthen executive marketing skills, develop marketing as a core competency, and improve financial performance.
- Created executive/employee development programs and modified human resource processes (compensation, performance appraisals, internal communications) to reinforce the desired culture.
- Developed and implemented a uniform strategic planning process that served as a model for other business units.

GENERAL MANAGER, MARKETING AND ACADEMIC EDUCATION (2005–2007)
Control Data Corporation, Minneapolis, Minnesota
Managed the marketing department of a business unit that promoted computer-based education in the academic marketplace. Analyzed the market, defined market segments, and developed a marketing strategy to meet the needs of each segment. Created formal criteria for advertising agency selection, interviewed agencies, and selected finalists to compete for the account.

- Instituted account planning processes and increased the sales force by 30%.
- Achieved 100% of goal and increased revenue by 152%.
- Developed a new marketing communication strategy with the ad agency that significantly increased product awareness in the market.

200

EXPERIENCE (continued)

GENERAL MANAGER, GOVERNMENT SERVICES DIVISION (2003–2005)

Control Data Corporation, Minneapolis, Minnesota

Provided direction for a division that marketed educational computer services and hardware to the government sector.

- Developed and implemented the division's first marketing strategy and restructured prices.
- Reduced the number of market segments covered to focus on those segments with a higher growth rate and where the company could provide more value.
- Created a program to retrain unemployed steelworkers in Pittsburgh, which was so successful that President Reagan visited the operation to show how government and the private sector can partner to improve performance.
- Succeeded in lobbying to change federal legislation for the industry from cost-based to performance-based pricing.
- Produced the first profits in the division's history, increasing revenue by 166% in the first year and 183% in the following year.

GENERAL MANAGER, LEARNING CENTER DIVISION (2000–2003)

Control Data Corporation, Minneapolis, Minnesota

Assumed full profit and loss responsibility for 52 education centers that delivered computer-based training programs to various market segments.

- Attained 130% of revenue objectives and improved the bottom line from a loss position to a 12% pretax profit.
- Promoted from General Manager of Field Sales Operations for the Business Center Division, which marketed computer hardware, software, and training programs to small-business markets.
- Built the division from the ground up, including leasing and renovating the facility and hiring staff.

GENERAL MANAGER, WESTERN REGION (1997–2000)

Control Data Corporation, Irvine, California

Managed four educational services divisions that included five Control Data Institutes, twelve computer-based learning centers, a consulting business, and a seminar business. Directed 175 full-time employees, as well as more than 100 supplemental employees and consultants.

- Took the region from the worst to the first region in the country by dramatically improving sales, profitability, and quality in all four divisions.
- Selected as the top regional manager; the region won 18 of the 23 top performance awards at the company's annual 100% Club event.

EDUCATION

MASTER OF BUSINESS ADMINISTRATION

Pepperdine University, Malibu, California

Graduated with a 4.0 GPA on a 4.0 scale

UNDERGRADUATE STUDIES IN ELECTRICAL ENGINEERING

University of Illinois, Chicago and Champaign-Urbana, Illinois

AFFILIATIONS

- Board of Directors, The Braas Company, Inc. (7 years)
- American Society of Training and Development, Current Member
- National Speakers Association, Current Member
- Colorado Speakers Association, Current Member
- American Marketing Association, Former Executive Member
- Sales and Marketing Executives International, Former Director
- Institute for the Study of Business Markets, Former Member
- The Pricing Institute, Former Advisory Board Member

PHILLIP W. SMITH

Home: (719) 555-1234 ▪ Cellular: (719) 123-4567 ▪ E-mail: psmith@protypeltd.com
1234 Fossil Drive ▪ Anywhere, Idaho 80918

SUMMARY
- Directed environmental services operations for regional medical centers with up to 300 beds.
- Developed and managed payroll and operating budgets from $500,000 to $3.4 million.
- Screened, hired, and managed staff as large as 95 employees. Delegated authority and assigned and prioritized duties. Counseled employees with discipline problems.
- Analyzed reports to track productive hours and made adjustments to schedules in order to maximize productivity.
- Attended daily staff meetings to ensure staffing levels were appropriate for each day's census.
- Developed and monitored operating standards, policies, and procedures.
- Conducted formal rounds with directors to discuss issues/concerns, and maintained positive relations with management.
- Conducted daily quality assurance audits of patient rooms to ensure the highest levels of cleanliness. Interviewed patients to determine their level of satisfaction with housekeeping services. Initiated 30-day action plans for ratings that fell below 80%.
- Developed and implemented effective safety programs. Conducted regular safety audits, analyzed problems, and developed quarterly training programs to correct deficiencies.

EXPERIENCE

2008–present

SODEXO, Denver, Colorado
Presbyterian St. Luke's Medical Center and RM Hospital for Children
Assistant Director of Environmental Services (300-bed combo of two hospitals in one)—Conducted weekly rounds of patient areas with managers to build cooperative relationships with other departments. Created a Patient Experience Coordinator position responsible for visiting newly admitted patients and gathering data on cleanliness and courtesy of staff. *Key Accomplishments:* Significantly improved patient perceptions of hospital care reflected in HCAHPS scores for environmental cleanliness, raising them from 35% to 68% in a single year. Selected as one of three hospitals to take part in 3M Clean Trace Certification, an experimental program using a new type of swabbing equipment to detect bacteria on surfaces. Implemented black-light inspections to detect bacteria left over after room cleaning. Reduced the time required to accomplish STAT cleaning of patient rooms by proactively monitoring computerized bed tracking data to capture orders and assign housekeepers; reduced the number of orders that exceeded the 30-minute standard from 35% to 2% in 90 days. Coordinated a 100 Fixes in 100 Days program—gathered a list of items needing repair from all departments of the hospital and fixed them all within 100 days. Implemented Sodexo's CARES training program (Compassion, Accountability, Respect, Enthusiasm, Service), which significantly increased patient satisfaction and employee engagement by making staff accountable for their actions. Developed patient amenity kits with assorted toiletries; created upgraded kits for mothers and babies.

2007–2008

SAINT ANTHONY NORTH, Westminster, Colorado
General Manager, Environmental Services Department (150-bed Centura Health hospital)—Managed 30 employees and ensured implementation of the highest operating standards. Conducted daily room inspections and quarterly safety audits. *Key Accomplishments:* Successfully passed a Joint Commission inspection with zero deficiencies.

2005–2007

SODEXO, Englewood, Colorado
Operations Manager, Environmental Services Department, Swedish Medical Center (300-bed regional medical center)—Managed the entire department in the absence of the director. Served as chair of the Safety Committee and member of the Standards and Values Committee. Edited the Kronus report to ensure accurate payroll. *Key Accomplishments:* Developed a monthly safety training program that resulted in zero workers' compensation claims for more than a year. Passed two successive JCAHO surveys. Raised patient satisfaction scores to the upper tenth percentile for all units.

2002–2005   **SODEXO**, Aurora, Colorado
Operations Manager, Environmental Services Department, Medical Center of Aurora (HealthOne hospital with 250 beds)—Member of the Safety Committee responsible for developing proactive solutions to hazards in the workplace. Served as the District Safety Coordinator responsible for improving the safety of all HealthOne hospitals in the Colorado and Wyoming district. Traveled to each hospital and conducted physical audits in preparation for Joint Commission inspections, including evaluation of eye-wash stations, safety boards, MSDS, and other safety requirements. *Key Accomplishments:* Succeeded in reducing accidents 50% throughout the district. Selected for the new Physician Satisfaction Team—helped to develop a survey instrument that evaluated the satisfaction levels of doctors with the appearance and cleanliness of the facility and to solicit ideas for improvement. Succeeded in building a sense of teamwork and consensus among a highly diverse staff from many different cultures.

2001–2002   **YWCA CHILD CARE SERVICE**, El Paso, Texas
Assistant Administrator—Helped to manage the operations of an organization that determined eligibility of child care providers and served as a resource/referral agency. Reviewed compatibility of a competing organization and helped to negotiate a merger. Developed and implemented directives, policies, and procedures approved by the Texas Workforce Commission's Upper Rio Grande Workforce Development Board and the YWCA Board. Prepared requests for proposals for child care contracts. Hired, trained, and supervised a staff of 35 in two departments. Managed operating budgets of $1.2 million, as well as state-allocated funding of $2.2 million. Served as a liaison between YWCA departments and the community. *Key Accomplishments:* Wrote a successful grant from the Texas Child Care Resource and Referral Association. Managed Young at Heart, a grandparent fostering program that provided health, education, and welfare services to youth with exceptional or special needs. Provided exceptional customer service to all constituencies.

2001–2002   **HOWARD PAYNE UNIVERSITY**, El Paso, Texas
Adjunct Faculty—Taught Introduction to Health Administration and Legal Aspects of Health Care Administration to undergraduate students at this private university. Designed learning environments to meet educational development requirements, adapting teaching methods to accommodate both individual and group learning styles. Developed curriculum materials to meet accreditation standards and lesson objectives, incorporating experiential learning when possible.

1995–1999   **SERVICEMASTER**, Denver, Colorado
Manager, Environmental Services, Kaiser Permanente
Manager, Environmental Services, Saint Anthony Central Hospital—Instilled a positive, service-minded attitude and a feeling of pride in a job well done by demonstrating a personal enthusiasm and team spirit. Maintained good public relations with patients, facilities personnel, administrators, and medical staff. Assumed responsibility for the department in the absence of the director.
Human Resources Specialist—Recruited, screened, interviewed, and hired for entry-level positions for a 250-bed facility. Ensured that all standards were met by managers handling personnel actions. Performed pre-employment drug testing and criminal background checks. Conducted new hire orientations, including OSHA requirements, infectious waste, hazardous communication, and personal protective equipment. Processed unemployment claims and handled workers' compensation cases.

EDUCATION

MASTER OF BUSINESS ADMINISTRATION (Emphasis on Health Care Management)
University of Phoenix, El Paso, Texas (2001)

BACHELOR OF SCIENCE DEGREE IN BUSINESS ADMINISTRATION
Regis University, Colorado Springs, Colorado (1995)

JULIE HARRIS, MS.Ed.

1234 Twin Gulch Court • Harrison, CO 80922
Phone: (719) 555-1234 • E-mail: julieh@protypeltd.com

PROFILE

NASP Certified School Psychologist who sets high standards and motivates students to achieve success. Well-organized professional with extensive experience in special education populations. Effective team player with proven listening, interpersonal, and communication skills. Knowledge of Windows, MS Word, PowerPoint, Excel, and computerized IEP programs.

EDUCATION

Ed.S. IN SCHOOL PSYCHOLOGY (August 2013)
University of Northern Colorado, Greeley, Colorado
Relevant course work: Psychological Testing and Measurement, Abnormal Psychology, Theories of Personality, Seminar in School Psychology, Community Psychology and Social Systems, Legal and Ethical Issues, Psychological Consultation—Theory and Practice, Evaluation of Psychological Services, Child and Adolescent Psychology, Behavioral Approaches to Professional Psychology, Theories of Counseling, Intellectual and Cognitive Assessment, Family Systems, Infant and Toddler Neuropsychology, Evaluation and Correction of Individual Reading Problems

MS.Ed. IN SPECIAL EDUCATION (2009)
Old Dominion University, Norfolk, Virginia
Emphasis on learning disabilities and emotional disabilities
Licensed Special Education Teacher K–12 (Colorado)

BACHELOR OF SCIENCE IN PSYCHOLOGY (2005)
University of Maryland, Heidelberg, Germany

CONTINUING EDUCATION

- Depression: Comprehensive Assessment and Treatment of Children, Adolescents, and Adults, Medical Educational Services, 8 hours (2013)
- ADHD: Beyond the Label—Assessment, Treatment, and Educational Interventions, Medical Educational Services, 8 hours (2013)
- Crisis Response and Intervention, National Emergency Response Team, 16 hours (2012)
- Threat and Suicide Assessment, CSSP, 8 hours (2012)
- Special Education Law, Law Advisory Council, 8 hours (2009)

INTERNSHIP

SCHOOL PSYCHOLOGY INTERNSHIP (2012–2013)
Harrison School District 2, Colorado Springs, Colorado
- Completed an intensive 1,200-hour internship in an elementary school, middle school, and alternative night high school program.
- Provided psycho-educational assessment, individual and play therapy, and direct/indirect consultation.

PRACTICUMS

- Cognitive Assessment, Gorman Middle School, Harrison District 2, Colorado Springs, Colorado (Fall 2010)
- Personality Assessment, Colleagues and Families, Colorado Springs, Colorado (Spring 2011)
- Individual Counseling, Buena Vista Elementary School, Colorado Springs District 11 (Fall 2011)
- Systems Intervention, The New Horizons Alternative School, Harrison District 2, Colorado Springs, Colorado (Spring 2012)

EXPERIENCE

SPECIAL EDUCATION COORDINATOR (2009–present)
The New Horizons Alternative School, Colorado Springs, Colorado
- Coordinate special education services for 7–12th-grade students with learning and emotional disabilities.
- Develop intervention, program, and transition plans.
- Write Individualized Education Plans (IEPs) and psycho-educational reports.
- Facilitate multidisciplinary team meetings and taught annual classes in psycho-educational assessment at the District 2 New Staff Institute.
- Supervise, train, and evaluate special education student teachers as a cooperating teacher for the University of Colorado at Colorado Springs.
- Serve as acting administrator in the absence of the principal.
- Certified ACT administrator and Accommodations Coordinator (2009–present).
- Member of the interviewing and hiring team for new teachers and paraprofessionals (2009–present).
- Member of the District Literacy Team responsible for developing a new literacy program, including curriculum and tests (2011–2012).
- Member of the District Transition Team that provided career and continuing education services to special education students between 18 and 21 years of age (2009–2010).

HONORARIUM INSTRUCTOR (2011–present)
University of Colorado, Colorado Springs, Colorado
- Teach Psycho-Educational Assessment to graduate students and professional educators in the Masters of Special Education Program.
- Developed and implemented a unique hands-on curriculum, examinations, and multimedia presentation materials.

SIED TEACHER (2008–2009)
Southeast Cooperative Educational Program, Norfolk, Virginia
- Taught emotionally disabled students in 7–8th-grade programs for the most at-risk students (expelled, violent, economically disadvantaged, and prison populations).

MENTAL HEALTH WORKER, TEACHER'S ASSISTANT (2008)
Southeast Virginia Training Center, Chesapeake, Virginia
- Worked with nonverbal adults in classroom and residential settings.
- Taught sign language to improve the communication abilities of adult autistic residents.

DISCIPLINE COORDINATOR, TEACHER'S ASSISTANT (2007–2008)
Chesapeake Bay Academy, Chesapeake, Virginia
- Served as an intervention specialist for this private school for learning-disabled and ADHD children. Investigated incidents, determined disciplinary actions, and developed classroom interventions to prevent future problems.
- Assisted in teaching second- and third-grade classes for the first half of the year before being promoted to discipline coordinator for the entire K–12 population.

AFFILIATIONS   • National Association of School Psychologists

Gloria R. Conner

PROFILE

- Experienced, hardworking flight attendant with a great customer service attitude.
- Able to foster cooperative relationships and generate enthusiasm.
- Skilled in taking the initiative—self-confident and conscientious.
- Traveled extensively in the United States, Hawaii, Mexico, and Europe.

RELEVANT EXPERIENCE

FLIGHT ATTENDANT
Frontier Airlines, Denver, Colorado (2003–2012)
Western Pacific Airlines, Colorado Springs, Colorado (2002–2003)

- Provided top-of-the-line service to airline customers during flights.
- Assured the safety and comfort of passengers on domestic and international flights.
- Greeted passengers, verified tickets, recorded destinations, and directed passengers to their assigned seats.
- Explained the use of safety equipment, served meals and beverages, and performed other personal services.
- Evaluated passengers for those who might pose a possible security risk, and ensured the safety of the flight deck and pilots.
- Interviewed candidates for flight attendant positions and made hiring recommendations.
- Certified for CPR, first aid, automated external defibrillator, and self-defense.

STAFF ASSISTANT, DRUG COMMISSION OFFICER
United States Anti-Doping Agency, Colorado Springs, Colorado (2005–2007)
United States Olympic Committee, Colorado Springs, Colorado (2002–2005)

- Assisted drug commission officers in the collection of samples to test for performance-enhancing substances in athletes who compete in Olympic, Paralympic, and Pan American games and/or train in the United States.
- Traveled throughout the U.S. to conduct doping controls both in competition and out of competition without notice.
- Monitored urine collection to ensure the integrity of samples, reduced the chances of sample contamination, and maintained the security of each sample up to shipment.
- Completed forms with personal data, drug use history, sport, and other information.

FOOD AND COCKTAIL SERVER
Maggie Mae's Restaurant, Colorado Springs, Colorado (2000–2002)
McKay's Restaurant, Colorado Springs, Colorado (1999–2000)

- Provided high-quality customer service in family-style restaurants.

PHYSICAL AND HEALTH TRAINER
Straub Clinic and Hospital, Inc., Wahiawa, Hawaii (1998–2000)
Darmstadt Military Community, Darmstadt, Germany (1995–1998)

- Taught aerobics and helped people reach their health and fitness goals.

EDUCATION

FLIGHT ATTENDANT TRAINING, Frontier Airlines, Denver, Colorado (2003)
- Completed three and a half weeks of flight attendant training

FLIGHT ATTENDANT TRAINING, Western Pacific Airlines, Colorado Springs, Colorado (2002)
- Completed three and a half weeks of intensive training

1234 Huaka Street • Kihei, Hawaii 96753 • Email: grconner@mail.com • Cellular: (720) 555-1234

Carol R. Florio

P.O. Box 1234 • Monument, CO 80132 • (719) 555-1234 • florio@protypeltd.com

PROFILE
- Experienced landscape artist with a strong background in these areas:
  - Xeriscape
  - Desert gardens
  - Water conservation
  - Low-water-use plants
  - Efficient irrigation systems
  - Wildlife habitats
- Proven ability to build trust and to sell new concepts to customers.
- Self-motivated professional with a strong work ethic and a passion for the environment.
- Effective team player with excellent communication and interpersonal skills.
- Knowledge of Windows, MS Word, Excel, Publisher, Outlook, and Internet Explorer.

EXPERIENCE

LANDSCAPING
- Certified Desert Landscaper, Phoenix Desert Landscape School, Desert Botanical Gardens.
- Experienced in the identification of low-water-use plants, appropriate maintenance of plants and irrigation systems, proper fertilization and weed control, and identifying and controlling plant diseases.
- Designed and installed a water-efficient landscape for a Habitat for Humanity property in Guadalupe, Arizona. Used xeriscape principles to design the landscape and installed an efficient irrigation system. Planted low-water-use trees, shrubs, and desert wildflowers.
- Renovated an old landscape to a new design compatible with the limited water supply of the Sonoran Desert.
- Recycled and relocated existing plants that were appropriate to the design and image of the new landscape.
- Removed high-water-use plants and installed new plants that functioned to provide shade, screening, privacy, seasonal interest, color contrast, and a wildlife habitat.
- Retrofitted the existing bubbler irrigation system to a drip system and upgraded it with an automatic timer to reduce water use.

SALES AND MANAGEMENT
- Successfully sold resale and new residential real estate. Licensed Real Estate Broker in Colorado.
- Consistently achieved annual Top Producer and won the Million-Dollar Producer awards.
- Built a client base through prospecting, referrals, cold calling, and direct mail campaigns.
- Demonstrated the features and benefits of properties and managed all of the details required to bring a transaction to successful close, including the negotiation of purchase offers and contracts.
- Accountable for long-range planning, profit and loss, budgeting, controlling costs, accounts payable, accounts receivable, operations, and customer service.

EDUCATION

CERTIFIED DESERT LANDSCAPER (2008–2009)
Phoenix Desert Landscape School, Desert Botanical Gardens, Phoenix, Arizona
Successfully completed three semesters to earn the CDL designation.

UNDERGRADUATE STUDIES (1990–1995)
Arizona State University, Tempe, Arizona
Completed three years toward a Bachelor of Fine Arts degree.

JONES SCHOOL OF REAL ESTATE, Colorado Springs, Colorado (2011)

WORK HISTORY
Real Estate Broker Associate, Prudential Professional Realtors, Monument, Colorado (2011–present)
Desert Landscaper, Phoenix, Arizona (2009–2011)
Real Estate Agent/Broker, West USA Realty, Phoenix, Arizona (2002–2011)
Real Estate Agent/Broker, ERA Realty, Scottsdale, Arizona (1997–2002)
Real Estate Agent/Broker, Coldwell-Banker Real Estate, Phoenix, Arizona (1985–1987)

Eric Thomas

4113 Anywhere Drive
Newtown, Colorado 80918
Phone: (719) 555-1234   Email: ericthomas@mail.com

PROFILE

+ *Dedicated manager with a strong background in service and consumer product industries.*
+ *Proven experience in business administration, event management, economics, and supervision.*
+ *Energetic team player with the ability to communicate clearly and work well with others.*
+ *Self-motivated professional with a demonstrated work ethic and dedication to lifelong learning.*
+ *Experienced international traveler (four continents) with an appreciation for other cultures.*
+ *Proficient in Windows, MS Word, Excel, Outlook, Access, Works, Netscape, and Telnet.*

EXPERIENCE

BUSINESS ADMINISTRATOR, Roche s.r.o., *Prague, Czech Republic (2009–2012)*

+ *Selected as a consultant for a contract to demonstrate Western business concepts for the Czech division of the third largest pharmaceutical company in the world.*
+ *Conducted an internal audit of executive, mid-management, and staff-level personnel processes and made recommendations to executive management to improve the company's organic growth.*
+ *Predicted a 7.2% growth in a shrinking market if recommendations were implemented.*
+ *Evaluated stock supplies and recommended actions to save $27,000 in overstock.*
+ *Designed the division's website to harmonize with corporate identity pieces.*

EXHIBITION COORDINATOR, Joly, *Prague, Czech Republic (2008–2009)*

+ *Recruited by the AIESEC for a six-month internship with this exhibition company specializing in hunting and fishing events.*
+ *Designed the layout and wrote the content for the company's website.*
+ *Planned and managed an event for 10,000 participants, including 40 international companies.*

RESEARCH ASSISTANT, Murdoch University, *Perth, Australia (2007–2008)*

+ *Conducted research on the Phillips Curve, working side by side with the noted Dr. Robert Lees.*
+ *Analyzed data, created formulas, and drew conclusions relating to the Asian crisis and its effect on Australian higher education for the Center for Labour Market Research.*

OWNER, GENERAL MANAGER, College Pro Painting, *Denver, Colorado (2006–2007)*

+ *Developed this franchise operation from the ground up, generating $80,000 in one summer.*
+ *Recruited, hired, and supervised three crews with a total of 13 employees.*
+ *Accountable for long-range planning, budgeting, controlling costs, collecting accounts receivable, and monitoring financial performance.*
+ *Scheduled, planned, and coordinated large projects, maximizing resources and ensuring customer satisfaction.*
+ *Developed new accounts through flyers, direct mail, referrals, and cold calling.*
+ *Achieved the highest customer satisfaction rate in the four-state mountain region as measured by surveys.*

PREVIOUS EXPERIENCE *(2003–2006)*

Foreman and Painter, *College Pro Painting, Colorado Springs, Colorado*
Volunteer Youth Soccer Referee, *Chargers Soccer Club, Colorado Springs, Colorado*

EDUCATION

BACHELOR OF ARTS, University of Colorado, *Boulder, Colorado (2004)*

+ *Major in Economics (Major GPA 3.6)*
+ *Study abroad at Murdoch University, Perth, Australia (Spring/Fall Semesters 2003)*

Cover Letters

16

The first rule of cover letters: Never use a generic cover letter with only "To Whom It May Concern." With tons of work on your desk, would you be interested in such a mass mailing? You would probably consider it junk mail, right? You would be much more likely to read a letter that was directed to you personally, and so would human resources professionals.

The second rule: Every résumé sent by mail or fax needs a personalized cover letter even if the advertisement didn't request a cover letter.

The third rule: Résumés sent by e-mail don't need a true cover letter. Use only a quick paragraph with three to five sentences telling your reader where you heard about the position and why your qualifications are a perfect fit for the position's requirements. E-mail is intended to be short, sweet, and to the point. Then, cut and paste your text résumé into the body of the e-mail message and attach your MS Word file (see Chapter 2 for detailed instructions on how to create and use an electronic résumé). Here is a sample cover letter for an e-mail message:

> I found your posting for a Customer Service Manager (Job #12343) on the Internet at Monster.com and would appreciate your serious consideration of my qualifications. I have more than thirteen years of operations management experience that included budget analysis and tracking ($13 million), expense control, staffing, training, and customer service. I have succeeded in significantly controlling costs and maximizing productivity in all my jobs. My team spirit, ability to manage multiple priorities with time-sensitive deadlines, and strong communication skills would be true assets to your customer service program.
>
> Pasted below is the text version of my résumé and attached is the MS Word document as your advertisement requested. I look forward to hearing from you soon.
>
> Sincerely, John Doe

This chapter will address several cover letter types. A letter to a recruiter requires different information from a letter in answer to an advertisement. A targeted cover letter that tells a story and captures your reader's attention is ideal when possible, but such letters

> *Never use a generic cover letter with only "To Whom It May Concern."*

aren't always practical (see the sample on page 227). Not everyone has the writing skills to produce an effective story, and the time involved in researching and writing the story would be impractical for mass mailings. A hard-hitting salesperson can write a dynamic cover letter, but not everyone is comfortable with that style, and a good cover letter doesn't have to be "pushy."

Before we get into specific styles, let's cover some general rules that apply to most cover letters. Most of the cover letters in this chapter follow the majority of these general rules.

1. Customize each cover letter with an inside address (do not use "to whom it may concern").

2. Personalize the greeting (Dear Ms. Smith). Try to get the name of a person whenever possible. A blind advertisement makes that impossible, but in other cases a quick telephone call can often result in a name and sometimes a valuable telephone conversation. When you can't get a name, use Dear Recruiter, Dear Hiring Manager, Dear Search Committee, or Dear Sir/Madam.

3. Mention where you heard about the position so your reader knows where to direct your résumé and letter. The first paragraph of your cover letter is a great place to state your objective. Since you know the specific job being offered, you can tailor your objective to suit the position.

4. Keep the cover letter sounding positive and upbeat. You can open your cover letter with a strong accomplishments statement or emphasize why you want to work for that specific company. Kim Isaacs, one of *Monster.com's* résumé experts, has written the following example: "Your company is truly a leader in health care information. You offer solutions that ultimately enhance the quality of health care delivery. I am excited about your mission and would be able to translate this excitement by providing top-notch administrative services to your team members."

5. Be a name-dropper. In the first paragraph, mention someone you know in the company. Hiring managers take unsolicited résumés more seriously when they assume you were referred by one of their employees or customers.

6. The second paragraph (or two) is your sales pitch. It is the perfect place to mention specific experience that is targeted to the job opening. This is your "I'm super great because" information. Here is where you summarize why you are absolutely perfect for the position. Really sell yourself and your passions. Your reader isn't interested in your life story. Hiring managers are inherently self-centered; they want to know what you can do for them. Show them that there is a direct match between their needs and

what you can deliver. Focus on relevant accomplishments and proven performance to convince the reader that you are worthy of an interview.

Pick and choose some of your experience and/or education that is specifically related to the company's requirements, or elaborate on qualifications that are not in your résumé but apply to this particular job. Research the company before writing your cover letter and become familiar with its mission, vision, and products or services. This will allow you to mention the specific needs of the company and your proposed solutions, which makes your letter more compelling to the reader.

When your cover letter is targeted, it becomes immediately obvious that it is not generic. Don't make this section too long, though, or you will quickly lose the reader's interest. Entice the reader to find out more about you in your résumé.

7. The closing should be a concise "call to action." Reach out to the reader, letting her know what you want—an application, an interview, an opportunity to call. If you are planning to call the person on a certain day, you could close by saying, "I will contact you next Tuesday [or a more general "next week"] to set up a mutually convenient time to meet." Don't call on Mondays or Fridays if you can help it. If you aren't comfortable making cold calls, then close your letter with something like "I look forward to hearing from you soon." And remember to say, "Thank you for your consideration" or something to that effect (but don't be obsequious, please!).

Story Letters

If you are planning a direct mail campaign to 50 or 100 or 400 companies, this type of letter is not for you. It just isn't practical. However, you will have to admit that the letters on pages 220 and 227 are great attention getters. For those dream jobs that require something special, this is the way to go. In a story cover letter, you must be able to tell a good story and write it well. If writing is not your forté, you can hire someone to write the letter, but you must still do the research and have a general outline of the story.

Letters to Recruiters

There are two types of recruiters: retained and contingency. The difference is that retained recruiters are hired by a company and are then paid by that company whether they ever find the right employee for the position or not. Contingency firms are also paid by the company but only when they find a good match and the job seeker is hired. Legitimate recruiting firms don't charge the job seeker a dime, which means they are working for their client companies and not *you*.

Because their mission is not to find the perfect job for you but to find the perfect employee for their client, they have little interest in communicating with you unless you are a prime candidate for a position they are seeking to fill *now*. Don't call recruiters; they will call you if they are interested. This affects both the beginning and ending of your cover letter. If you don't have a person's name, use Dear Recruiter. You should resign yourself to waiting for the recruiter to call you, so "I look forward to hearing from you soon" is an appropriate closing for a recruiter cover letter.

In addition to the "I'm super great because" paragraph(s), you need to add another paragraph just before the closing that tells the recruiter your ideal position title, industry, salary, and geographic preferences. Check the cover letter on page 229 as an example.

Dynamic Letters

Job openings that require a certain amount of dynamic spirit—like sales—deserve a more dynamic letter. This can be accomplished in the opening paragraph. The rest of the letter is written like a standard cover letter but with a little more energy than usual. The last paragraph can be a bit more aggressive—you call the hiring manager instead of waiting for him/her to call you. See pages 217, 219, 224, 226, 228, and 230 for examples of cover letters that exude confidence and power.

Thank-You Letters

According to a recent survey, less than 20% of applicants write a thank-you note after an interview. Of the recruiters surveyed, 94% said that a thank-you letter would increase the applicant's chances of getting the job, or at least help him/her stay in the running, provided the applicant is otherwise qualified. Fifteen minutes of your time and a first-class postage stamp are very inexpensive investments in your career!

A good thank-you letter continues the conversation you started during the interview. It simply thanks the interviewer for his or her time and reiterates some of the important things you learned about the company in the interview, which helps the interviewer remember who you are. Add some key qualifications that you forgot to mention in the interview, or emphasize some of the more important things you discussed. If the interviewer shared some information that gave you an insight into the company and its culture, build on it to prove you would be a good fit.

Your thank-you letter should "connect" you to the interviewer. Put yourself in your interviewer's shoes and ask, "What would enlighten, delight, or inform me?" Find an article in a newspaper or magazine that would interest your interviewer and enclose it with your letter. It can be related to the industry or to your interviewer's hobbies and interests. Ideally, you "connected" with the interviewer on a personal level by noticing things in his or her office that you can mention in your letter.

A thank-you letter should be short—three paragraphs at the most. Don't try for the hard sell. You had your chance in the interview. The thank-you letter just reinforces what you have already said and provides information you might have promised during the interview.

To be effective, your thank-you letter should be mailed as soon as possible after the interview. I recommend no longer than seven days but preferably the day after the interview. Use the same letterhead as your résumé with a common business format and send it by snail mail. If the company and interviewer were very informal or you have received e-mail correspondence from the person before, then you can send a thank-you letter by e-mail. E-mail might also be quicker if the candidate will be selected soon. Generally, a hard-copy letter is preferable. See the examples on pages 231 and 232.

Letterheads

It is so easy to create a letterhead all your own and to make it match your résumé. Just copy into a new document the name and address you have already created for your résumé. It couldn't be simpler! It makes a very sharp impression when your cover letter and résumé match in every respect from paper color to font to letterhead.

Paper Colors

Color, like music, creates an atmosphere. Everyone knows that different colors evoke different feelings. Red can make a person feel warm, whereas blue does just the opposite.

Of course, you wouldn't want to use red in a résumé—although an artist could get away with just about any color. As a general rule, résumé papers should be neutral or light in color. After 27 years in the résumé business, I have discovered that brilliant white linen paper is still the most popular, followed closely by a slightly off-white and then by shades of light gray.

Today, the vast majority of résumés are sent to recruiters and human resources via e-mail or e-forms on websites, so paper résumés might seem like a moot point. There are still uses for paper résumés, and you should always have some on hand when you are actively job seeking. The most prominent uses for paper résumés today are for handing to a contact at a networking event, meetings with mentor(s), job interviews, and anywhere you will meet a contact in person. That means your paper résumé isn't dead yet! For those times you need your résumé printed, here are some suggestions.

Make sure that the color of the paper you choose is representative of your personality and industry and that it doesn't detract from your message. For instance, a dark paper color makes your résumé hard to read.

There is another reason to avoid dark-colored papers and papers with a background (pictures, marble shades, or speckles). Often companies will photocopy résumés for hiring managers, and dark colors or patterns will simply turn into dark masses that make your résumé difficult to read. If a company has multiple locations, the original résumé may even get faxed from one site to another and the same thing happens.

The type of paper (bond, linen, laid, cover stock, or coated) isn't as important, although it also projects a certain image. Uncoated paper (bond, linen, laid) makes a classic statement. It feels rich and makes people think of corporate stationery and important documents. Coated stock recalls memories of magazines, brochures, and annual reports. Heavy cover stock and laid paper can't be successfully folded and don't hold the ink from a laser printer or copier very well, so they must be handled gently. All of these factors play a part in your paper choice.

Regardless of the paper you choose, mail your résumé flat instead of folded. It costs a few extra cents in postage and a little more for the 9-inch by 12-inch envelope, but the impression it makes is well worth the extra cost. Thank-you letters and other follow-up letters can be folded in standard No. 10 business envelopes. Even if you e-mail your thank-you letters, always follow up with a hard-copy mailing.

Experienced Sales and Marketing Professional
Project Management – Data Analysis – Sales Support

Market and Business Analysis – Project Management – High-Impact Presentations
Copywriting – Training – Vendor Management – Database Marketing

▶ **Charlotte Johansen**
12345 Carmel Creek Rd.
San Diego, CA 92130

cjohansen@protypeltd.com
619.555.1234

October 15, 2012

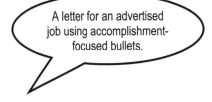

A letter for an advertised job using accomplishment-focused bullets.

Mr. Alan Robinson
National Aviation, Inc.
P.O. Box 456
Ft. Collins, Colorado 80522

Re: Manager of Vendor Performance

Dear Mr. Robinson:

Whether challenged to create a sales support program from scratch, hire and train a high-performance team in a matter of weeks, or create effective training programs and compelling presentations, I have repeatedly delivered stellar results. Examples include the following:

- ➤ Increasing sales up to 300% by conceiving and executing novel cross-merchandising strategy.
- ➤ Leading multiple top-performing internal and third-party teams.
- ➤ Improving management capabilities by adopting leading industry practices and innovating proprietary data analysis tools.
- ➤ Optimizing CRM by streamlining data management systems and practices.
- ➤ Defining and succeeding in newly defined positions and building specialized teams.

Your search for a **Manager of Vendor Performance** caught my eye because of your desire for a candidate who can launch a complex vendor quality program from scratch. Defining and implementing performance-oriented tools and processes involving multiple players is my expertise. I would welcome a personal meeting to learn more about your needs and discuss my potential contributions.

Thank you for taking the time to consider my candidacy.

Sincerely,

Charlotte Johansen

Charlotte Johansen

Enclosure

[Letter contributed by Kim Mohiuddin, kim@movinonupresumes.com]

215

James Pitt
PRODUCTION MANAGER

Address: 12345 Park Way, Piedmont, CA 94611
Phone: (510) 555-1234
E-mail: pitt@protypeltd.com

July 22, 2012

Skill-focused, cold-calling letter with no job advertised.

Talent Acquisition
St. John Corporation
122 Armstrong Avenue
Irvine, CA 92614

Dear Recruiter:

I am an exceptionally talented, award-winning, and self-directed production management professional who has made a mark in various facets of web-based project environments, including team recruitment and management, user interface direction, executive production, client relations, sales, and budgetary control. I am passionate and energetic and can quickly analyze complex projects in high-paced environments, establish priorities, and formulate effective solutions to consistently exceed expectations with timely and cost-effective results.

As an outstanding resource-builder, I will not rest until the project is completed to the highest possible standards. My technical understanding and hands-on abilities in the areas of web-based strategies will make me an invaluable member of your organization.

My experience supports this passion and I am proud to have delivered notable projects and solutions across a diverse yet integrated landscape. My notable skills encompass work flow and process improvement, video production, web interactive production on usability design and improvement, 15 years of Photoshop familiarity, experience in location photography, and color correction processes. I invite you to read more about my accomplishments in my attached resume.

Furthermore, I am recognized as an energetic motivator and communicator who is consistently acknowledged by colleagues, clients, and stakeholders alike as an intuitive problem-solver, an excellent leader, and a dedicated professional with the talent and experience to deliver measurable results in high-volume web production platforms.

I will follow up with you in a few days to answer any questions you may have. In the meantime, you may reach me at the above phone number or via e-mail. I look forward to learning more about your company's goals and how I can contribute to your continued success. Thank you for your time and consideration.

Sincerely,

James Pitt

James Pitt

Enc: Résumé

[Letter contributed by Sandra Ingemansen, singemansen@gmail.com]

Eric T. Pryor

1015 Kent Street
Chicago, IL 88997

713-987-06543 or 713-687-5678
pryor@protypeltd.com

August 28, 2012

Ms. Michelle Stone
Chief, Human Resources Analyst
Sampson Human Resources Consulting Corporation, Inc
6655 Kumis Boulevard
Chicago, IL 22665

SUBJECT: "Personnel Operations Manager" listed on your company website on August 27, 2012

Dear Ms. Stone:

 Based on each of our professional objectives, today could ultimately prove to be a lucky day for both of us!! In response to the employment opportunity listed on your Web posting, I am submitting this cover letter and accompanying résumé for consideration. Evidenced by my employment history and career enhancement training are skills that demonstrate in-depth business acumen, industry-specific intellect, distinctive qualifications, and accomplishments related to the following:

- ✓ **Performing special reviews and surveys in conjunction with manpower and management analysis surveys to identify problems in alignment, supervisor/employee ratios, delineation of duties and responsibilities, career-enhancing opportunities in the organization structure, employee retention, and delegations of authority.**
- ✓ **Making full use of special employment programs for students, youth, veterans, people with disabilities, women, and minorities.**
- ✓ **Strategizing and executing quality assurance initiatives that define problems, analyzing alternatives, and recommending solutions to assess effectiveness of programs.**

As requested, my previous positions commanded an average annual salary of $100K in addition to a full benefits package. I have no doubt that your company offers a salary that is both fair and competitive and therefore open for discussion.

I welcome being able to discuss my qualifications and this employment opportunity further. I will follow up with you early next week to discuss arranging a mutually agreeable time. Thank you in advance, for both your time and consideration.

Respectfully yours,

Eric T. Pryor

Eric T. Pryor

ATT: Résumé

A dynamic letter using an innovative graphic to grab the reader's attention.

[Letter contributed by Phyllis Houston, phyllis_houston@msn.com]

August 16, 2012

Unsolicited letter to create a job.

Ms. Nancy Waite
COO, Executive Vice President
Ports of Call
3333 Quebec Street, Suite 9100
Denver, Colorado 80207-2331

Dear Ms. Waite:

Carol Ingwersen recommended that I forward a copy of my résumé for your review. I am very interested in returning to the travel industry in a sales capacity and would appreciate an opportunity to sit down with you to talk about the unique ideas I could bring to your sales process.

As you can see in my résumé, I have extensive sales and customer service experience, but what you can't see is that I have worked for travel clubs twice in my career. I succeeded in selling 450 memberships in only three months for The Diplomats in Des Moines, Iowa, and I worked as the membership director for the Texas Air Travel Club during my early career. With its own private jet and 2,500 members, the Texas Air Travel Club was very similar to Ports of Call. I developed some innovative ways of increasing memberships that would be valuable to your company.

Even though you don't have any current openings, I think you will find my ideas worthy of a trial even if you have to create a position for me. I will give you a call next week to see if there is a mutually convenient time we can get together to talk about the possibilities. Thank you for your consideration.

Sincerely,

David Kovach

David F. Kovach

Enclosure

STEPHEN L. JOHNSON

ACCOUNT EXECUTIVE / SALES MANAGER

12345 Elizabeth Avenue, Pfafftown, NC 27040
Home: (336) 555-1234 • Cell: (336) 555-1234
johnson@protypeltd.com

November 15, 2012

Ms. Shelly Brockheimer
Human Resources Manager
Wachovia Bank
301 N. Main Street
Winston-Salem, NC 27101

A dynamic cover with a strong accomplishment focus.

Dear Ms. Brockheimer:

As a key account diplomat and sales manager, I am equipped with a commanding track record in finding and optimizing winning business ideas while driving solid company expansion within fast-paced, highly competitive landscapes.

You will notice one common thread throughout my career—I am a lateral-thinking negotiator and problem solver who knows how to identify new business opportunities, negotiate rewarding and mutually beneficial contracts based on detailed assessment of client requirements, and close the deal through masterful presentations and appropriate recommendations of products and services tailored to client business objectives. With this dynamic approach, I have successfully gained recognition for consistent first-ranking achievements in sales, superb management of the retail planning process for Hanesbrands, Inc. (a multi-billion-dollar company), achievement of high-level product penetration percentages, facilitation of multi-million-dollar sales results, and forging a multitude of referral client relationships from my devoted reputation for service delivery to the fullest.

Purposefully scrutinizing operational processes, including inventory flows and shipment statistics, I dedicate all efforts to functional superiority. Emphasis on precision forecasting, troubleshooting, initiation of process, and planning improvements in addition to report preparation and presentation are all indicators of my unyielding follow-through and dedication.

Furthermore, I am a respected administrator, motivator, and mentor who has garnered trustworthiness and commitment across multitalented groups of highly skilled professionals from internal staff and client teams alike. I have trained staff in sales and marketing techniques as well as demonstrated appropriate product and service features to customers for assurance of business enrichment.

I encourage you to read more about my notable achievements in my attached résumé, as I am confident that I can deliver similar results for your company. My geographic preferences center on the southeastern United States, and I am quite willing to relocate for a mutually acceptable offer. I look forward to a discussion with you regarding your future goals and how I can contribute to their realization.

I will follow up with you in a few days to answer any questions you may have. Meanwhile, you may reach me at the above phone number or via e-mail. I look forward to our conversation and thank you for your time and consideration.

Sincerely,

Stephen L. Johnson

Stephen L. Johnson

Enclosure: Résumé

[Letter contributed by Sandra Ingemansen, singemansen@gmail.com]

"Steve's strong customer relationships have been instrumental in maintaining client satisfaction through some difficult operational challenges. He is extremely client-focused and is always in our clients' operating reality."
— **John Truliant, Executive Vice President, Flexible Payroll Solutions**

CAROLINE KAZYNSKI

12345 LINCOLN AVENUE, MILWAUKEE, WISCONSIN 53203
414-555-1234 / kazynski@protypeltd.com

January 15, 2013

Mr. and Mrs. Harvey Fredericks
12345 Sunnyside Lane
Milwaukee, WI 53203

Dear Mr. and Mrs. Fredericks:

It has always been my pleasure to work at Home Expo and to provide valuable design services for homeowners like yourself who made the decision to let us help with their remodeling plans. I trust that you are enjoying your new kitchen and receiving many compliments from visitors to your home. As you have probably heard by now, Home Expo has, unfortunately, closed all of its stores because of the downturn in the economy. However, I want to thank you for the confidence you had in me as your designer and to let you know that I am still available to answer any questions you may have.

I have now started my own business venture, representing many fine lines of stock and custom cabinetry. Together with my team of two talented design consultants, we have more than 30 years of combined experience as well as the services of skilled contractors I personally know would work hard to achieve a beautiful result to any project. Enclosed is a copy of my current résumé that will provide a more comprehensive summary of my background and achievements. My major strengths include the following:

- Building relationships by listening carefully to clients' ideas and communicating through each step of design and installation to turn their visions into reality.

- Creativity and forward thinking in all project areas, with a special flair for creating eye-catching designs that meet customers' financial and aesthetic needs.

- Exceptional project management, budgeting, and organizational skills honed from a heavy workload and fast-paced, highly competitive environment that demands quality performance and timely completion.

- The ability to turn around adverse situations—including difficult building conditions both anticipated and previously unforeseen—to meet project demands without cost overruns.

Please take a few minutes to think about possible needs among your friends or acquaintances who may benefit from our design talents and pass along one of my enclosed business cards. I would be happy to arrange a meeting with them at no cost or obligation to discuss their kitchen and bath remodeling needs, no matter how large or small. Your continued support is greatly appreciated.

Sincerely,

Caroline Kazynski

Caroline Kazynski

Enclosures: Résumé and business cards

[Letter contributed by Melanie Noonan, peripro1@aol.com]

MEREDITH STRUNK, MGA

12345 Tunnel Road, Palo Alto, CA 94301 • 650-555-1234 (mb) • strunk@protypeltd.com

January 1, 2013

Human Resources
PricewaterhouseCoopers
1234 Avenue of the Americas
New York, NY 10013

Dear Hiring Team:

I am writing to express my interest in the ***Senior Business and Technology Analyst*** position you announced on Monster.com. I believe I am uniquely qualified for the position, offering 12 years of experience as a trusted partner to senior managers and stakeholders on high-stakes technology consulting projects.

From my days at Ernst & Young to my current role at Citigroup, I have built a career hinged on the principles of information technology and Web software development, centered on using analysis and improvement methodologies to efficiently execute business and user goals. My strengths include the following:

- **System Design and Revision Lifecycle Management:** Striking a balance between technical decisions and end-user experience, particularly relating to problem solving / alternative solutions; user vs. business system requirements; testing, training and acceptance criteria; and information handling and reporting.

- **Constituent Relations and Project Leadership:** Building and managing relationships with internal and external stakeholders, including senior executives, IT managers and staff; vendors, consultants, and clients.

- **Technical Optimization and Efficiency Setting:** Analyzing core business objectives and technology solutions against multi-industry standards and best practices. Includes technology investment and feasibility advisement, system utilization, and documentation requirements facilitation.

Most importantly, I help organizations anticipate and confront roadblocks early in the project life cycle, bringing to light weaknesses and potential risks while identifying areas for improvement. I thrive in ambiguous environments, with a practiced ability to align contributor and stakeholder expectations.

My résumé is enclosed for your review. Citigroup's IT division is moving out of state, and I am looking forward to exploring a new role with a company like yours. Please reach me any time at 650-555-1234 or strunk@protypeltd.com. I look forward to meeting you soon.

Sincerely,

Meredith Strunk

Meredith Strunk

Encl: Résumé

Ingrid Hägglund, M.A.

Influential • Analytical • Pragmatic • Resourceful • Tenacious • Inspiring • Engaging

August 14, 2012

> *"Ingrid was a valuable contributor to our department and we miss her ... exceptional interpersonal skills, determination, intellectual curiosity, ... upbeat outlook."*
> – Robyn Stone, PhD
> Clarkson University

Roslyn Smith, M.S.
Community Programs Manager
Barrington, Inc.
2268 North Fountain Avenue
Milwaukee, WI 53201

Dear Ms. Smith:

I am writing to express my considerable interest in the ***Program Specialist, Milwaukee*** position announced by **Barrington, Inc.,** on TheLadders.com. With more than nine years of part-time and university-based professional experience, I believe I am uniquely qualified for the role.

As you may appreciate, I am searching for the right fit, which means returning to work in a team-oriented, part-time position after a family sabbatical that included U.S. relocation with my husband as he undertook a new assistant professorship at the University of Wisconsin.

Barrington's mission parallels my pursuit of a second master's degree in counseling psychology. Assisting the organization's staff would be an ideal environment to jump-start my work and education in the world of family resource planning and assistance.

The enclosed résumé outlines the skills and experience I would bring to Barrington, Inc., in the areas of outreach and internal program support. Additionally, I offer a strong professional ethic; intellectual curiosity, warmth, and instinctive reasoning; and adaptability, critical thinking, and goal-directed diligence.

I am open to working during the times specified in Barrington's job description and look forward to having an opportunity to meet with you in person to discuss the position. Please contact me any time at 414-555-1234 (mobile) or hagglund@protypeltd.com.

Sincerely,

Ingrid Hägglund

Ingrid Hägglund

Encl: Résumé

A letter answering an online advertisement.

[Letter contributed by Jared Redick, jredick@theresumestudio.com]

1234 Grove Street, Milwaukee, WI 53208 • 414-555-1234 (mb) • hagglund@protypeltd.com • Green Card Holder

JAMES D. KENT

222.777.7676 ★ jkent@protypeltd.com

October 12, 2012

Judy Benner, Chief
HR Department
Craddock Enterprise
1301 Fifth Avenue, Suite 4000
Seattle, Washington 98101

A letter answering an ad and associating the company's needs with the writer's qualifications.

Dear Ms. Benner:

I was excited to learn of your need for a **Sales Representative** through your advertisement on Indeed.com. I believe my skills and unique background will be a tremendous benefit for you in developing, sustaining, and exceeding your sales targets.

My passion for servicing customers and strengthening my professional relationships has driven my success throughout my career. I savor the customer focus and contact, value each challenge, and thrive on exploiting new business opportunities, whether in additional sales or untapped niches.

Let me point out three good reasons to consider me for the position:

YOUR NEEDS	MY SKILLS
Driven, Self-Motivated Individual	In my most recent position as Sales Representative, I increased my company's market share and revenue 40% by developing a partnership with another firm.
Client Relationship Management	Throughout my career, clients have commented on the "special consideration" paid to them, which resulted in repeat business, referrals, and clients who requested my services and personal attention year over year.
New Business Development	In my most recent position, as well as in my personal businesses, I have multiplied the customer base anywhere from 25% to 50% in the first year.

I know I can deliver the same results for Craddock Enterprise, and I would welcome the opportunity to speak with you in more detail. I will call your office at 9:00 AM on Wednesday, October 22, to speak with you further. Enclosed is my résumé for your review. Thank you for your time and consideration.

Sincerely,

James D. Kent

James D. Kent

Enclosure: Résumé

[Letter contributed by Jasmine Marchong, jmarchong@therightresume.biz]

Tamara Lynn Beckham
Certified Wedding Planner

~~~~~~~~~~~~~~~~~~~~~~~~~~~~~~~~

55 Westminster Avenue, London, W10 6LM
Tel: (020) 8072 9261 or (079) 4972 4323
tamara@protypeltd.com

~~~~~~~~~~~~~~~~~~~~~~~~~~~~~~~~

January 31, 2013

A dynamic letter broadcast to all wedding shops in town to create a job.

Mrs. Valerie Davidson
Proprietor
The Wedding Shoppe
101 Chamberlain Road
London SW1 6RF

Dear Mrs. Davidson:

If you could delegate work to someone who would do it right the first time, would you increase your business, your profits, and your own free time?

As a recent graduate of The Wedding Planning Institute, I can effectively assist you—quickly and with a minimum of training—on a full-time, part-time, freelance, or short-notice basis.

I offer solid organizational and clerical skills gained from employment as a front-line customer service professional, office supervisor, bookkeeper, and administrator. Also, I have successfully planned and delivered two events. In addition, my referees will attest to my abilities to stay calm, cool, and collected during "crisis" situations. Using well-honed customer service skills gained in the hotel industry, I'm able to defuse escalated customer complaints, act when others hesitate, and remain professionally polite under all circumstances.

Perhaps most importantly, I'm a cheerful and confident lady who wins the trust and confidence of clients. I deliver on my promises by being very well organized, meticulously detail oriented, and 100% serious about doing every job to the best of my abilities.

Thank you for taking the time to read this letter and enclosed résumé. If you could use a trusted and capable assistant, please call or e-mail me at your convenience. I would especially appreciate the opportunity to meet with you so that we can discuss precisely how I could help you deliver a perfect wedding day to your clients.

Sincerely yours,

Tamara Beckham

Tamara Lynn Beckham
Certified Wedding Planner
Diploma, Event Management

Enclosure: Résumé

[Letter contributed by Debra Mills, dmills@pro-cv.co.uk]

Susan Madigan

5511 West Main Street
Pittsburgh, Pennsylvania 12345

(888) 555-1111
smadigan@protypeltd.com

October 6, 2012

Joan Baker, Vice President
ABC Mortgage Services
123 First Avenue
Pittsburgh, PA 12345

Subject: Senior Risk Manager, Credit and Counterpart Risk, #22594

Dear Ms. Baker:

Given the country's current financial crisis, I have been compelled to offer my expertise in the banking industry, particularly in the area of risk management. During my 15+ years tenure in loss mitigation, quality control, and due diligence, I have acquired the reputation for increasing staff efficiency, establishing and maintaining project standards and compliance, and minimizing risk.

Some of my key accomplishments include the following:

- Reduced loan rejection rate from 40% to 3%.
- Established automated comprehensive mortgage risk database, increasing productivity by 50%.
- Revitalized, reorganized and trained staff to ensure regulatory compliance for four organizations.

After the unfortunate downsizing of Wachovia Bank, I would welcome the opportunity to speak with you about how I can help ABC Mortgage Services meet their current challenges head-on. Please contact me at your earliest convenience to arrange an interview. Thank you in advance for your consideration.

Sincerely,

Susan Madigan

Susan Madigan

Enclosure: résumé

[Letter contributed by Ginger Korljan, ginger@takechargecoaching.com]

SARAH JOHNSON, RN
28549 Cloverfield Drive
Agua Dulce, California 91350
sarah5289@yahoo.com

Residence: 661-471-6501   Cellular: 661-295-8015

November 15, 2012

Ms. Melanie Duff
Reliable Home Nurses
23589 Sue Drive, Suite 350
Studio City, California 91605

Dear Ms. Duff:

In this modern world, there is a new model for a successful career—a series of lateral moves that keeps a person involved in new tasks while using the same set of skills. The employee gets the satisfaction of variety and of doing something well, and the employer gets the benefit of a staff member with extensive related experience.

Having worked as both a registered nurse and an office manager in a dental practice, I find that my passion now lies in working as a clinical nurse.

Total commitment to the patients in my care and to the achievement of the objectives of the facility and medical staff is my primary focus. You will find me to be quick to learn and eager to initiate self-directed work when appropriate.

As my résumé details, I can ensure doctor's orders are implemented, that the patients have the needed supplies and meds, and evaluate nursing care. I excel at evaluating patient needs as they change such as physical therapy and nutritional evaluations. Equally strong is my aid with activities of daily living.

Unlike most clinical nurses, I have a strong background in business. You will find me unequalled in following up on appointments, willing to work for private duty shifts, being extremely flexible with days and hours, and being a valuable partner in your expansion to the Santa Clarita and Antelope Valleys. Of course, I would not neglect the San Fernando Valley.

A good fit seems to exist between your requirements and my experience. As such, I would greatly appreciate a personal interview to further explore a mutually beneficial relationship. Thank you for your time and consideration.

Sincerely,

Sarah Johnson

Sarah Johnson

Enclosure

[Letter contributed by Myriam-Rose Kohn, myriam-rose@jedaenterprises.com]

JOSE CASTELLANOS

E-mail: josecastellanos@mail.com • www.linkedin.com/in/jcastellanos

1234 Bell Road, #567 • Phoenix, Arizona 85123 • (602) 555-1234

June 26, 2012

A story letter that tugs at the heartstrings of the reader.

Ms. Cindy Smith
College Relations Manager
Hallmark Cards, Inc.
P.O. Box 123456
Kansas City, Missouri 64141

Dear Ms. Smith:

It was in my hometown of Bogotá, Colombia, that as a teenager I came into contact with Hallmark for the first time. Even though I was not aware of the vision, effort, and commitment of resources that had gone into the Mother's Day card I had purchased, I was a happy customer. I never thought to wonder about the logistics of how that card had gotten to that small store or why a company more than 3,000 miles away was able to appeal to me, a kid from another country, culture, and language.

Hallmark's aggressive market penetration in more than 100 countries and its striving to provide employees with a supportive and challenging environment to best develop and apply their individual skills demonstrate to me that Hallmark is a company well worth entrusting with my career. In addition, I am impressed and attracted by Hallmark's commitment to supporting the communities in which it operates.

In light of Hallmark's international interest, you may be interested in my background. I started a small business in Colombia, which tested my energy, creativity, and initiative. The business quickly grew to be competitive as a result of innovative marketing and operation strategies. I have since learned to speak English, obtained a Bachelor of Business Administration from a U.S. university, and worked in several countries in varied positions, successfully adapting to both the people and management styles of these countries. Furthermore, in order to be better prepared for today's complex business environment, I am pursuing a Master of International Management degree, which I will complete in December.

It is my hope that my solid academic and cultural backgrounds, business experience, and interest in the international arena will convey to you that I have the qualifications to make a valuable contribution to Hallmark's efforts to remain the worldwide leader of the social expression industry.

I would like to be part of the Hallmark team that once helped me express myself through that card I gave my mother, and to take part in expanding the company to reach even more people all over the world. I would appreciate the opportunity to interview with you during your upcoming visit to Phoenix and hope that you will give the enclosed résumé favorable consideration. Thank you for your attention.

Sincerely,

Jose Castellanos

Jose Castellanos

Enclosure

227

HAROLD STEVENS

1325 Richards Road, #53 ▪ Seattle, WA 98117 ▪ (206) 555-1212 ▪ E-mail: harold.stevens@protypeltd.com

January 30, 2013

A dynamic letter graphically highlighting the applicant's strengths.

David Kosar
Network Manager
Qwest Communications
1256 Main Street
Seattle, WA 98118

Dear Mr. Kosar:

I take quite seriously my core responsibilities to identify and protect against security vulnerabilities and to provide best practice solutions that can be executed rapidly and reliably. My goal is to continuously refine my skills as a network security expert. I keep up to date on the latest techniques, policies, and practices in information security management. I enjoy my work and take great pride in the results that I produce.

My history of increasingly responsible roles is demonstrated by accomplishments in designing and maintaining secure systems. Highlights include the following:

Accountability—Monitor business and information management activities to ensure appropriate authentication of user accounts.

Integrity—Prevent unauthorized access by corrupted systems or individuals by maintaining the integrity of the data architecture and regularly conducting vulnerability assessments of critical systems.

Confidentiality—Foster good working relationships with business units. Conduct information sessions to discuss security policies and best practices for maintaining the organization's information assets.

Availability—React quickly to system anomalies; reduce downtime and unavailability caused by overused or poorly configured security controls.

Thank you for your time and consideration. I would welcome the opportunity to interview for this position, and I look forward to hearing from you.

Sincerely,

Harold Stevens

Harold Stevens

Enclosure

[Letter contributed by Jennifer Hay, jhay@ITresumeservice.com]

1234 Bridle Trail
Pueblo, Colorado 81005

Phone: (719) 555-1234
polacek@protypeltd.com

November 17, 2012

Letter to a recruiter. Note the third paragraph that is unique in letters to headhunters.

Mr. Stefan Smith
President
Management Search, Inc.
1234 S. Cook St., Suite 12
Barrington, IL 60010

Dear Mr. Smith:

Is one of your clients looking for a Human Resources or Labor Relations Manager with a proven track record of success in both manufacturing and high-tech services industries? Then you will want to review my qualifications.

As a successful human resource generalist with extensive labor relations experience, I have become well known for my ability to improve employee morale and increase trust between unions and management. I have negotiated and administered several collective bargaining agreements and was often called in to diffuse stalled bargaining processes. My dynamic leadership style motivates change within the corporate culture and builds support from within the ranks. These skills, plus many more, would be true assets to any company whether they are unionized or not.

My target job is at the middle-management level with an innovative company that could challenge my skills in human resource management, employee relations, and compensation and benefits administration. I have no geographic preferences and would be open to relocation. My salary requirements would of course depend on the city, but I would anticipate a base salary in the area of $60,000.

Should one of your clients have a current or emerging need for a member of their human resource management team, I would appreciate your serious consideration of my qualifications as outlined in the enclosed résumé. I am free to meet with you at your convenience and look forward to hearing from you soon.

Sincerely,

Tony Polacek

Tony Polacek

Enclosure

John G. Warren

First Avenue #4C • Long Island City, NY 11106 • Cell: 407-555-1234 • Home: 212-555-5678 • E-mail: johnwarren@protypeltd.com

September 12, 2012

A dynamic letter for a senior management position.

Florida Hotel & Resort
3138 Terry Brook
Winter Park, Florida

Dear Employment Manager:

You need impeccable guest services, tenacious management, and a sincere desire to fulfill expectations to cement memorable experiences for customers in the hospitality industry. As an experienced General/Senior Manager with more than 10 years of experience ensuring excellent operations, propelling profits, and delivering superb service, I now offer you my assistance as your new General Resort Manager.

In order to annihilate your competition, retain your existing clientele, and win new ones, your hotel must service above the standards of your competitors and make an impression with competent and professional people. In addition, your facility must invite your existing and prospective guests with pleasing aesthetics and seductive comfort. Above all, every person in your team MUST exceed the expectations of every guest with whom they interact. I offer to secure these essentials for your hotel and continue to uphold the professional image Florida Hotel & Resort exudes.

With an accomplished history under my current employer, I now seek an opportunity to contribute in the hotel industry with an upscale establishment like yours. Please review my attached résumé, and allow me to highlight the following.

- ✓ Turned low-performing locations into profitable establishments that pleased directors, owners, and customers.
- ✓ Enhanced already successful establishments and produced in areas overlooked by other managers.
- ✓ Led large staffs by motivating them, infusing them with confidence, and leading them by example.
- ✓ Communicated with corporate and non-corporate personnel using language that is clear, sensible, intelligent, and persuasive.
- ✓ Developed a valuable reputation with a highly demanding clientele by delivering on promises and anticipating their comfort and service needs.
- ✓ Generated millions in annual gross by overhauling departments and decreasing expenditures.

The value I will bring to your hotel is not limited to the above. In me, you will gain a manager who can forecast financial, operational, and guest needs accurately, prioritize and manage intelligently, and own all responsibilities in your organization, which will lead to your continued success.

Thank you in advance for your time and consideration. I look forward to hearing from you.

Sincerely,

John Warren

John G. Warren

[Letter contributed by Rosa Vargas, rvargas@creatingprints.com]

SALLY RENE STEWART

5000 West 5th Street
Lubbock, Texas 79400
(806) 555-1234
srs@protypeltd.com

September 20, 2013

Ms. Jane Young
The Design Center
Merimax Interiors, Inc.
234 Waukegan Road
Lubbock, Texas 79402

A thank-you letter reiterating why she is perfect for the job.

Dear Ms. Young:

Thank you for the time you extended me during our interview last Tuesday. Our discussion was enlightening and enjoyable. I am sincerely interested in a designer position with Merimax Interiors, Inc., as I was impressed with your company's culture, growth options, and mission to provide creative yet functional interior designs to clients in the medical care industry.

As you may recall, my particular strength is a positive approach to my work and a commitment to excellence in any endeavor I attempt. The honors I attained during my college career at Texas Tech University reflect my quest for distinction. The prospect of putting my color and design knowledge to work in a business environment such as yours at Merimax Interiors, Inc., is thrilling.

If you have additional questions, please feel free to contact me at (806) 555-1234. I look forward to hearing again from you in the very near future.

Again, thank you for your interest in my qualifications for your designer vacancy.

Sincerely,

Sally Stewart

Sally Rene Stewart

[Letter contributed by Edie Rische, earische@suddenlink.net]

David M. Hudson

4321 Oakmoore Avenue NE
Massillon, OH 44646
330-555-1234

February 10, 2013

Mr. Randall Killian
Manager, Prototype Operations
Topco Industries Inc.
4231 Seabrook Ave. NW
North Canton, OH 44720

Dear Mr. Killian:

I would like to take this opportunity to thank you for the interview Thursday afternoon at your office and to confirm my strong interest in the CNC Machinist position.

After we spoke, it became increasingly clear to me that the position we discussed would be a good fit for my skills and interest. I recognize that this is a busy department with a demanding schedule and a need for accuracy and the ability to meet deadlines. I believe my background, experience, and skills will allow me to make a positive contribution in this department. I hope you will consider me for this position.

In closing, I would like to again thank you for sharing your valuable time with me. I am excited about the possibilities of this position and remain even more convinced of the potential for a good match. I would consider it a privilege to be an employee of a company with an excellent reputation such as Topco. I look forward to a favorable outcome.

Sincerely,

David M. Hudson

David M. Hudson

[Letter contributed by Barbara Kanney, bkanney@abcdocuments.com]

MATT C. LINCOLN
8899 First Place – Lubbock, Texas 79416
(806) 555-1234
mattlincoln89@protypeltd.com

February 18, 2013

The letter every job seeker can't wait to write.

Mr. Jack Preston
Vice President
Cox & Preston Advertising
9986 Avenue G
Lubbock, Texas 79401

Dear Jack:

It is with mixed emotions that I present this letter of resignation. As you know, my parents have been ailing for the last three years. Considering their poor health, I have secured a position with Braxton and Braxton in New York City to be near them. I will relocate to that area in two months. However, it is my intention to remain in the office for at least two to four weeks to ease the transition in filling my vacancy.

I want to express to you that my ten years with you and David have been rewarding and beneficial to my growth as a layout artist. You have both been great associates and mentors. I only hope my position with Braxton and Braxton will bring me as much job satisfaction.

Please let me know if there is anything else I must do to complete the resignation process.

Sincerely,

Matt Lincoln

Matt C. Lincoln

[Letter contributed by Edie Rische, earische@suddenlink.net]

Index

246